ONE
✝
HEART

The Story of the Osage Monastery Forest of Peace

SALLY DENNISON

Pointer Oak / Tri S Foundation

© 2024 by Sally Dennison

Distributed by Millichap Books

Photographs courtesy Osage Monastery, Osage Forest of Peace, and Teresa Matyniak except where noted.

Book and jacket design by Carl Brune

ISBN 978-1-937462-51-2 (hardback)

ISBN 978-1-937462-52-9 (paperback)

Printed in the USA

millichapbooks.com

The human race needs those among us who are willing and happy to live the mystery of the sacred with the greatest possible interiority, in that infinite space within the heart.
—Sister Pascaline Coff, OSB

© MARY JANE MATTHEWS

CONTENTS

ACKNOWLEDGEMENTS	IX
INTRODUCTION	1

1976–1980

Beginnings : 1976–1980	5
India : 1976 & 1977	7
BSPA Monasteries : 1977 & 1978	25
Tulsa : 1978 & 1979	39
Osage Forest : 1979 & 1980	57
Osage + Monastery : 1980	87

1980–2022

Forest Dwellers : 1980–2008	109
Tibetans : 1981–1996	123
Pushback : 1989 & 1990	137
Father Bede : 1979–1993	143
Trustees : 1991–2022	159
Epilogue	179
INDEX	183

ACKNOWLEDGEMENTS

Like the Osage+Monastery Forest of Peace itself, this book owes its existence to many who share a common vision of a more conscious humanity and peaceful world.

I had visited the Osage Monastery several times over the course of its decades in existence, had prayed in its chapel, seen Sr. Pascaline's slide presentation there, sat at the feet of Father Bede Griffiths there, and, many years later, toured those grounds with out-of-state visitors and friends. Until I began to write the history of the place, however, I had little knowledge of the magnitude of its ministry.

In the course of my research, the worldwide scope of this place's history emerged and a deep sense of gratitude took root in me — gratitude for the Osage Forest and the people who inspired it, built it, took care of it, lived and shared it, saved it and are now extending its ministry to a new generation. Gratitude, too, for having been given the privilege of telling this story. I've learned that a small place can be a force for enormous good in the world if it is called into existence by Spirit, as the Osage Forest surely has been.

The Spirit's call came first to a Congregation of Catholic nuns, the Benedictine Sisters of Perpetual Adoration, among them, Sister Pascaline Coff. To them, and to her, we who now enjoy the peace of the Forest owe a debt of gratitude. I am also personally indebted to the BSPA Sisters, and to Sr. Pascaline in particular, for so much of what is in this book. In interviews, photographs, documents she saved over the decades, her timelines, her articles, her speeches, her letters and emails, as well as the chronicle books she meticulously kept day-by-day, she and her BSPA Sisters provided me with the beating heart of the story and enough details to fill a shelf of books.

The Archivist at the BSPA monastery in Clyde, Missouri, Sr. Colleen McGrane was immensely helpful in providing me access to many of these documents, as was Sr. Pascaline herself. The Sisters welcomed me into their monasteries in Tucson and Clyde where I was able to hear the O+M story from Sr. Pascaline herself and even visit with Sr. Priscilla Trost before her death. During the editing process, the BSPA Congregation's Prioress General, Sr. Dawn Annette Mills, and BSPA Sr. Sarah Schwartzberg read through a draft, fact-checked my work and saved me from many mistakes. Whatever errors remain here are solely mine. I stand in awe of these remarkable women; this story points to the vital role the BSPA Congregation has played in the current resurgence of contemplative Christianity.

I am also deeply grateful to my lifelong friend Bob Doenges for the faith he showed in me by encouraging me to create this book, as well as for his willingness to share deeply about his own journey. My friend and business partner Paulette Millichap was, as is often the case, a catalyst for this project. It was she who first brought me to Osage Monastery Forest of Peace. I thank her for her encouraging

ACKNOWLEDGEMENTS

and guiding input on the manuscript and for helping to shepherd this project all along the way.

Many former Forest Dwellers at Osage generously shared their memories with me, including Don and Karen Chatfield, Fr. Brian Pierce, Sr. Maryann Greenwald, Sheila Lazier, Sr. Jane Comerford, Laurie Larson, and Fr. James Conner. The voices and perspectives of former Forest of Peace Trustees were also essential to this story, including Bob Doenges, John Douglas, JoAnn Huber, and Michaela Lawson. Archbishop emeritus Eusebius Beltran, Monsignor Gregory Gier and Fr. James McGlinchy were also generous with their time and their memories. They are examples of the deep truth the Osage Forest whispers to the world: We are all One Heart.

Judson Trapnell's study of Bede Griffiths and Sr. Mary Sheridan's 1999 interviews of Srs. Pascaline and Priscilla were invaluable sources. Fabrice Blée's book in English translation, *The Third Desert: The Story of Monastic Interreligious Dialogue*, was key to my understanding of the Catholic Church's inter-monastic dialogue movement. Greta Reed's inspirational memoir, *Sacred Enticement*, depicted life at Osage so eloquently that I begged to reprint passages here. I'm humbly grateful to both of these authors for permission to quote their writing.

Osage Forest of Peace oblates and Friends of the Forest were supportive friends to me as well; Barbara Schneeberg shared her memory about the Survivor Tree. I thank them all.

Support, encouragement and valuable input came from several others who read early drafts of the book in manuscript. Joli Jensen added her helpful suggestions. Input also came from readers Cheryl Dobbins, Sally Mahe, Christine Booth and Nona Charleston, and the women in my writers group, all of whom I greatly admire.

Carl Brune's elegant design and photo research were essential in completing and presenting the story told here. Photographer Mary Jane Matthews' beautiful work, that of Teresa Matyniak, Scott Thompson, John Douglas and Rosemary DeLucco Alpert display a love for this place that many can share.

My chief supporter—spiritually, emotionally, and materially—was for over 52 years my husband, Gene Dennison, who passed away two days after the passing of Sr. Pascaline. To her memory, and to his, I dedicate this book.

© MARY JANE MATTHEWS

© SCOTT THOMPSON

INTRODUCTION

"Things come together in the heart—at the center."
—Sister Pascaline Coff,
OSB, One+Heart

For over 40 years, the Osage Monastery Forest of Peace has welcomed hermits and holy men, Buddhist monks and nuns, Catholic bishops and Presbyterian ministers, addicts and angels, teenagers and octogenarians, Hindus, Muslims and atheists, tinkers and tailors and at least one Indian chief. They have come for retreats, services, and special programs. They have come to get help and to give help. They have come to hike or hang out or just to see the place.

Born out of Catholicism's post-Vatican II opening to the riches of other faiths and traditions as well as a desire among a Congregation of Benedictine Sisters for greater interiority, the Osage Monastery Forest of Peace became a centering place for spiritual seekers from around the world, people of many faiths, those seeking faith, or hoping to recover their faith. It was an investment in renewal, where a small handful of Benedictine Sisters of Perpetual Adoration lived out their vows of fidelity to God and each other through monastic holiness and obedience to the voice of God discerned in prayer, while building and operating a Center that became a centering place for the world.

The life there has been rich, aesthetically and intellectually as well as spiritually. The Sisters would learn about Christian meditation, but also about Buddhism, Hinduism, Native American cosmologies, Jungian archetypes and transpersonal psychology, all the while practicing the Liturgy of the Hours, celebrating the yearly round of Catholic feast days, personal birthdays and saints' days. They would welcome retreatants and they would cook, clean, plant, weave, sew, create art and pottery, teach, write, publish, build, and greet guests from all over the world, along with children from the neighborhood. Mondays were set aside as Forest Days, when Eucharist was celebrated in silence and then each spent the day in quiet prayer and contemplation.

On other days the screen door of the main house swung open and shut repeatedly with drop-in visitors, retreatants arriving and leaving, the Sisters coming in for chapel or for meals, preparing observances, cooking, and always welcoming visits from their Prioress General and Sisters from their monasteries in Clyde, Missouri; St. Louis; Kansas City; Tucson; and San Diego. In the earliest days, their Bishop Beltran of the Tulsa Diocese liked to drop by with prominent guests to show off the Monastery, while priests, monks, and Catholic Sisters of other orders came for celebrations and hermit days, spiritual direction and retreats. Taking care of all these visitors could have been a full-time job for a hotel staff, but Sr. Pascaline Coff and her four or five

INTRODUCTION

Sisters seemed to handle it with joy and grace, still having time for their own hermit days, their daily rounds of Catholic observances performed with Eastern fire, and the study of the scriptures of both East and West.

High school and university classes came *en Mass* to experience this strange phenomenon in the Osage woods outside Tulsa, Oklahoma — a Catholic monastic ashram. The word soon got out beyond the Catholic community and Protestant clergy and laity began showing up, looking for spiritual renewal in this interfaith retreat.

Each visitor seemed to bring a gift of some sort, from canned goods and pies to carpentry skills and spiritual teachings. Sister Pascaline, up at 5 AM to prepare for her day and the early-morning meditation gathering, would end each day near midnight, dutifully entering the events of that day — the comings and goings, activities, celebrations and dharma lessons — in the chronicle book. There is one for each of the Sisters' years at O+M.

From the first, there was a sense that something world-changing was happening here in this Forest of Peace. There was, and is, a sense of the numinous in the very peace of it, a Power that emanates from this Center, that somehow encompasses and transcends whatever ceremonies and theologies people bring here.

Here, one senses, is something essential, the still point of the Infinite at the Heart of all that is.

© MARY JANE MATTHEWS

© SCOTT THOMPSON

Beginnings
1976–1980

INDIA

1976 & 1977

The monastic dimension is one constituent which every human being has and must cultivate in one way or another.
—Father Raimundo Panikkar

An oxcart stacked with hay, pulled by a single white bullock, lumbers through the streets of Kulithalai in South India, along the banks of the meandering Kavery River. It is not yet dawn, and the streets are dark. Perched on the cart behind the wiry old Indian driver sit two middle-aged American nuns in loose-fitting white dresses.

The August day is already steamy, even before the summer sun rises. Sister Pascaline Coff, BSPA, feels the heat and is glad that she no longer has to wear the traditional habit of her Benedictine monastic order — black robe topped by a black veil layered over a white wimple. The BSPA stands for Benedictine Sisters of Perpetual Adoration. Her tall, red-headed companion, Sister Maurus Allen, is suddenly jostled against her shoulder by a hard sideways lurch of the oxcart, which now jerks to a stop.

The oxcart driver can be heard shouting, and as the two nuns twist around to see what is happening at the front of the cart, they see him raise his long whip and snap it over the head of the ox. The poor animal has collapsed in the road.

"Oh, great!" Sr. Maurus exclaims.

Now the driver jumps from the cart and lashes the flesh of the beast repeatedly with the whip.

"Stop that!" Sr. Maurus shouts at the driver. But the driver persists, cruelly pummeling the boney back of the white ox.

"Stop! Please, stop! You're going to kill the poor animal."

To Sr. Pascaline's horror, though not to her surprise, Sr. Maurus slides down off the oxcart and makes for the driver with his whip. "We will walk the rest of the way."

"No, Memsahib." The driver's tone is sharp, and his words are punctuated by another sharp crack of his whip. Standing in the cart, Sr. Pascaline can see red whelps rising on the poor animal's white rump.

"We can't walk," she tells Sr. Maurus. "We don't know the way."

But Sr. Maurus is around at the front now, arguing with the driver. "Just quit beating that poor animal and tell us the way to the ashram. We will walk."

Sr. Maurus seems oblivious to the fact that she is in a strange place on the far side of the earth from home, and the Indian cart driver is not afraid to use his whip. Her face blazing, she points to the fallen ox, the mass of flies now crawling on its neck and face.

"That ox isn't getting up," she shouts at the man. "It's dead."

But now, as if by some miracle, the white ox begins to rise, jerking the little cart sideways, so that Sr. Pascaline has to sit down quickly to avoid being thrown off. As the ox gets two front legs under its body, Sr. Maurus sprints back up onto the cart and somehow they are again underway.

The two nuns are Benedictine monastics, and they are indeed far from their respective motherhouses back in the United States of America. In this Year of Our Lord 1976, Sr. Pascaline, at age 49, has lived since age 22 in various cloisters of the Benedictine Sisters of Perpetual Adoration in the American Midwest, where she has spent several hours each day chanting the scriptures and observing the Holy Offices. Oddly enough, she and Sr. Maurus have come to India not in spite of their devotion to prayer, but because of it. India is known for its interiority, and they have come here to go within, to find the still center where the heart opens to the Infinite — to learn how to meditate.

Sr. Pascaline Coff was born January 20, 1927, in St. Louis, Missouri, and christened Margaret Mary ten days later. Margaret and Mary were the names of her two grandmothers, but Margaret Mary was also the name of a Catholic saint and mystic who in the seventeenth century had received a vision in which she was instructed to initiate the adoration of the Sacred Heart of Jesus. When Margaret Mary Coff was still an infant, her mother "carried me up to the Visitation Monastery on one of her mission nights and had me consecrated to the Sacred Heart."

Looking back on her Catholic upbringing and spiritual development, Sr. Pascaline would say of Saint Margaret Mary, "Oh, I loved her, and I certainly loved the Sacred Heart. I always went to the Sacred Heart statues in our school or wherever. We had one at home too. I loved Corpus Christi. My first Holy Communion was a real special day for me. From there on, I loved and was devoted to the Eucharist. I made visits, and wanted to be close to Jesus in the sacrament of His love, the sacrament of His body, which He left to us ... So I was delighted years later to find a community devoted to adoration, to the presence of Jesus in the Eucharist."

As a seventh grader Margaret Mary decided to attend Mass every morning during Lent. "Then when Easter came, it just didn't seem right to stop. It wasn't a penance, it was a gift, so I kept that up all through high school and all through college until the day I entered Clyde"—the Monastery of the Benedictine Sisters of Perpetual Adoration in Clyde, Missouri.

This didn't happen until Margaret Mary had celebrated Mass daily for almost a decade. The knowledge of her vocation as a nun came at age 18, when she was about

to graduate high school at Ursuline Academy in St. Louis. Along with three other senior girls, she made a private retreat. Kneeling on an improvised prie-dieu before a monstrance that the girls had set up on the coffee table in their retreat apartment, she felt the now-familiar sense of peace settle over her. Soon, she knew, the weekend would be over and it would be time to get back on the streetcar and return home to the Coff family. A lifetime later she would say of this retreat, simply, "I never wanted to leave."

Certainly, there was love in her home as well, with a family of boisterous, teasing older brothers and older and younger sisters. With six children, the Coffs' house was bursting at the seams with love and life, but offered little peace. Her father was a red-headed Irish real estate man and her mother, the daughter of German immigrants, kept the large household running. Both were talented, sensitive people who had had to give up educational opportunities to take care of the day-to-day needs of their large family.

Margaret Mary was an outstanding student and eligible for a scholarship to enter college in the fall. But here was something better than any book knowledge — this love of God infusing her directly from the heart of Jesus, His body, His blood. She remembered the Corpus Christi celebrations of her girlhood when, clothed in her white First Communion dress, she led the procession through the streets and into the church, strewing rose petals before the monstrance enshrining the Host — the love of God incarnate in the sacrificed body of His Son. Above all else, she wanted to study this love. College would not teach it to her. Family life would only distract her from it. This contemplation, this adoration was the only way to know the Sacred Heart better, and life as a Benedictine nun would be centered on this very thing.

MARGARET MARY WITH HER BROTHERS.

FONTBONNE COLLEGE GRADUATION IN 1948 WITH MOTHER BERNICE.

She spoke to the priest and nuns about her vocation; they encouraged her, but sent her home to discuss the matter with her parents. Her mother, far from encouraging, burst into tears at the thought of her academically bright daughter locked away in a cloister. "What about college? The nuns won't give you a scholarship."

"Wait five years," her father advised. "See some of the world before you lock yourself away from it for the rest of your life."

How ironic it is, thinks the middle-aged Sr. Pascaline Coff, OSB, PhD, as she sits jostling on the bullock cart through the streets of this village in India. To please her parents, she did wait, took the scholarship and graduated college. But it was the Benedictines who sent her through graduate school at St. Mary's at Notre Dame, one of the first women to be awarded a doctorate in theology from that famous university. She did wait the five years, but didn't see much of the world in that time. She's certainly seen it now! She and Sr. Maurus have just spent the past night on the train across India, sitting up on a wooden plank that swung from a rusty chain in the jostling boxcar that passed for a sleeping car.

Now, with the strange sounds and smells of the South Indian morning rising up around her with the gathering light, Sr. Pascaline smiles to herself as she sends up a prayer for the life and health of the white ox. St. Louis to Bangalore to Kulithalai. ... She has seen more of the world in the past month than her dad saw in his lifetime. And now Shantivanam, the Forest of Peace, will be home for the next eleven months. Fresh from six years as Prioress General of her Congregation in the United States, and then Prioress in Kansas City, she has traded her Benedictine Sisters' monastery for a South Indian ashram, still seeking that deeper love that called her as a girl in St. Louis — a fuller communion with the Sacred Heart of the divine.

FR. BEDE GRIFFITHS

When Sister Pascaline and Sister Maurus arrived at the gate of the Shantivanam Ashram, a man greeted them. He wore the saffron robe of the Hindu sannyasi renunciant, though he was, like them, a Roman Catholic Benedictine monastic. He was Father Bede Griffiths, OSB, an Englishman, and in the predawn grey he greeted the two American nuns in the cultured accent of an Oxford don. His greeting was warm and welcoming, and Sister Pascaline felt instantly that here was a kindred spirit.

Indeed, Father Bede had important things in common with Sr. Pascaline. He had come to India for much the same reasons when he was about the same age, after having served his Benedictine Congregation in several of the same capacities as she had, including novice director and prior. He had become a Benedictine monk in order to live a life of contemplative prayer, then had been assigned to a role that involved him in many administrative duties and personnel problems. Wrote Sr. Pascaline later:

> I delighted to find in his autobiography, his own initial confusion about monastic life being a "contemplative life." On the contrary, he experienced, like all of us, the atmosphere of incessant activity, the whole day being taken up in a constant round of duties, in the choir, in the house, in the garden, workshops, etc., which left little time for leisure, the leisure of contemplation.

Bede felt called to India for its interiority — the ashram, the ancient practice of meditation — but it was only when he moved to Shantivanam, Saccidananda Ashram, in Tamil Nadu that Bede found his Christian faith enriched by the Eastern forms of worship and prayer.

Now almost 70, Father Bede's heartfelt greeting to the two Benedictine Sisters at the gate was at least in part due to his need for a monastic community. Sr. Pascaline had never seen Father Bede before, but had seen his picture in the newsletter of her BSPA congregation. It was a small picture of the monk celebrating a tea ceremony in his ashram, but it had been enough to capture her interest and set her on the path to his gate.

An article written by Bede Griffiths accompanied the photograph, explaining:

> The aim of the ashram from the first was to establish a form of contemplative life based alike on the traditions of Christian monasticism and Hindu sannyasa. It is a way of life based on the Rule of St. Benedict and the monastic tradition of the Eastern Fathers of the Church. Hindu doctrine and methods of prayer and meditation are studied as well. In this way the monks hope to enrich their life with the treasure of Hindu doctrine and spirituality to assist in the meeting

between these two great religious traditions at the deepest level of prayer and contemplation.

A Christian ashram must be a place of genuine prayer and contemplation where the search for God takes precedence over everything else.

Sr. Pascaline had read the writings of the Trappist Monk Thomas Merton of the Abbey of Gethsemani in Kentucky, and shared many of his teachings with novices when she was Novice Mistress of her BSPA congregation and Postulant Director in St. Louis in the 1960s. She first became aware of the inter-monastic movement when she heard of Merton's accidental death on December 10, 1968, while he was attending an interfaith conference between Catholic and non-Christian monks in suburban Bangkok, Thailand. Merton, whose work and focus on international peace she admired so much, had been on a tour of the East, exploring Hindu and Buddhist contemplative practices.

THOMAS MERTON

In 1968, Sr. Pascaline had been elected by her Sisters to be Prioress General of the BSPA Congregation. During her six-year term, "six of the most difficult years for all [Catholic] religious," she "was called … by other Benedictines to be chairperson of the American prioresses."[1] These were challenging years in monasteries because Vatican II had called upon them to reexamine all their time-honored traditions, to reinvigorate the monastic experience. "Beginnings were slow and difficult because many sisters required more preparation for change," Sr. Pascaline would write a decade later. "The pyramid-shaped structure, in which only a few were trained and thought capable, gradually gave way as the gifts and potentials of each individual were made available for the good of the Church and community."

As Prioress General, Sr. Pascaline was an agent of such changes for which many BSPAs were not prepared, so she should not have been surprised when the BSPAs elected someone else Prioress General in 1974. "In 1974, the chapter of elections was a very emptying experience for me. Actual lightning and thunder during the evening confirmed the storm I was feeling. The emptying was from so many angles at one time that I felt it had to be from the Lord himself."

When Sr. Pascaline, now no longer Prioress General, found the article by Father Bede in her BSPA congregation's publication, she immediately wrote to Father Bede, asking three questions:

"Do you take women? Is it possible to come for a year? How much will it cost?"

---

1 She served as president of the Association of American Benedictine Prioresses in 1972-3 and traveled to Europe with Sr. Joan Chittister to represent American Benedictine sisters as "observers" at the 1973 Congress of Abbots.

Fr. Bede's answer to the first two was a warm, welcoming "yes." There was no charge, he said. A dollar a day would be okay.

In 1975, about the time Fr. Bede's letter arrived, Sister Maurus Allen from Sacred Heart Convent in Cullman, Alabama, came to teach yoga to the Sisters at the Kansas City BSPA monastery where Sr. Pascaline was now Prioress. During that visit, Sr. Pascaline would later recall that she and Sr. Maurus were sitting and talking outside on the steps. "She said she was so despondent with monastic life. She said, 'It just isn't going anywhere.' I said, 'Well, I haven't told anybody this, but I wrote to Bede Griffiths in South India, and he said, yes, I could come.' She got so excited, and she wanted to know if I would write and ask if she could come. So I did, and he said, yes."

SISTER MAURUS ALLEN

Sr. Pascaline asked her superior if it would be possible for her to go to India for a year. The superior told her it would help her cause if the Abbot Primate were on board. She wrote the Abbot Primate to inquire about Father Bede and was warned against this monk. "He said he would not recommend it at all, because Father Bede was in trouble with the bishop, with the clergy, and with his community."

Fr. Bede's problem with his bishop in India was that the bishop "had this big thing about foreigners" coming to India and adopting Hindu-style monasticism. Catholicism in India needed to be made more Indian in custom and form, while still conveying the heart of the Christian faith, apart from its European trappings. But when Fr. Bede invited the bishop to an event at Shantivanam Ashram, the bishop sent Fr. Bede's emissary away angrily. "The bishop hit his fist on the table, and he said, 'Indianization must come to India, but only by sons of the soil.'"

Many Westerners had a problem with Fr. Bede because he was an outspoken proponent of dialogue with Eastern religions, and that didn't sit well with some in the Church. Wrote Judson B. Trapnell in the *The American Benedictine Review*, "Bede Griffiths as a Culture Bearer":

> In the midst of a time of profound change in the Church, it was perhaps inevitable that groups attempting to respond to the call of Vatican II and new interreligious realities would be misunderstood and criticized by those who were resisting such a call. Over the years, Griffiths and Shantivanam were indeed the focus of sharp criticism.[2]

---

2 Judson Trapnell, "Bede Griffiths as a Culture Bearer: An Exploration of the Relationship Between Spiritual Transformation and Cultural Change," The American Benedictine Review, 47:3 (Sept. 1996): 272.

By the time Sr. Pascaline received this discouraging letter from the Primate General, she had already asked for and received permission to leave her post as the Kansas City Prioress and go to India. "Then I got this letter back from the Abbot Primate, and he said he would not recommend it at all. He didn't say what he would recommend. I was really disappointed. I sent a copy of that [letter] to Sr. Maurus."

Sr. Maurus Allen, five or six years older than Sr. Pascaline, was not to be dissuaded. She challenged Sr. Pascaline, who was now almost 50, in words Sr Pascaline would always remember: "Are we going to let men run our lives forever?"

"I said, 'No.' She said, 'Why don't we go over and find out for ourselves?' I put that letter from the Abbot Primate in the files somewhere. Nobody but me has ever seen it."

And she and Sr. Maurus went to India.

"We left the USA in early June [1976], headed by plane for Bangalore, the garden spot of India, having been advised it would be easier weather-wise to spend our first month with the Benedictine Sisters at Shanti Niyalam," Sr. Pascaline recalled. Fr. Bede had also begun his Indian life in Bangalore, 21 years earlier. He found this garden spot too westernized to give him the longed-for immersion in Eastern meditation.

Sr. Pascaline would later write: "In June 1976, Sister Maurus Allen and I were hosted on our arrival in India by six young Indian Benedictine women who had just returned from eight years in England where they were totally westernized from their garb to their Gregorian chant."

Once they set out on the train from Bangalore to Kulithalai in South India, however, the American nuns began to see what it was like to leave Western conveniences behind. They had booked a berth in a sleeping car for the overnight railway journey. Instead of the beds that one might expect in the Pullman cars in the USA, the sleeping car in South India provided two narrow wooden planks, one above the other, swinging from rusty chains. Afraid to use the top "bunk" for fear the chain wouldn't hold, Sr. Pascaline and Sr. Maurus sat up all night on the lower board as the train swayed and lurched southward from India's "garden spot" in Bangalore to the town of Kulithalai in the state of Tamil Nadu on the banks of the Kavery River.

Staggering off the train in the predawn darkness, they were immediately faced with the question of how to get themselves and their bags from the station in Kulithalai the three kilometers east to the Christian ashram in the little village of Tannirpalli. No worries. Suddenly, out of the darkness emerged a pack of Indian men, shouting and vying for the chance to transport the travelers. The nuns chose one driver more or less at random after he grabbed their bags, and followed him to his conveyance, a cart pulled by a white bullock.

Now, after the long train ride and the frightening experience on the bullock cart, Fr. Bede Griffiths' bearded, welcoming face at the gate was a heartening sight.

SHANTIVANAM

Said Sr. Pascaline, warmly remembering her first meeting with Bede that day, "When we finally got to the monastic ashram, here was Father Bede waiting for us with a smile."

Sister Pascaline's year with Father Bede Griffiths in India would be the pivotal moment in her life, and in a way, it would be pivotal in Catholicism. It led directly to the establishment of the Osage Monastery, an inter-spiritual ashram in America, a unique center for inter-monastic dialogue and practice.

Thirty-five years later, Father Brian Pierce, a Dominican monk, would say, "Thomas Merton's Gethsemani monastery in Kentucky was a very important signpost. After that, Osage Monastery was next in importance. These were the two lights of true interreligious dialogue in the USA. They touched thousands of people; their influence has lasted many, many years."

Resting on a table by the front door of the Osage Monastery for many years were copies of the "Declaration on the Relation of the Church with Non-Christian Religions" from Vatican II, *Nostra Aetate,* which says in part:

> The Catholic Church rejects nothing that is true and holy in these religions. She regards with sincere reverence those ways of conduct and of life, those precepts and teachings which, though differing in many aspects from the ones she holds and sets forth, nonetheless often reflect a ray of that Truth which enlightens all men.

Like Shantivanam, the Osage Monastery would actualize in daily practice Catholicism's post-Vatican II opening to the riches of other faiths. Established and built for this purpose by the Benedictine Sisters of Perpetual Adoration under Sr. Pascaline Coff's leadership, this monastic ashram, tucked back in a crosstimber forest in Osage County, Oklahoma, embodies in wood and stone the very heart of interspiritual monasticism.

Another Vatican II document had much to do with the founding of the Osage Monastery. That document is Perfectae Caritatis, in which the bishops addressed "the life and discipline" of Catholic religious orders. This one document, which encouraged efforts at renewal among monastics, would have a profound effect on religious orders throughout Catholicism.

The spirit of Vatican II was one of openness — a new openness to different ways of doing things — and the founding of the Osage Monastery would be part of this.

For years before Sr. Pascaline's sojourn at the ashram in India, she and her Sisters had been discussing new possibilities for their congregation. What did they have to offer young people who were longing for a life with purpose and meaning? And, when those who came and entered the monasteries later left, what was it they had failed to find? In 1971, while Sr. Pascaline was Prioress General, the BSPAs had initiated an in-depth study for "Sisters desiring experimental forms of living."

"We were talking about smaller groups as a way to simplify. We started a little newsletter before I left to go to India to see if our Sisters were interested in a smaller community."

Sr. Helen Mercer edited the newsletter, "Hello Out There," which went out to the entire BSPA congregation. In it, a questionnaire asked for feedback about the Sisters' hopes and aspirations for the future of the BSPA. In 1973, during Sr. Pascaline's time as Prioress General, the Prioresses Council began active investigation into what might be the "future thrust" of the Congregation, to coordinate the findings of the questionnaire. Srs. M. Dolores and Helen were appointed to write up the results. As Sr. Pascaline recalled decades later:

> We had a good 22 Sisters on the list who were interested in small group living. We asked, "What do you mean by simple living?" "What do you mean by small group?" "What do you mean by poverty?" People had opinions across the board, but there were certain concepts that could be identified.

Later that year, the Clyde Guesthouse was used for an experiment in small group living. Small support groups were also set up at Clyde. Then, in the spring of 1974, while Sr. Pascaline was still Prioress General, a small group lived together in Payson, Arizona, for what was to be a five-month experiment that ended in disharmony after three months. Decades later, Sr. Pascaline would say of that experiment:

> I wanted so much to select the people. But the Council pushed to select all those who asked. It was a disaster in communicatons [and] interpersonal relations. And

Sr. Helen had not had any training as far as leadership. A couple of people were older than she. Sr. Helen is very laid back. She'll do something herself rather than ask somebody to do it.[3]

The inability of a handful of BSPA Sisters to live together happily for even a few months would bolster those within the congregation who were reluctant to fund such a permanent living arrangement in the future. Sr. Pascaline remained committed to the idea, however. She would later say of the experiment: "I had to go out [to Payson] and help bring it to a happy — I don't know how happy it was — close. I kept trying to tell Sister Helen and the others, 'This is a good first step. It's not a disaster, it's a learning.'"

And so it would prove to be. The later success of the O+M community would come as a result of the BSPAs having learned from the Payson experiment. For instance, they would require a careful discernment process before individual Sisters would be chosen to live at Osage. Also, the little community would invest significant time and energy in group-building and in learning communication skills.

In 1975, however, the whole idea of such a departure from the large convent norm remained controversial. Sr. Pascaline, no longer Prioress General, was appointed to study small monastic lifestyles among Benedictine congregations that might have been tried in the decade since Vatican II. Father Jim Conner, a Trappist monk and Thomas Merton's former assistant at Gethsemani in Kentucky, also had a keen interest in small monastic communities. He recalls meeting Sr. Pascaline when he was living at the little Benedictine monastery, Christ in the Desert in New Mexico. She and Sr. Maureen visited and told him that "she was hoping to establish some kind of a small, simple monastic community very similar to what we were doing at Christ in the Desert."

The BSPA Prioresses Council meeting in February 1976 heard reports and recommended more research, but tabled any action until a new infirmary wing could be completed in the St. Louis house and the priory at Mundalein closed.

By then, Sr. Pascaline was making preparations to go to India to learn what she could from Eastern sources. "And I certainly was not disappointed."

Shativanam was also known as Saccidananda Ashram of the Most Holy Trinity.

"*Sac* is Being, *cid* is Consciousness, *ananda* is Bliss," Sister explained.

Located in the village of Tannirpalli, Tamil Nadu, India, it had been founded in 1950 by two European monks, Abhishiktananda (Father Henri le Saux), OSB and Father Jules Monchanin. Bede Griffiths had moved there from a more Westernized monastery in India in 1968, after Monchanin had died and Abhishiktananda moved to a hermitage in the Himalayas. Some five or six young native Christians formed community with Father Bede.

---

3   Sr. Mary Sheridan recorded extensive interviews with Sr. Pascaline and Sr. Priscilla at O+M in 1999. Transcripts of these are held in the BSPA archive, Clyde, Missouri.

When the two nuns arrived at Shantivanam, "there were four of us Benedictines who had come from afar: Father Bernadino, a Camaldolese Benedictine from Italy, Father Vincent Cooper from Ealing Abbey in England, and Sister Maurus and I, two nuns from America." In addition to these four that made up Bede's Benedictine community, spiritual seekers would visit Shantivanam for a few days or weeks at a time.

After greeting them at the gate, Father Bede showed Sisters Pascaline and Maurus to their huts, separate rooms arranged side-by-side, each with a cot and a place to hang clothes. Sr. Pascaline set her bag on the cot and followed Father Bede to Eucharist and breakfast.

"At breakfast he rose up in the dining hall and poured his curds on our plates. All were sitting on straw mats. After breakfast he told Sr. Maurus and me to 'come along' to the porch of his hut where he asked us questions about America and told us much about what was happening there at the ashram."

When Sr. Pascaline returned later to her room, the bag that she had left there was full of holes. "Rats," Father Bede told her, and he "accompanied me in discovering the situation and graciously offered to move me to another of the guest cabins, built more like motel rooms all hitched together but open at the tops from one room to the next. So the little beasts had free run from one to the next, sniffing at whatever was intriguing enough for them to descend and investigate." After this, Sr. Pascaline kept a flashlight to ward off rats and also bats that roosted inside the open thatched-roofed hut, flying in and out at night.

Sister Pascaline would later write:

[We] listened to the sacred Scriptures of both East and West in Father Bede's liturgies, incorporating the rich symbolism of the East into the Western tradition. … Under the picturesque coconut trees next to the Kavery, Father Bede gave daily sharings to the ashramites on the Upanishads, and Gita, and Christian Contemplation.

Father Bede's wisdom and great love for the Scriptures, both East and West, shed tremendous light on the Word for all of us. He gave homilies daily, during Eucharist and at Vespers, on the Epistle and Gospel for the day. He radiated a deep joy whenever he opened the scriptures for others. He honed in immediately to the mystical meaning beneath the Word. Each afternoon from 4 until 5 PM, Father Bede expounded on the Upanishads and/or the Bhagavad Gita … over the course of the year.

We always had the ancient Eastern Fire blessing, the Arati (with camphor) and then kumkum was passed so each could dip into the dish and make the third eye on their forehead: yellow to welcome the Bridegroom at Mass; red at noon.

One of the first things Sr. Pascaline learned was that the third eye was the "inner eye which sees beyond the outer externals."

At night he would [offer] ashes with talcum powder in the ash. The symbolism was so rich. "Remember, O man, that thou art dust, and unto dust thou shalt return," like what we have on Ash Wednesday. But this was every night. You just took it yourself and put it on, making the sign of the cross.[4]

She later described a typical day:

They would ring a bell; we were sleeping under a mosquito net. We would rise about 5:15, wash, and go to the temple, which was open. It didn't have any windows or screens. They would light candles and sing bhajans, like Krista jaajaya. They would sing that over and over for about 10 minutes. At the end of that, you could either stay there, or go down to the riverbank, or go back under your mosquito net. And the mosquitoes were bad, because there was the Kavery River very close by. And then after an hour, it was time for Eucharist and the bell would ring again. And every day Father Bede would give a homily on the Gospel during Mass.

So after Mass, we would all go to the refectory. In the East, they have water outside, before you go in. So you'd wash your hands, and then go into the refectory and sit on the floor. We each got a little metal pan, no spoon. Sr. Maurus used to always get up and go out to the kitchen. She'd say, "No lady should eat with her hands," so she'd bring out spoons for me and for her. That was for the first while; she finally got used to it.

We'd [prepare] vegetables, help cut up things, and wash things, right after breakfast. Then we'd be free until noon prayers. Sometimes we'd go into town to buy oranges, or a bucket to wash your clothes in, something like that. In the afternoon it was very, very warm, and people could take a siesta. We had like motel rooms, linked onto one another. Outdoor toilet, outhouse, and the showers were common at the corner. There were spider webs inside.

At about three o'clock we'd have tea. At noon, he handed out the mail, then at teatime, anything anybody would bring by way of food or cookies or fruit or something would be considered Prasad, like they do in the temples. They brought it to the head person to be blessed and it was put out in the middle of the table, available for everybody. They'd cut up an apple in about 16 pieces. It was interesting. There was also a big vat of boiled water so you could fill up your own little bottles daily.

For an hour every afternoon, he would teach us from the Bhagavad Gita or the Upanishads, bringing Christian light on the Eastern Scriptures. In the afternoon at Vespers, he would give a homily on the Epistle.[5]

---

4   Sr. Pascaline Coff, "Bede Griffiths — Icon of Integrity," (May 13, 1994): 1
5   Sheridan interview.

For the next nine months, the nuns would spend all their time at this monastic ashram, with occasional outings to parish conferences or nearby villages. Recalled Sr. Pascaline: "Several times, we, Father's community, accompanied him to the Catholic seminary at Trichi or to the Benedictine monastery in Bangalore where Father Subash Anand and others shared the riches of the East."

Bede's afternoon talks under the palm trees, his ashramites sitting around him in a circle on mats, "were very helpful for those of us wanting an understanding from an Eastern point of view. The West had become more materialistic and secular. He spoke on transformation and transcendence, quoting both Christian scriptures and Indian. At the time, in much of Western Christianity, anything Eastern was suspicious."

Bede used the Gayatri mantra, a hymn from the Rigveda, to invoke Christ's presence: "Let us meditate on your glorious splendor, O Divine Giver of Life ... May you illuminate our meditation.[6]"

He performed the Arati fire ceremony, waving a flame around the blessed sacrament. He added a Hindu flower ritual during Eucharist.

For Sr. Pascaline, the Hindu scriptures became accretions that "gathered like incense around the Host."

The experience of living in Bede's ashram, being part of this small group of contemplatives immersed in India's culture of interiority, changed Sister Pascaline's spiritual life and deepened it. "Father Bede was a great teacher by example of his humble loving presence. He radiated the Lord. Contemplation was the basic dynamism of his life and he believed it was meant to be the aim of all human life. He knew how to go beyond silence to stillness of heart where silence bursts into flame."[7]

Bede was continuing to write and publish during those years, and both he and his publications were celebrated by the ashramites and villagers around him. Sr. Pascaline would recall that when the first copies of Bede's book *Return to the Center* arrived, its publication came just in time for Bede's 70th birthday celebration:

> Thomas, the guest master, made a lovely design on the temple floor of seven petals, one for each decade of Father's life, then placed small boats on four of the petals in honor of the years since Father's ordination. In the center was Bede Griffiths' newly released volume *Return to the Center*. Village girls came and filled small oil lamps so that the entire temple was aglow.
>
> The birthday celebration was beyond any I had ever experienced. Drummers began at 5:30 AM in the temple as Father Bede himself was being accompanied down to the bank of the Kavery River for a special Indian puja (ritual), during which his feet were washed and he was incensed and garlanded. He was truly loved, not only by those within the ashram but by many Harwijan villagers who came to do him homage. He often went to their villages on Hindu feast days.

---

6   Bede Griffiths, *The Marriage of East and West* (Tucson, AZ: Medio Media, 1977): 53.

7   Sr. Pascaline Coff, "Bede Griffiths, The Man, the Monk, and the Mystic."

Bede accepted the gifts of the villagers in the spirit of love with which they were given, just as they recognized that Bede, though English and Christian, was also sannyasi in the best Indian tradition, a renunciate, living in radical simplicity, but fully dedicated to embodying the divine love of the Holy One for each villager. Years later Sr. Pascaline would write:

> We all had the blessing of experiencing Father Bede living sannyasa as he taught the Upanishads and the Gita passages that touched on sannyasa.
>
> The Presence, the witness, the life of the Indian monastic, the sannyasi is more needed in our world than ever … The human race needs those among us who are willing and happy to live the mystery of the sacred with the greatest possible interiority, in that infinite space within the heart.[8]

Although she returned from India when the year was up and, unlike Father Bede, didn't wear the saffron robe of the sannyasi, Sister Pascaline carried the communion of East and West within her heart, and then with her sisters at the Osage Monastery Forest of Peace. They would provide a welcoming presence, listening heart, and spirit of joyful thanksgiving for all who came to experience its atmosphere of peace, contemplative meditation and prayer.

---

8   Sr. Pascaline Coff, "Reflections of My Experience of Sannyasa and Its Contemporary Relevance," in Ashrama Aikiya Newsletter, no. 31 (April 1996) 15–16.

SR. PASCALINE COFF, OSB

BSPA MONASTERIES
1977 & 1978

I humbly ask permission to initiate a small community with a simplified monastic style of life, somewhere apart from our present structures and grounds . . .

—Sister Pascaline Coff,
Letter to the BSPAs, 1977

As Sister Pascaline's planned year in India neared its end, she felt reluctant to leave, but, after prayer and discernment, realized that taking a second year would be unfair to her BSPA Sisters. She and Sister Maurus began planning their journey home, making several stops along the way.

The first stop was Calcutta to visit Mother Theresa who was in a private retreat at a convent where Srs. Pascaline and Maurus also stayed. "She graciously appeared at our door soon after we arrived," Sr. Pascaline recalled. "She was delighted and delightful. After introductions we explained our plan to return to the States as our year was ending and we asked her to write something for us to carry 'home.' She very graciously opened a drawer in the room where we were, pulled out two holy cards with some words of Cardinal Goodier, and wrote a tiny message for each."

Srs. Pascaline and Maurus's trip home took them to Israel and Mt. Sinai before they returned to the United States.

They landed in New York on June 14, 1977. Coming off the airplane, Sr. Pascaline waited patiently at the baggage claim rack for her suitcase. And waited ... and waited. It never arrived.

Years later, she would be well-known for telling those who came to her for spiritual guidance, "Pray for surprises." Now, fresh from her year experiencing the spiritual treasure of sannyasi poverty, it was a shock to find herself suddenly divested of her one rat-chewed brown cloth bag and all its contents.

She and Sr. Maurus turned from the empty luggage rack and began looking frantically around at the crowded baggage claim lobby and the mass of people coming down the corridor from the gates. Everything was in that bag, including her treasured note from Mother Theresa!

Suddenly, there was another surprise. As they searched the airport looking for someone who might be carrying the brown bag, "our eyes rested on Mother Theresa herself, coming down the runway carrying only one small see-thru plastic bag and smiling at all the attendants and eventually at the two of us! We smiled and waved as crowds kept moving."

The suitcase was never found, and Sr. Pascaline returned home to Kansas City with nothing but the clothes on her back. Meanwhile the contents of the bag were discovered in a wastebasket in the men's room of an airport in another part of the country. The man who found them realized that they must belong to a religious sister, "so they were given to a priest going to Tulsa, Oklahoma, who agreed to contact the owner," Sr. Pascaline recalled. "The airline reimbursed for the suitcase and all was well."

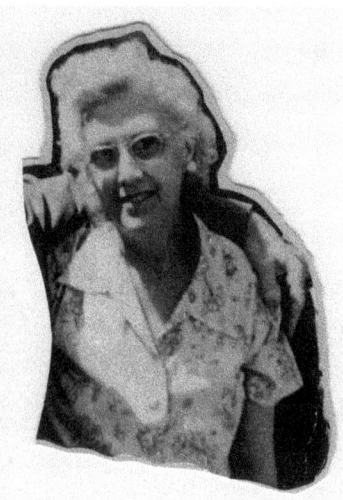

AGNES NEWSHOM COFF

Sr. Pascaline was met at the Kansas City airport by her Prioress General, Mother Audrey, who had another surprise for her.

She said that the AID Intermonasteries wanted to have somebody to do secretarial work for them in the United States. They were also starting a "working group" for East-West dialogue. Because I had been in India, they wanted me to go in the car [to St. Louis] with M. Audrey the next morning. I had been on the plane many hours, and my bag had been stolen! But if I would go back to St. Louis in the car, this monk from France would be there, and he would explain to me what they wanted. I did not go.

Arriving back at the BSPA house in Kansas City, "on 'holy hill' at the turn in Paseo Avenue above 'The Landing,'" Sr. Pascaline had yet another surprise waiting; her 81-year-old mother, now widowed and living in a Catholic rest home in St. Louis, had fallen and broken her hip. A few days later, Sr. Pascaline's mother, Agnes Newsham Coff, died.

Sr. Pascaline, in a 1999 interview with Mary Sheridan, remembered how she had refused to go back to St. Louis with Mother Audrey. "If I had gone, I would have been there when my mother died."

"I always ran to my mother," Sr. Pascaline would later recall. Her mother had been the one to lay the cornerstone for Sister Pascaline's devotion to God. "She taught us to love God with our whole heart, mind, soul, and strength. By the time I started first grade, I already knew to bow my head at the name of Jesus."

After Margaret Mary had graduated from Fontebonne University and worked in the publicity department at Webster College for a year, she still felt the call to the convent, and her mother joined in making the decision as to which religious order Margaret Mary might enter. In guiding her daughter's choice, Agnes consulted Father George Gottwald, who was a close family friend. He was the "priest who came for supper every Sunday night," Sr. Pascaline recalled, "a great friend of the family who later became a St. Louis Bishop."

Father Gottwald received the magazine *Spirit & Life,* published regularly by the

BSPA MONASTERIES
1977 & 1978

I humbly ask permission to initiate a small community with a simplified monastic style of life, somewhere apart from our present structures and grounds . . .

—Sister Pascaline Coff,
Letter to the BSPAs, 1977

As Sister Pascaline's planned year in India neared its end, she felt reluctant to leave, but, after prayer and discernment, realized that taking a second year would be unfair to her BSPA Sisters. She and Sister Maurus began planning their journey home, making several stops along the way.

The first stop was Calcutta to visit Mother Theresa who was in a private retreat at a convent where Srs. Pascaline and Maurus also stayed. "She graciously appeared at our door soon after we arrived," Sr. Pascaline recalled. "She was delighted and delightful. After introductions we explained our plan to return to the States as our year was ending and we asked her to write something for us to carry 'home.' She very graciously opened a drawer in the room where we were, pulled out two holy cards with some words of Cardinal Goodier, and wrote a tiny message for each."

Srs. Pascaline and Maurus's trip home took them to Israel and Mt. Sinai before they returned to the United States.

They landed in New York on June 14, 1977. Coming off the airplane, Sr. Pascaline waited patiently at the baggage claim rack for her suitcase. And waited ... and waited. It never arrived.

Years later, she would be well-known for telling those who came to her for spiritual guidance, "Pray for surprises." Now, fresh from her year experiencing the spiritual treasure of sannyasi poverty, it was a shock to find herself suddenly divested of her one rat-chewed brown cloth bag and all its contents.

She and Sr. Maurus turned from the empty luggage rack and began looking frantically around at the crowded baggage claim lobby and the mass of people coming down the corridor from the gates. Everything was in that bag, including her treasured note from Mother Theresa!

Suddenly, there was another surprise. As they searched the airport looking for someone who might be carrying the brown bag, "our eyes rested on Mother Theresa herself, coming down the runway carrying only one small see-thru plastic bag and smiling at all the attendants and eventually at the two of us! We smiled and waved as crowds kept moving."

The suitcase was never found, and Sr. Pascaline returned home to Kansas City with nothing but the clothes on her back. Meanwhile the contents of the bag were discovered in a wastebasket in the men's room of an airport in another part of the country. The man who found them realized that they must belong to a religious sister, "so they were given to a priest going to Tulsa, Oklahoma, who agreed to contact the owner," Sr. Pascaline recalled. "The airline reimbursed for the suitcase and all was well."

Sr. Pascaline was met at the Kansas City airport by her Prioress General, Mother Audrey, who had another surprise for her.

She said that the AID Intermonasteries wanted to have somebody to do secretarial work for them in the United States. They were also starting a "working group" for East-West dialogue. Because I had been in India, they wanted me to go in the car [to St. Louis] with M. Audrey the next morning. I had been on the plane many hours, and my bag had been stolen! But if I would go back to St. Louis in the car, this monk from France would be there, and he would explain to me what they wanted. I did not go.

AGNES NEWSHOM COFF

Arriving back at the BSPA house in Kansas City, "on 'holy hill' at the turn in Paseo Avenue above 'The Landing,'" Sr. Pascaline had yet another surprise waiting; her 81-year-old mother, now widowed and living in a Catholic rest home in St. Louis, had fallen and broken her hip. A few days later, Sr. Pascaline's mother, Agnes Newsham Coff, died.

Sr. Pascaline, in a 1999 interview with Mary Sheridan, remembered how she had refused to go back to St. Louis with Mother Audrey. "If I had gone, I would have been there when my mother died."

"I always ran to my mother," Sr. Pascaline would later recall. Her mother had been the one to lay the cornerstone for Sister Pascaline's devotion to God. "She taught us to love God with our whole heart, mind, soul, and strength. By the time I started first grade, I already knew to bow my head at the name of Jesus."

After Margaret Mary had graduated from Fontebonne University and worked in the publicity department at Webster College for a year, she still felt the call to the convent, and her mother joined in making the decision as to which religious order Margaret Mary might enter. In guiding her daughter's choice, Agnes consulted Father George Gottwald, who was a close family friend. He was the "priest who came for supper every Sunday night," Sr. Pascaline recalled, "a great friend of the family who later became a St. Louis Bishop."

Father Gottwald received the magazine *Spirit & Life*, published regularly by the

MONASTERY OF THE THE BENEDICTINE SISTERS OF PERPETUAL ADORATION IN CLYDE, MISSOURI.

BSPAs at their monastery in Clyde, Missouri, about 350 miles from St. Louis in the northwest corner of the state. It was he who suggested this option to Margaret Mary and her mother. They sent for a booklet from the BSPAs and liked what they saw. "I wrote to them," Sr. Pascaline recalled. "They were gracious. They wrote back asking how soon could I come and enter."

Margaret Mary was ready to enter the convent at Clyde immediately, but they wouldn't be able to take her until early June, several weeks away. Meanwhile, a neighbor, on hearing that Agnes' daughter was joining the BSPAs, phoned Agnes. "At least you should go look at the place first. Would you let your daughter marry a man you'd never met?"

"We got Father Gottwald to drive us up to Clyde, and I loved it."

Now, in June, 1977, it was Bishop Gottwald who offered the funeral Mass for Sr. Pascaline's mother, just a week after Sr. Pascaline's return from a year in India.

Sr. Pascaline had lost her father, Ed Coff, fourteen years earlier, in 1963, the same year both Pope John XXIII and President John F. Kennedy died. If her mother had been the one she ran to, her red-headed Irish dad, who sold real estate for a living and wrote poetry for fun, had been the man dearest to her heart. Together they had been Margaret Mary's primary supporters emotionally and spiritually as she sought out the fulfillment of her religious vocation; her father had written Sister Pascaline monthly after she entered the BSPA congregation.

MARGARET MARY AND HER FATHER, 1950.

Now, with both parents gone and freshly returned from a deeply fulfilling year with Father Bede in India, Sr. Pascaline, age 50, settled back into the Kansas City monastery to meditate about what might come next for herself and her BSPA family. She had gone out to India to experience the interiority of ashram life. Within weeks Sr. Pascaline's new role began to open before her. It would be the role of a change agent, of a consensus builder for a new monastic paradigm within the BSPAs and ultimately within Catholicism and throughout the world.

During Sr. Pascaline's six years as Prioress General and in the two years since, some of the BSPA Sisters had repeatedly expressed a desire for a more simple monastic lifestyle, with more time given to contemplation and prayer. Her months in India had answered Sr. Pascaline's own deep need for a more complete immersion in the contemplative life for which she had chosen to become a nun. Mother Audrey requested that she go around to the BSPA Priories and share with the sisters a bit about the year in India. She decided that the best way to do so would be to give them a taste of Hindu practices like she had experienced at Bede's ashram, such as the arati ceremony with burning camphor.

> When visiting our sisters at our priory at Mundelein, I had forgotten to pack a little arati dish (used in liturgies in India when chanting) and some of the small camphor squares easily available in India. Good Sister Regina suggested I use a glass ashtray and try some mothballs since they are made of camphor. All went well until the mothballs began emitting flakes that ascended and then descended over our heads. One dear elder sister from Germany cried out: "I knew it! I knew it! It's the devil."

It was a difficult adjustment coming back, because there was no way to share with others what [that year] really was.

There was no one formal moment when the idea of the BSPAs creating a Christian ashram like Father Bede's Shantivanam came up, Sr. Pascaline would later say, but shortly after returning from India, she became involved in a new organization that would soon make such an idea seem not only plausible, but the inevitable next step. That organization was the North American Board for East-West Dialogue.

In honoring Sr. Pascaline on the twenty-fifth anniversary of the Board's formation, Sister Mary Margaret Funk, OSB would recount:

> Staying at … Shantivanam Ashram, Sister [Pascaline] also read many of [Henri le Saux] Abhishiktananda's writings on dialogue and accompanied Father Bede and his ashramites to local interfaith encounters. On the anniversary of the death of the two founders of Shantivanam, Father Jules Monchanin and Abhishiktananda, Sister Pascaline took part in inter-monastic dialogue conferences hosted at the ashram. Then, near the end of her year abroad, she visited some of the Hindu ashrams in and around the holy city of Rishikesh.
>
> … At the June 1977 meeting and conference of Inter-Religious Dialogue, held at Maria Assumpta Academy in Petersham, Massachusetts, there was set up a working group; to explore the possibilities of East-West dialogue.[9]

Sr. Pascaline was still en route home from India at the time, and did not attend that Petersham meeting. The "priest or monk" who had wanted to meet with her in St. Louis the next day was from Aide Inter-Monastique (AIM). Sr. Pascaline would summarize in a letter the following spring that AIM was "a secretariate of the Confederation of Abbots in the West, especially created to assist the poor in the impoverished third world countries."

The meeting at Petersham, under the auspices of AIM (or AID, as it was also known) had been attended by Benedictine monks and nuns, university scholars, Buddhists, Hindus, laypeople from various Christian backgrounds, and a representative of the United Nations, and was widely publicized in the USA. A number of proposals were floated. One was "to establish loosely organized centers of Christian meditation (on the model of an ashram) to respond to the need to offer Christians, Buddhists, and Hindus the possibility of coming together for the study of meditation. These centers would be open to receiving lay people who would like to live there for a time. In order to accomplish this the proposal was made that [Catholic] monasteries be asked to provide financial help and trained personnel."[10]

The Petersham Conference has been seen by historians as different from other contemporary interreligious events in that it "marked the beginning of a long-term project." This would be in great part due to the work of Sr. Pascaline and her BSPA Sisters at the Osage Monastery Forest of Peace. It would be they who would take the

---

9   Funk, "Sister Pascaline Coff, OSB; MID Board Member," in Monastic Interreligious Dialogue, no.60 (Aug. 1998).

10   Fabrice Blée, *The Third Desert: The Story of Monastic Interreligious Dialogue*, trans. William Skudlarek with Mary Grady (Collegeville, Minnesota: Liturgical Press, 2011): 68-69, Google Play Books.

seeds of this new spiritual consciousness, plant them in the center of North America, and nurture them with prayer and service, bringing together spiritual giants of their time to discover this new thing at O+M, cross-fertilize it, grow it, and send it out again to the world.

Three months or so after her June 14 arrival home from India, Sr. Pascaline recalls, "About six of us monastic men and women in the United States received [a letter] from the AIM outside of Paris. This was the Abbots' Confederation, and they wanted to start a working group, both in Europe and the United States, for the Secretariate in Rome on the Church's relations with other religions."

Sr. Pascaline was invited to join the working group, no doubt because of her experiences with East/West dialogue and exchange in India with Father Bede.

Twenty-five years later, Sister Pascaline wrote that: "Prior to being invited to this inter-monastic working group I had never thought of becoming involved in interreligious dialogue." She accepted the AIM invitation to be part of a "working group" with enthusiasm, feeling, no doubt, that her AIM work might well be of benefit to her Sisters who shared her desire for a simpler lifestyle.

FOUNDING OF NABEWD AT RICKENBACH. 1978

Sr. Pascaline was soon in charge of planning the organizational meeting of the AIM working group, to be known as the North American Board for East-West Dialogue (NABEWD). The meeting would be held January 6–8, 1978, at Rickenbach Center at the BSPA monastery in Clyde, Missouri.

Planning and facilitating this meeting meant that Sr. Pascaline became the unofficial corresponding secretary of the working group, as well as their liaison with AIM in Europe. This new American AIM Board would need a central office somewhere, she saw, a place where records could be kept and regular newsletters edited and distributed. A new BSPA small-group living arrangement could become such a secretariat office with their work supported in part by a modest salary from AIM. It could be an East-West center, and more — a "monastic ashram" much like Bede's Shantivanam, located ideally somewhere in the middle of the United States.

In late 1977, Sister Pascaline began to draft a formal request to her BSPA Sisters, a letter to be sent out to Mother M. Audrey and the Prioresses Council on Christmas Day. Years later she would write: "One thing I do recall clearly is that we were trying to make this request for a new small foundation and have the request arrive on Dec. 25th, Birthday of our Savior. ... It would be, if allowed, a 'new birth within our Congregation' with God's coming anew in our midst."

The letter began:

> Sanctuary of the Holy Spirit
> *Christmas, 1977*

Dear Mother M Audrey and Councillors,

After much prayer, discernment, advice and patient waiting, and in virtue of the reasons listed below, I believe the Holy Spirit is urging me to make the following formal request on this day of Christ's BIRTH:

> I humbly ask permission . . . to initiate *in common with our Congregation* and in behalf of it, a "small community" with a simplified monastic style of life, somewhere apart from our present structures and grounds, with sufficient freedom for birth and growth, life, death and resurrection.

Sr. Pascaline went on to list the purposes for establishing such a small community in a "natural contemplative setting that would lead the way into smaller communities for us" with more freedom for contemplative prayer in an "atmosphere conducive to spiritual growth, joy and love flowing from a common faith-vision."

She followed up her Christmas letter to the BSPA Prioresses with a New Years Day letter to the "A.I.M. Secretariat (Members of the 'Permanent Working Group,')" proposing an "East West Monastic Center USA."

> PROPOSAL: That the East West Monastic Center begging to be born at the call of the Church in our monastic milieu in 20th Century America — be, from the beginning, a real Center of God's presence on earth, nurtured by a new 'small community' in communion with a larger monastic family but with efforts at a more simplified monastic life-style, where East and West can embrace and become One Heart! And that this be somewhere apart from present structures and institutional grounds, with sufficient freedom before the Lord for birth, growth, life, death and resurrection.

Sr. Pascaline's letter went on to list several purposes for the new center: It would be the primary "locus" for a dialogue that witnesses to the Christian life of faith while recognizing the value of Asian religions. She noted that it would "aid in the recovery of the West's own contemplative and mystical tradition." It would also "proclaim with an unarguable witness that poverty is not the world's problem, so much as it is the answer that must be given immediately by us monks to the injustice and self-centeredness of our race."

The new Center would make this witness by its presence and atmosphere. It would be a place where the lifestyle would be a simple one of prayer and study. Here people might taste and share the treasures of Eastern interiority through liturgies, shared silence and dialogue.

The proposed center would be a sign of hope and an expression of new life within the world — a place where all people — not just monks and nuns — might have a "foretaste of ultimate union" with each other and with the Divine.

Sister Pascaline ended her proposal by stressing that "tangible encouragement from the Working Group and the BSPAs in the form of letters of approval" would be "essential to the success of [the] venture."

Six monastics attended the organizational meeting of the NABEWD at the Clyde Monastery on January 6, 1978. Sr. Pascaline later recalled:

> That was kind of a historic meeting, but I still didn't have permission to begin this effort with a small community. I called Mother Audrey, who had just been with Cardinal Cody of Chicago. I told her that they were asking me if I could be secretary for this board. I still didn't want to say 'yes' until I knew whether or not we were going to be able to do a community of people on board with this. She gave permission and we were going to work out the details later.

At the meeting Sr. Pascaline was elected to a five-year term on the new NABEWD Board and a three-year term as Executive Secretary. The letter of "tangible encouragement" from the NABEWD to the BSPA leadership came the following week. Along with gratitude for BSPA having hosted the meeting of the Board, the newly elected Chairman, Martin J. Burne, OSB wrote:

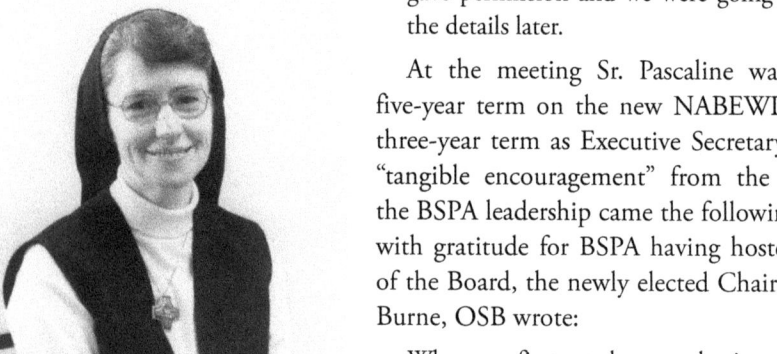

MOTHER AUDREY JONES

> When we first sat down to business, most of us learned for the first time of Sister Pascaline's proposal for the establishment of a monastic center for certain of the purposes envisioned by the Board. We had resolved to write you, Mother, to endorse Sister's idea and to encourage you to promote the establishment of such a center if it seemed to you and your Council at all feasible.
>
> In the middle of our deliberations on Saturday your welcome telephone call came, and Sister Pascaline related to us the very good news that you and your Council were willing that the center be established, given, of course, the necessary personnel and means requisite for such a venture. We are much heartened by your decision, and we wish to thank you, as a Board, for the immense help afforded by your decision.
>
> We are grateful, too, Mother Mary Audrey, for your willingness that Sister Pascaline should serve as Executive Secretary for the Board, a task for which she seems especially well equipped.

Sr. Pascaline was indeed well equipped for the duties of the Board's Executive Secretary, both by experience and by temperament. Beyond her year with Fr. Bede in India, she was a proven administrator and even had experience in communications from her year in the publicity department at Webster College before she entered

January 25, 1978

Dear Sisters,

On this last day of the Week of Prayer for Christian Unity, I want to give you further information about developments which have taken place concerning our Congregation's involvement with another outreach of the A.I.M. As you may have learned from the Minutes of the recent meeting of the Executive Board of the East-West Dialog Center which met at Rickenbach Center at the beginning of January, Sr. M. Pascaline has accepted the position as Secretary of the Center which at present is not set up in a <u>place</u> but wherever the Secretary is. The Council encouraged Sr. M. Pascaline to accept the position as it seems from the knowledge we now have to supply a need toward East-West dialog that is supported by the Church as a good for the Church. The participants in the Inter-Religious Dialog held at Petersham, Massachusetts, June 1977, assembled under the sponsorship of the A.I.M., recognized as one of their goals, "To <u>take</u> the <u>initiative</u> in promoting inter-religious dialog with <u>Asian</u> monks and <u>Asian</u> <u>religious</u>, as requested by the Roman Secretariate for Non-Christian religions." We feel that our having the opportunity to enter more directly into this ecumenical endeavor offers our Congregation a new and unique way for us to express Eucharist.

Sr. M. Pascaline's experience during her year's stay in India has been an excellent preparation for the position she has accepted. Because of her commitment to the members of our Kansas City community as their delegate to our General Chapter, she will remain at that priory until the completion of her responsibility. Permission has been given, however, for her to search out a possible location for a small group living experience. No details have been worked out as yet, but Sister has been asked to draw up what she envisions. As the A.I.M. will pay a salary to the Secretary, a means of support has in part been made available.

The Council sees this indeavor as another response to our Congregation's own expressed openness to such an invitation: "The Congregation shall remain open to experimental forms of living." Acts #26, Gen. Chap. 1974. As soon as I have any more definite information for you, I will be writing to you again, but for now, I commend the project to your prayer. Throughout the developments which take place, may the Lord be glorified and our Congregation become a humble, simple instrument for the strengthening of faith relations between East and West, North and South, that Christ may be All-in-all.

In the Lord,

Mother M. Audrey

the BSPA Congregation. She was well connected within American Catholicism as a former Superior of her Congregation and president of the Benedictine Prioresses.

A letter from Mother Audrey to the BSPAs on January 25, 1978, shared the news of what had transpired with the East-West Board: "The Council sees this endeavor as another response to our Congregation's own expressed openness to such an invitation." By the time Mother Audrey's report went out, Sr. Pascaline had already begun her work as Executive Secretary, creating the first NABEWD Bulletin from news of the Board's organizational meeting at Clyde. As she recalled 25 years later:

> This first issue [of the Bulletin], only four pages long, was dated January 9, 1978. It was printed on a mimeograph machine at Hogan High School next door to our monastery, then run off by hand on a copy machine and assembled on the floor of my cell in our Kansas City monastery. The community all helped with the mailing to our first 250 potential readers. I loved creating the Bulletin from the beginning.

Within a few weeks, she also began a search for a place to build the new East-West monastic center. First she had to get permission from a local bishop. On March 10, 1978, Sister Pascaline wrote a one-page letter to ten bishops in the midwestern United States on the letterhead of her monastery:

> *To whom it may concern:*
>
> The world is on the verge of turning to contemplation, its primal vocation! There is the "hidden monk" in every man. Do you want to be involved in the effort to support this turning?

She went on to explain who she was and describe the new monastic community that was, she wrote, a "response to the call of the Church for E-W dialog, preparations to include prayer, study and integration of dual spiritual traditions and mystical sources!"

> *Location:* needed! 10-15 acres of farmland, ranch or wooded area with natural setting suitable and conducive to a contemplative atmosphere, anywhere in the USA, especially mid-West.
>
> *Self-support:* Full-time salary: Ex. Secretary of Board (3 yrs.); hospitality, limited guest quarters shared; directed retreats on small scale.
>
> *Chaplain:* needed! Priest with similar faith vision.
>
> *Initial outlay:* dependent on the mercy of God and those who find contemplative prayer a priority and believe in the treasures of God's truth disbursed in both East and West and desire to see communion begin in the heart of a small community nurturing this.
>
> *When?* Search underway with view to begin September, 1978.
>
> If you desire to contribute to the Church in her work of renewal and in her outreach in a world on the verge of turning East and West to contemplation, contact the writer at your convenience with suggestions, questions and support, be it ever so humble.

A number of the bishops responded, encouraging the effort, but saying that they already had small-group-living experiments going on in their dioceses and wanted to wait and see how those turned out.

Meanwhile, the effort to find a place for the BSPA ashram was accompanied by Sr. Pascaline's effort to build support within the BSPA congregation before their General meeting scheduled for August, where the delegates from all the Houses would meet to vote on issues and leaders. As Sr. Pascaline went around to the various BSPA houses to share some of the experiences of her year in India and talk about East-West inter-monastic dialogue, she was also looking for Sisters who were ready to join in pioneering the new community:

Sr. Pascaline seems to have had little trouble pulling together the small group for the new venture. Several had been praying and advocating for this for years. They soon settled on five.[11]

Meanwhile, Sr. Pascaline's Benedictine friend in Tulsa, Sr. Jan Futrell had told Sr. Pascaline her new Bishop might well be open to an experimental small group monastery, so one copy of the letter "To whom it may concern" went to Bishop Eusebius Beltran in Tulsa.

The new Bishop of the Tulsa Diocese was already acquainted with the BSPAs. "I got to know that community in my travels up to Kansas City," Archbishop Beltran recalled many years later. "Bishop [John] Sullivan, formerly of Tulsa, took me by the BSPA House in Kansas City and that's when I first met the community. Then I also went to St. Louis and met the community there. At one of those visits I must have heard about Sister Pascaline, but then she contacted me."

ARCHBISHOP EUSEBIUS BELTRAN

On April 28, Bishop Beltran responded that he was "greatly interested in having contemplatives in his diocese," and invited the BSPA Sisters to come visit with him.

"We drove down there the very next day," Sr. Pascaline recalls. She and Sister M. Benita made the drive from Kansas City to Tulsa together — eight hours round trip in the car — for a one-hour meeting with Bishop Beltran.

"I was delighted when they contacted me," Archbishop Emeritus Beltran remembered decades later. "She and another Sister came to Tulsa and met with me and described what they had in mind. I liked what I heard. I felt they were very sincere women — very good religious women — and so I encouraged them and told them I would welcome them."

On April 28, when he answered Sr. Pascaline's letter, Eusebius Beltran himself was new in Tulsa, having been consecrated on April 20.

Sister Priscilla later recalled the Bishop saying, "We'll grow up together." And, she added, "That's what we did."

---

11 The five were Sr. M. Monica Sanders from the San Diego monastery; Sr. M. Trinitas Nordhaus from the Tucson monastery; and Srs. M. Priscilla Trost, M. Christine Bonneau and Sr. Pascaline from the Kansas City monastery.

In May, Sr. Pascaline and her Kansas City sisters issued the second NABEWD Bulletin, an eight-page affair packed with news of E-W dialogue activities planned and underway. Her first year's salary from AIM had been placed in an interest-bearing account to be used for the new monastic ashram when the time came. On June 5, Sr. Pascaline wrote Mother Audrey to report on the progress of the "new life style" initiative. "Bishop Beltran asks that I come and stay longer than an hour next time so we can look around at locations near the city but removed some distance."

Sister Pascaline would later report she visited Tulsa four times with various ones of her group that summer to search out a possible site for the monastic ashram.[12]

She met with Bishop Beltran on the first three of those visits and reported that on "June 27th Bsp. Beltran drove Sisters around the diocese to see locations and learn trends of growth, prices, etc." She quoted him as saying, "'Tell your chapter we are anxious to have you Sisters come. We need you to pray for the Diocese.' He was also happy about the chaplain [Father Jim Conner] as the Diocese is short on priests."

Father Jim, the Trappist monk Sr. Pascaline had met in 1975 while he was living at Christ in the Desert, was a native of Tulsa. As a high school junior, he had entered Gethsemani, in Kentucky, and, "After I was ordained, [Thomas] Merton had become Novice Master and I was appointed as Sub-master."

By 1978, Father Jim recalls, he was doing studies at Berkeley at the Jesuit facility at GTU.

> While I was there I got a letter from Sr. Pascaline telling me that she had returned from spending a year in India with Bede Griffiths and had just gotten permission from her chapter to try to begin something similar to that someplace here in the States, and asked me if I'd be interested in being a part of that or not. I wrote back that, yes, I'd be very interested.
>
> We corresponded back and forth. The first letter I got from her, she told me that the first bishop she'd heard from that was sort of interested in the place was Bishop Beltran in Tulsa. I told her that was certainly a coincidence because I was born and raised in Tulsa and my family still lived there.

In a letter to M. Audrey, Miriam and Council on June 29, Sister Pascaline reported:

> By now Sister M. Rachel has shared the good news of the recent trip to Tulsa and interview with Bishop Beltran. He was so gracious and happy over the possibility of the new contemplative community in his diocese. He has formed very recently a property commission for the diocese and this search for property for us is one of their priorities.
>
> In about 15 minutes he clarified a few points about the direction of our effort, location, contemplative status and asked what the community is prepared to spend. In answer to his questions as to whether we would want to own the place or have the diocese own it, I am happy I said we usually own our own.

---

12 "April 30: SM Benita and Pascaline – 1 day; June: S. David and Pascaline – 2 days; Aug.: SM Priscilla & Pascaline – 3 days; Sept.: SM Christine, Trinitas & Pascaline – 4 days."

He was happy to learn we have been blessed with some furnishings from Mundelein, including a car. He showed us all the territory surrounding Tulsa and gave much information on values, growth tendencies, etc. so he really had done his homework. His own choice was country property with hills only 15 minutes from his own residence. It is called Osage Hills and was a favorite of the Indians!! He seemed delighted to know that we sort of agreed on what he was to look for. He now has two real estate men combing the countryside. He was even more enthused when he heard we may have five instead of two or three. He asked what our means of income would be and I told him we already had the full-time salary[13] in the bank for the first year. Then the group would decide how it could best support itself from there on. Retreat requests have been sufficient this year to promise some hope for next year.

At any rate, it was a very promising visit and blessed in so many ways.

Sr. Pascaline also reported that "Grants have been requested from 6 charitable foundations benefiting Catholic organizations of non-profit origin."

In early August 1978, delegates from all the BSPA houses convened in St. Louis for the Ninth General Chapter, where leaders would be elected and important issues would be discussed and voted upon. Sr. Pascaline gave a "progress report on Tulsa and questionnaire returns with names of core group ok'd by General Council."

At last the way was clear for the little group of BSPA Sisters to make the move to a new home in the Tulsa diocese. Their "monastic ashram" could now become a reality … as soon as they could find a place to live.

---

13   From AIM.

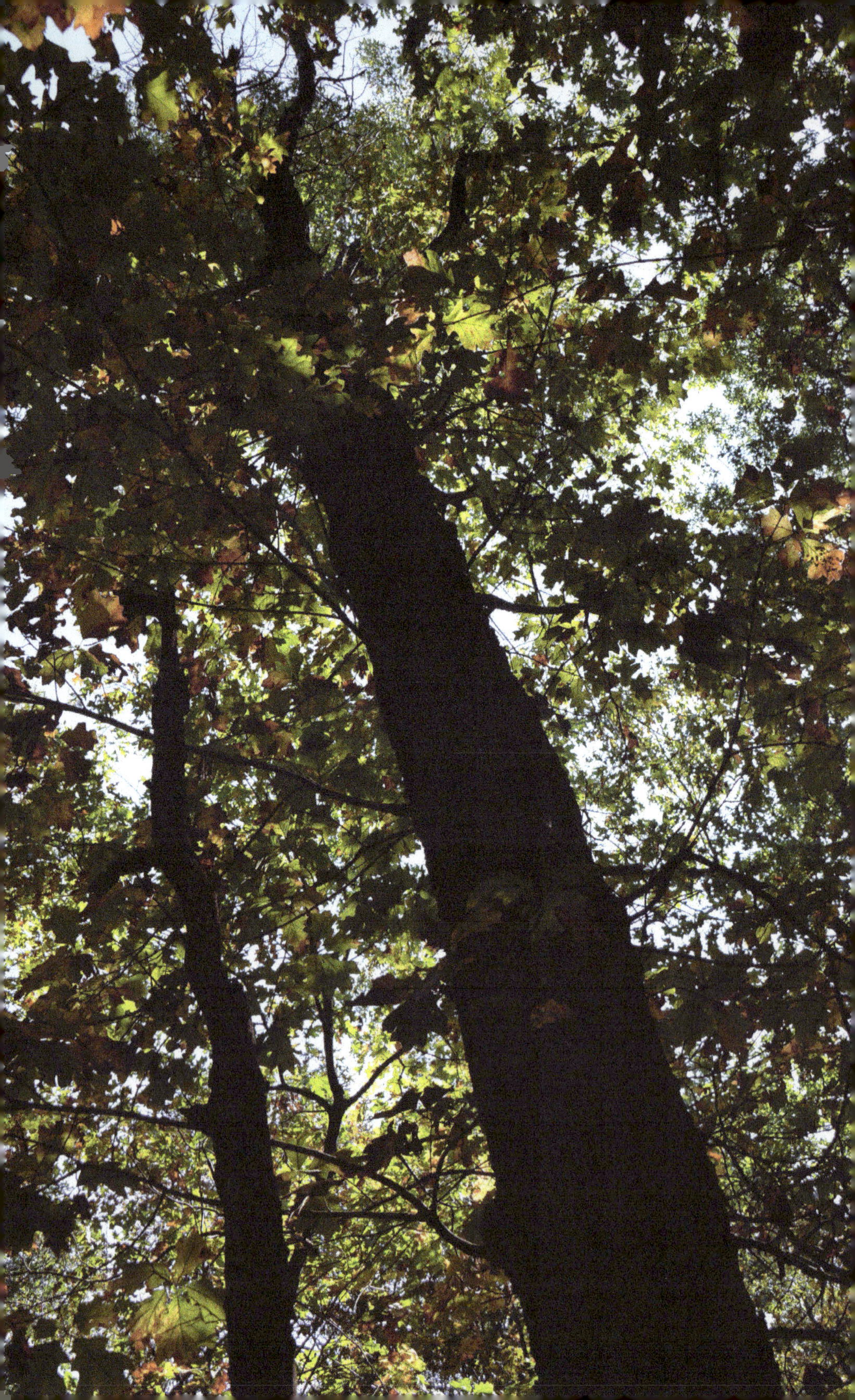

TULSA

1978 & 1979

"Trees, trees, plenty of trees, even a little crick."

—Sister Priscilla Trost

Within days after the General Chapter meeting, Sr. Pascaline made the drive to Tulsa again, this time with Sr. M. Priscilla Trost, one of the BSPA Sisters planning to move there with her and help establish the new monastery.

Sister Priscilla was almost a decade older than Sr. Pascaline and had grown up a protestant headed for the missionary field when, as she said later, "God sent a Catholic priest across my path. Each week for a year I went to Father for spiritual direction. It was during this time that my desire to be a missionary changed to being a contemplative nun."[14]

She had developed sewing as one of her useful skills; the BSPAs supported themselves in part by making habits, stoles and other garments for Catholic religious. She enjoyed this work, along with passing along the kind of spiritual direction she had received from the good Father who had brought her into the Church. She had prepared for the move to Tulsa by spending a month at a Catholic "prayer farm" in Easton, Kansas.[15]

Sr. Priscilla was destined to become the "heart" of the Osage Monastery, supporting, with her quiet practicality and loving friendship, Sr. Pascaline, who was its "head."

On August 27, Srs. Priscilla and Pascaline met with Bishop Beltran in Tulsa, just before he left for a month in Rome. Sister Priscilla remembers it was Bishop Beltran who advised them to move to Tulsa while still searching for the land to build the new monastic ashram. "He said come down and find someplace to live and then see about your property. Do all of that together."

The Bishop appointed a Catholic Realtor and Chancellor "to care for us during his absence so there would be no delay in finding a suitable place," Sr. Pascaline reported. They stayed three days, looking at land and land prices.

Temporary quarters for the five BSPA Sisters were easier to find. The Chancellor and Vice-Chancellor were consulted. They soon found an "empty but furnished rectory belonging to the Benedictines of St. Joseph's convent."

This rectory was a house that backed up to a Catholic girls' school, Monte Casino,

---

14 She joined the BSPAs at Clyde on the day the Japanese bombed Pearl Harbor, December 7, 1941.

15 Founded by Fr. Ed Hays, this Catholic retreat center was called Shantivanam in honor of Fr. Bede's Shantivanam in India.

2125 E. 22ND PLACE

founded by the Benedictine Sisters in a good residential area in midtown Tulsa. The house, at 2125 E. 22nd Place, "... has four bedrooms, a very small kitchen, and a hole in the roof which the Sisters will have fixed. It will be free except for utilities."

Planning for the move went into high gear. "We agreed to move in on Friday, Sept. 22nd," Sr. Pascaline reported.

And so it began.

St. Michael's Day 1978
Tulsa, Oklahoma!

Dear Mother Audrey and all our Sisters,

This is the day the Lord has made! He has called Pope John Paul to eternal life and simultaneously gives new life to our congregation in the green hills of eastern Oklahoma. By midnight all five of the small community will be together for the first time. Sister M. Monica will be picked up at the airport around 2:15 PM coming from San Diego. And Sister M. Christine is arriving the long way by minibus from K.C. around 9 PM. Sister David and Judith will bring a few more of our things along in the minibus. There is more room in the little house than we imagined.

Bishop Eusebius Beltran graciously welcomed us to the Diocese of Tulsa just before he left for a month of new theology in Rome. He returns Sunday night unless he will stay longer for the funeral of Pope John Paul. His Chancellor and Vicar General have been exceedingly good to us, finding us this empty rectory belonging to the Sisters of St. Joseph convent, Benedictines who have welcomed us as their own. We have the loan of the house and need to pay only for utilities and groceries, although they want us to feel free to share any of their meals. We have been Eucharistic with them daily but Father Dorney, the Chancellor, stopped by yesterday to say he will be happy to offer the Eucharist here whenever we are set up and then can reserve the Lord in his special presence, giving permission for all of us to be Eucharistic ministers on the spot.

Of all the properties we have seen the one we felt was closest to our possibilities turned out to be owned by the Diocese but it has a Cherokee Indian attached to it who thinks he owns it! Needless to say the Diocese is investigating the deed which was given to them as a gift many years ago. Meanwhile we are searching elsewhere.

The Lord has come in so many unexpected ways to celebrate this first day of community here. One of the Benedictines in Tulsa came this AM to ask if there is anything we could use, since they have a high school cafeteria that has been closed. She returned about 3 PM with some mixing bowls, two chickens, butter, syrup and boxes of pancake mix, canned goods, etc. They left a "raincheck" for supper some evening at their humble home.

Sister M. Monica arrived right on time at 2:15 and came beaming down the ramp from the plane, carrying the love of all our sisters in San Diego, and their sunshine.

The Diocese of Tulsa is only 3% Catholic. The city is about 80% Baptist with some Methodists. Our Protestant neighbor said he has lived here 16 years and this is the first time he has seen a resident of this house working on the front lawn! Sr. Trini gave the place a good cleaning, windows and all, for three days before we arrived. We started taking turns cooking and preparing liturgies. Each afternoon we have tried to have a quiet hour between 5 and 6 PM before we start supper and preparing for evening liturgy. Adoration is before and after Eucharist each AM.

Father Jim Conner, our chaplain, is in Israel until October 3. After a visit at Snowmass he promises to be with us. We are finding suitable chapel appurtenances at the Salvation Army for a little altar and Sister M. Trinitas is designing and making a tiny tabernacle.

M. Audrey, Srs. Mary Jane, Benita, Miriam, and on down the litany of each of you! We are so deeply grateful for all that has been done and given, for all that is and is being done, and for all that will be and will be done! Even now the K.C. minibus is wending its way loaded with all your goodness and love.

Let us pray for each other that we may continue to become the One we've been called to be.

Lovingly, Sisters M. Pascaline, Trinitas, Priscilla, Monica (Christine en route)

1976–1980

Of the five BSPA Sisters who moved to Tulsa in 1978, Sister M. Trinitas, or Trini, was the first to arrive and would be the first to leave. She was 50 at the time, a year younger than Sr. Pascaline, a Kansas farm girl from a large Catholic family. She was an artist, designer, and writer, and had been one of the 12 who founded the BSPA monastery in Tucson in 1954. She had moved into the house on 22nd Place on the Friday before the others arrived, claimed one of the three little upstairs bedrooms for her own, and for three days cleaned house from top to bottom, even washing the windows.

Sister Monica Sanders, at age 55, was as handy and mechanically minded as Sr. Trini was artistic. During WWII she had trained as a machinist and worked as a parts inspector in various military plants. She also had a great love of the outdoors. The beaming smile she exhibited on arrival in Tulsa would last through all the years she was a part of the Osage Monastery community. Later she would say that she had loved "that little place in the woods" where she could enjoy nature, maintain the cabins and grounds, and spend her days in prayer. First, however, she would have to settle for a cramped bedroom up in the eaves of the house and help with its maintenance as the group searched northeastern Oklahoma for land.

For the rest of her life, Sister Priscilla would remember the move to Tulsa. The house on 22nd Place had four bedrooms and five residents, each of whom had chosen to come, expecting the space for prayer and study in her own monastic cell. Rather than make two of the five double up in one of the bedrooms, Sister Priscilla converted the dining room into her bedroom, sleeping on a pile of mattresses on the floor. She remembered:

> We set the date of 29 September, which is the anniversary of our whole congregation coming here [to America] from Switzerland. And so we got what we had together of our things at Kansas City and of all things I put my sewing machine in! A friend drove us down in her station wagon. We piled everything we could in, a couple of mattresses, the sewing machine, until the driver could not see out of the back of the car. But we had to leave enough space so the driver could see [out the front]. So we came down, late at night, and landed in Tulsa with the sewing machine and the mattresses and a few benches. That's all we could get in the station wagon.

Sister Christine Bonneau, at age 65 when she arrived in Tulsa

SR. PASCALINE COFF

SR. MONICA SANDERS

SR. PRISCILLA TROST

in the Kansas City minibus, was the eldest of the pioneering group. She was a "down to earth" Kansas farm girl, and once said of herself, "I think the farmer in me has a very important role. To love everybody, all living things, the sun, the rain, the sky, the clouds and good mother earth. ... God's gift to my heart, mind, and being, is growing into love, deep love."

Sister Christine "was really a cook," Sr. Priscilla recalled, and in fact she was the last to arrive in Tulsa on September 29 because she had to finish her cooking duty at the Kansas City monastery. She would become the chief cook in Tulsa. "The kitchen was very small," Sr. Priscilla remembered. "If she was in the kitchen, hardly anybody else could be in the kitchen. ... Sr. Christine had the one big bedroom on the first floor."

That a group of late-middle-aged nuns should choose — and be chosen — to pioneer an ashram in the rugged Oklahoma Cross Timbers might seem odd, except that a certain amount of maturity was an asset when it came to living in such a small group, and the BSPA leadership knew this. Each of the pioneers was in good health, had talents to contribute to the effort, avidly shared the goal of a simpler lifestyle that was more in tune with the natural world, and had a willingness to give up a certain amount of comfort and convenience to make this experiment work.

Sr. Pascaline remembers the move to Tulsa and the spirit of joyful excitement that accompanied the Sisters as they gathered to begin their new life together:

SR. TRINITAS NORDUS

SR. CHRISTINE BONNEAU

> As best I can recall, we each had "all" our belongings from 30-40-50 years winter, summer and in between.
>
> Then, some of us had notebooks, retreat offerings, etc. So — some needed much more space than others. We also brought with us donated equipment (typewriter, mimeograph, etc.). We were so happy to be there and to be there together at last — to begin the new "way of life."
>
> Vatican II had suggested several ways of having Perpetual Adoration so we had asked permission of our Prioress General for that and received a happy o.k. We chose to have a communal time during our early morning prayer, counting one of the 30 minutes periods as our Adoration together.
>
> Sister Priscilla was delighted with the pile of mattresses in the dining room and I kept some of her things in the room I was using on the 2nd floor. Sister Trini already had staked out one bedroom as she was there earlier than the rest of us, who

were driven down by a Sister of Charity of Leavenworth, Sister Gloria Solomon, in her van.

We celebrated with the little we had on hand as if it were New Years Eve, and for us it was: a New Year with Himself!

We made a tiny chapel out of a small step-down room off the Living Room and it became well used by the time we moved to larger, more spacious quarters in the Forest.

The Benedictine Sisters at St. Joseph's Monastery were exceedingly good to us, permitting us to share daily Eucharist with them plus some of our early meals until we got adjusted.

Sister Priscilla would also remember that there were unexpected challenges when they got to Tulsa, not the least of which were the sleeping arrangements. It isn't clear where (or if!) Sr. Priscilla slept that first night, but converting the dining room into her bedroom required the Sisters to move the dining room table and chairs into the little kitchen. This made it difficult for the group to work together on cooking or dishwashing.

Another challenge was doing the laundry. The house on 22nd Place had no laundry facilities. "We found a laundromat," Sr. Priscilla recalled. "So we went once a week, took all our wash, sheets and things, to the laundromat. ... Sr. Christine and I took care of that."

True to his word, Father Dorney came to offer the first Eucharist celebrated in the little sunroom chapel the next Tuesday, October 3, and was surprised by a winged visitation of symbolic significance. As Sr. Pascaline recalled:

Sister Priscilla somehow managed to bring with her a white dove from Father Ed Hays' Shantivanam in Easton, Kansas, where she spent a few months in preparation for this new lifestyle. The first morning one good pastor came to offer Mass for us in our little "chapel," and, as he patiently waited on the screened back porch, Sr. Priscilla's dove flew up on his all-but-bald head. You can imagine his astonishment.

The five Sisters divided their time among a number of new challenges: one of which was publishing the NABEWD's fall Bulletin.

Bulletin #3, eight pages in length, typed single-spaced on the one typewriter in the 22nd Place house, was packed with information about East-West dialogue, past, present, and future. One item announced: "Father Bede Griffiths has been invited by the A.I.M. for East-West to be a roving guest lecturer, visiting Benedictine and Cistercian houses from east to the west coast this coming summer. He aims to give a comprehensive understanding of Indian spirituality for which his last twenty years as a sannyasi in India well equip him."

Another item discussed plans for the Thomas Merton Commemoration at Columbia University in New York, December 5–7. Sr. Pascaline herself was listed as a speaker for a program on the State of East-West Religious Dialogue with Father

Thomas Berry and others, and part of a panel discussing Contemplation and Feminism. "This program segment of the greater commemoration for Merton at Columbia is being co-sponsored by the A.I.M. North American Board for East-West Dialogue," the item concluded. Sr. Pascaline's correspondence about and preparations for the event could not be neglected in the midst of all her other concerns during this busy autumn of 1978.

On October 11, Father Jim Conner returned from Israel, moved in with his mother in Tulsa, and began celebrating daily Eucharist with the Sisters at the house on 22nd Place. The next day, October 12, the group sat down together for their first "Community Reflection" on the topic of "Simplicity." This exercise was their first attempt at community building, and it showed that the group's coherence was a priority. As Sr. Pascaline would report a few weeks later, "In between our diligent search for a suitable place to begin our new simplified lifestyle, we have had a community day of corporate reflection on simplicity and what it means to each, which was rich and challenging."

In a letter to Mother Audrey a week later, Sr. Pascaline wrote:

> Our chaplain, Father Jim Conner, arrived back from Israel a week ago and has offered Eucharist for us three times. We scheduled a prayer day and he joined us for the beginning of it but there is really no place for him to sit privately once Eucharist is over …

FATHER JAMES CONNER, OCSO

The search for land for the monastic ashram that had been going on since June hardly paused long enough for the group to move into their Tulsa house, and by the second week in October it seemed to have borne fruit. The Sisters had located a large tract of wooded, rolling hills near Pawhuska, Oklahoma, in Osage County, over an hour away by automobile from Tulsa. The land belonged to the Immaculate Conception Parish in Pawhuska and Bishop Beltran believed that the parish corporation might be willing to donate it for the monastery.

The little group, after two weeks of living together in the house in Tulsa, were delighted to have found this land and wanted to move out as soon as possible. However, the move was repeatedly delayed.

Sr. Pascaline wrote back to her Prioress General, Mother Audrey, on October 19, saying about the Pawhuska land:

The GIFT is going round and round. Because of Sisters in the past selling property given by the Indians and making money on it later there is hesitancy regarding gifts to Sisters. The Bishop thought a good solution might be to lease the land to us on a longterm basis, renewable in 25 or 30 years. Since the Parish Corporation is still in process of deciding if they want to sell it to the Diocese or give it to them, or whatever, we are praying and waiting for the Lord.

Perhaps the name "Osage Monastery," with its initials spelling the omkara, sacred mantra and mystical sound of Dharmic religions, dates from this 1978 hope that the little group would soon be able to settle on the acreage in Osage County, near Pawhuska, the headquarters of the Osage Nation. Decades later Archbishop Emeritus Beltran remembered, "They were looking for a place and they had this dream of being with the Indians and Pawhuska being an old Indian town and a number of Osage still live there. They very much were interested in that."

The Osage are a Siouxian language people who had at the time of first contact with Europeans controlled trade west of the Mississippi River in lands between St. Louis and the Rocky Mountains. Following the Louisiana Purchase, they had been forced to sell their claims to all their lands in exchange for part of what is today Kansas, and then fifty years later again were forced to sell Kansas and buy a 2,304 square-mile reservation in northeastern Oklahoma. Notably, the BSPA monasteries in St. Louis; Clyde, Missouri and Kansas City were all located on what had once been the Osage homelands.

Unlike the citizens of Tulsa, the Osage people were predominantly Catholic in 1978. They had first been evangelized by the famous French Jesuit missionary explorer Father Jaques Marquette in 1673, and Jesuit priests had been serving the Osages continuously since the mid-nineteenth century. When the Osage Nation was removed to Oklahoma, the Church arrived in their new lands with them and they established a Catholic boarding school at Pawhuska that, during the early 20th century, all Osage children in the area attended.

The Osage Nation, about 6,400 strong in 1874 when they were removed to Oklahoma, had diminished to 2,229 individuals a generation later when they were forced to accept allotment of their entire reservation into privately owned acreages — 640 acres to each Osage man, woman, and child on the tribal rolls.

The rights to the minerals under the land were another matter. In the 1906 allotment, the Osage Nation managed to hold all of the mineral rights in common, with some of the mineral lease proceeds benefitting Osage education and other tribal goods and the rest being paid out in quarterly headright checks to each Osage allottee. Oil was discovered in great quantities in what was now Osage County, and the Osages became, for a time, the richest people on earth.

The fact that Tulsa was known as a wealthy Catholic diocese was almost entirely due to the Oklahoma oil boom in the early twentieth century, and Osage Catholics

PAWHUSKA'S IMMACULATE CONCEPTION CHURCH,
THE "OSAGE CATHEDRAL": THE OSAGE WINDOW

certainly played a large part in that. Up until 1978, Osage mineral headrights could be sold, deeded or willed to whomever the owner wished, and a large number of these passed into the hands of Catholic institutions.

Thus, in 1978, the parish corporation of Pawhuska's Immaculate Conception Church, the "Osage Cathedral" with its famous stained-glass windows depicting French priests sharing the Gospel with Osage people, had in its possession a 120-acres tract of undeveloped land just two miles outside Pawhuska, perhaps a donation from one of the Osage allottees or heirs. It was raw land, mostly wooded, with a rocky ravine running through it and no road, electricity, phone lines, or gas lines nearby; a "running spring" but no other water, sewage infrastructure, or fence. Much would be needed in order to develop it into a monastic ashram where the five BSPA Sisters and Father Jim could live in relative poverty and welcome retreatants and visitors.

For the Prioresses Council meeting at the Kansas City monastery in November, Sr. Pascaline and the "New small community and secretariate" prepared a formal financial proposal to immediately develop the new monastery on the land near

Pawhuska. They proposed to live there together in two prefab buildings, 70' x 40' and 30' x 40', without plumbing but flanked by a pair of outhouses. The group had already nicknamed their proposed outhouses "East" and "West." Instead of a water line, they wrote, "Water can be carried for drinking from the Parish Hall for the present. The Pastor is due to be moved but is eager now to do any and everything for us."

As the letter explained, "The five in the small community are excited about the possibility of really starting simply. This is what we came for and desire so much. ... The neighbors are good people and we are all happy with the possibility in Pawhuska of beginning at last, after searching the entire eastern corner of Oklahoma in the proximity of Tulsa."

Sister Pascaline's report to the Prioresses on the progress of the Tulsa community, in November, plead the case for this plan, saying that the five Sisters were:

> ... neither "fish nor fowl." Buildings and lifestyle and community all need to grow together, simply and humbly and the sooner the better. "You keep doing things over and over and time is wasted in useless things because it is only temporary and there is no place for anything."
>
> All five agree that it would be unhealthy not to move ahead into the desired lifestyle while building community. None believe it would help to wait to see if one or another is going to leave the group. It will happen anytime anywhere and cannot be 'awaited.'

The "desired lifestyle" would not materialize "sooner," as hoped. As the proposal to buy or lease the Pawhuska land was being discussed, the Tulsa group spent the entire week of Thanksgiving in lengthy discussions and sharing on a personal level about "the basic fundamentals of our call." The following week Sr. Pascaline attended the Merton Conference at Columbia University in New York, co-sponsored by AIM, where she spoke at two sessions.

Meanwhile, as Tulsa Catholics got word of the proposed monastic retreat center, enthusiasm for it began to grow. Requests began to pour in for retreats, requests that the "Tulsa five" struggled to fulfill in the little house on 22nd Place. Sr. Pascaline reported:

> Requests are coming by mail and by phone. Just this week the major superior of the Notre Dame sisters in St. Louis asked if we would be ready, after her term of office ends in June, for her to take several months of prayer and quiet in our new small community. Another Kansas City Sister asked for a year, a CSJ.
>
> A 36-year-old lay woman from the Tulsa diocese wrote that she read the article about us in the *Eastern Oklahoma Catholic*. She is mother of three small children and wrote: 'As a lay person who is active in the church and very much involved in the secular world, I value prayer as the area most important in my life and have longed for a 'house of prayer' within this diocese for many years. We have no

renewal center, no retreat house and very little is offered to laypeople on PRAYER. Godspeed your task of finding a suitable tract of land! —Sincerely, PS'

Soon, the local Catholic community also weighed in on the notion of "Tulsa's" monastic ashram being placed so far away from the city in Pawhuska. Pascaline reported that "Sister Janice Futrell, OSB, visited and begged us not to get 'too far out of the Tulsa area' for the sake of the religious who would want to come for retreats and spiritual direction." The view that the Pawhuska land might not meet the needs of Tulsa Catholics gained traction, even as the Sisters pushed forward with their plan to acquire the property. Bishop Beltran quickly became one with strong reservations.

A survey of the property was delayed by winter ice, snow, and extremely cold temperatures. No doubt the idea of roughing it in temporary metal buildings and hiking to outhouses began to seem much less appealing to the little group of nuns now than it had the month earlier in the autumn sunshine. Father Jim, who had been living with his mother in Tulsa, agreed to temporarily pastor the little church in Bristow, 36 miles from Tulsa in the opposite direction from Pawhuska.

Years later, Sister Priscilla would recall that, when they moved into the house on 22nd Place and she made her bed on the dining room floor, "we thought we would be out of there in six weeks, six months." The last week in December, as Sr. Pascaline traveled to the BSPA convent in St. Louis for the second annual meeting of the NABEWD, she no doubt believed that the move out of the little house would happen before summer, 1979. Instead, the Tulsa "campout" would continue for another year and a half.

Two days after New Years, Bishop Beltran, just back from a winter vacation, "phoned and said several Sisters begged him not to let us go so far out from Tulsa." Beltran strongly urged looking again for land closer in, where there might already be roads and utilities nearby so that the move to the property could happen sooner. Since the property in Pawhuska had not yet been surveyed, maybe this was the time to take one last look at something nearer." And so the search continued.

The nonprofit bulk mailing permit was transferred to the Tulsa address in time for the February mailing of Bulletin #4. One of the unexpected benefits of editing the Bulletin was that the little group received review copies of new books on monasticism and East-West dialogue from publishers hoping for publicity in the Bulletin. They did indeed publish lengthy reviews written by Sr. Pascaline, Fr. Jim and others. Such review copies were the genesis of the Osage Forest of Peace's unique library of books and recordings about Eastern and Western contemplative practice.

All this time, Pascaline and the "Tulsa Secretariate" had also been hard at work writing and publishing the Bulletin, and planning for Bede Griffiths' roving lecture tour of monastic houses in the United States the following summer. They reported in the Bulletin, "From more than fifty requests, the two visiting monks from S. India [Father Bede and Brother Amaldas] will be hosted by twenty-five houses …" across the country. One of the select few on this list was, of course, "A.I.M. Secretariate in Tulsa."

> Other monasteries will cluster with one or another of these twenty-five houses. The itinerary prepared by the Board, from New York to California, has been sent to all Cistercian and Benedictine Houses with a cover letter suggesting stipend, travel arrangements, timing, scheduling and dietary considerations.

This itinerary and the mailing were apparently prepared and sent by the Tulsa five, a job that was followed by the work of composing, typing, mimeographing, assembling and mailing the eight-page Bulletin itself. Meanwhile, spiritual retreats were hosted as best they could be, given the cramped quarters the Sisters shared.

By February, one of the "Tulsa five" BSPAs was unhappy and preparing to leave. On February 4, Sister Trinitas had begun negotiations to move to the Kansas City monastery. Sr. Pascaline's letter of February 15 to Mother Audrey reported, "I fear her multiple sclerosis may be flaring up again." The following month Sister Trinitas would move to the monastery in Kansas City.

In their March report, the Sisters would explain that, "Father Jim Conner, our chaplain, has offered to help the Diocese while waiting for us to settle into our own place. [On] February 12th he was appointed Administrator at St. Joseph's Parish in Bristow." Sr. Pascaline wrote to M. Audrey:

> We went out to his new rectory and church yesterday to clean. It was beyond dirt. We really shoveled bushels of dirt out of every room. Srs. Priscilla and Monica did a good job on the Sacristy and High Altar and Father ordered two new vestments from Sr. Priscilla. She of course is thrilled but never made one!! She got some lovely material this AM with the money the other priest gave her for her first two stoles. Nice!

Thereafter, Father Jim would live in Bristow and drive to Tulsa twice a week for Eucharist with the Sisters, and for "confessions, spiritual direction and his class on mysticism, which is excellent. He has been and is a real gift."

By the end of February, Sr. Pascaline and the Tulsa group, having finally abandoned the plan to build on land near Pawhuska, were back to square one. She reported:

> Weather cleared and search began again. Mr. Hoey gave 2 days' time to accompany us to four or five pieces of property, within a twenty-five mile radius of Tulsa. He spent much time estimating a metal building for a common house according to our simple description. He finally came up with an amount when completed with insulation.
>
> His suggestion after hearing our situation: Contact the Corp of Civil Engineers and request a 100-year lease on some lake frontage for the House of Prayer. The Tulsa Corps have done this for other religious groups: Baptists, etc. The sum would be anything from $1.00 to $100.00 for the hundred years. The community would be open to following through on this.

Hand-in-hand with the search for land to build the new BSPA ashram went the need for the group to firmly agree upon the goals of this new venture. Why had they left the comfortable cloisters of the BSPA monasteries with their beautiful chapels to come to Oklahoma looking to build something new? In the group's March, 1979 report, under the heading of COMMUNITY, Sr. Pascaline reported, "All 5 are making real effort at contemplative atmosphere: peace, non-violent heart, gentleness, sensitivity to others, quiet, prayerfulness, prayer time, and communion through communication."

Both Srs. Trini and Pascaline have turned down at least five requests for retreats or other talks necessitating long trips from the community at this time.

—New Form of Adoration: the group has chosen a common period of adoration both morning and evening during that time, sacred in the East, when darkness changes to light and light changes to darkness. Before Praises a Eucharistic bhajan (antiphon) is sung several times, then all enter into silence, adoring the Father with Jesus, and pondering his gift and his call to be Eucharist. The periods conclude with the ringing of the bell and/or a repetition of the initial bhajan. The same is done after the Marian Anthem at night with the glass tabernacle recently made by Sr. Trini.

Other times of adoration are offered in the afternoon or night. Several pray during the night. Many rise early, long before Praises. During the wait for more permanent quarters this mode of adoration has been chosen as fitting and "right" for all concerned. Some consider it profound.

Under the heading of Forming Community, Sr. Pascaline reported Sr. Trini's request for a transfer out of Tulsa, adding, "The group was unanimous in wanting to lovingly and prayerfully support Sr. Trini in her present need." Sr. Pascaline also reported:

Sharing the atmosphere and prayer on a limited basis with the Congregation, diocese, etc. has not been possible, although a Passionist priest and a Franciscan nun made 6-day directed retreats and Srs. M. Lupita and Judith visited.

Secretarial work for the A.I.M. North American Board has continued and is full-time, even when shared because of Bulletin, mailings, etc. We agree with Mother Audrey that it, too, really is our 'unique way to express Eucharist.'

The search for land continued through March, April and May, 1979. Sister Priscilla remembered:

We went to so many places, some were given as a gift, more or less, but had [only] one tree on it. We knew what we wanted, trees, trees, plenty of trees, even a little crick – creek. But it was all flat many places we went. One place was a nice place, but it was on Keystone Lake and there would be motorboats coming all the time. After the boats were there awhile we said no, no matter how much would be given us of this property, we couldn't take it.

1976–1980

The season of Lent brought requests for Sr. Pascaline to speak to various Catholic groups about contemplative prayer, and it was at one of these that she first met Mary Vance, a real estate agent who would become a great friend of the Tulsa group. Mary joined them in the hunt for the right property.

During Holy Week, Abbot Tholens, the Benedictine monk from Amsterdam who had helped found AIM and organize its boards in America and Europe, arrived to spend Easter with the Tulsa group and "celebrated East-West liturgies for Passover."

As April turned into May, the search continued, along with preparation of the May Bulletin. The publication was expanded to 12 pages with this issue and carried Part 1 of a long interview with Abbot Tholens. There were also two book reviews, one by Father Jim; and one, of Bede Griffiths' *Return to the Center*, by Sr. Pascaline.

In early June, Sr. Pascaline traveled to St. Louis to attend a BSPA congregation workshop. Here she reported on the Tulsa experience. Afterward, Sister Matthias returned with her to Tulsa to help in the search for land. They spent a fruitless week of looking. Finally, Sr. Matthias boarded a Greyhound bus back to St. Louis.

She left just before the "Eureka moment." Within days, Sr. Pascaline phoned from Tulsa with the news that another piece of land had been shown them, and she felt sure it was exactly what they had been looking for.

By this time, the friendly real estate lady, Mary Vance, had become a frequent visitor to the house on 22nd Place, along with her friend Elva. Visiting with the Sisters, showing them various properties, and even sharing some of their anthems and bhajans, Mary and Elva had gained a very clear idea of what Sr. Pascaline and the group were looking for.

As Sr. Priscilla would later recall:

Such beautiful people ... the ladies that helped us find this property. We call them cofounders with us. Mary Vance was one ... She asked her son about it and he said, "I know just the place [Sr. Pascaline] would like." And so he brought her out and as soon as she saw it, that was it.

The land was in the southeast corner of Osage County. It was being developed for rural residences near the community of Sand Springs, just a twenty-minute drive west of Tulsa. Like the Pawhuska land, it was wooded and had hills, views, a creek and privacy. The nearest houses would be a mile away down a country road.

The land had originally been part of the 1906 Osage allotment and later the homestead of Edward Anderson and his wife and four daughters. Anderson was 1/16 Osage, and at age 21 was issued a certificate of competency by the US Department of the Interior so that he could make use of his allotted property however he wished, without a guardian, as would have been required had he been a half-blood or more Indian. The Andersons farmed on a nearby piece of the homestead, and it isn't hard to imagine the four Anderson sisters growing up and hiking in those woods and playing along that creek, just as would the Benedictine Sisters in a later era, when

© SCOTT THOMPSON

this became the Osage Monastery Forest of Peace.

The search that had begun more than a year before was over. The date when Sr. Pascaline first saw the place where she would spend the next 30 years of her life expressing Eucharist was June 16, 1979, two days after the Feast of Corpus Christi. Three days later, the group celebrated Eucharist at Bishop Beltran's home and then "visited the 'Forest' with joy."

Sr. Pascaline's first impression that this was "it" was confirmed, and Sisters Miriam and Kathryn were sent from the BSPA motherhouse to look over the property and make a down payment, which they did on June 22, another date propitious from Sister Pascaline's point of view, the Feast of the Sacred Heart.

The preliminary agreement they signed was to purchase "40 acres, Osage County, Sand Springs, Oklahoma." On June 30, the shape of the property was changed by the developers at the Sisters' request, as they began serious planning for building on the land. They hoped to finish construction on the main building and two little cabins (one for Father Jim and one for a visitor or retreatant), before winter. On July 11 the developers finalized the sales agreement. Sr. Pascaline sent it on to St. Louis, along with a letter to Mother Audrey and her Council.

A few days earlier, Sisters David and Benita had arrived from St. Louis with a truck and camper for the Tulsa group. "Thank you for that conveyance," Sr. Pascaline wrote. "There is no way to drive over the meadows at present without a truck." They had walked the "entire piece" several times.

The letter also shared with the Council news of a new member in the Tulsa community. "We received the gift of a puppy two days ago and named it Vedanta (joy). It is a brown and black shepherd which we hope will grow up with us so that when we get to the woods he will be able to bark and be brave." The "pup," actually a German shepherd/doberman pincher mix, was quickly nicknamed "Nandi."

Mother Audrey signed the sales contract on July 16, and shared the news with the BSPA congregation in a letter:

Dear Sisters,

On this feast of Our Lady of Mt. Carmel it was my privilege and joy to sign the contract which transfers to our congregation the 40-acre tract of land upon which, God willing, the Tulsa community will begin to establish the new small foundation approved by the general chapter. Undoubtedly you will be hearing directly from Sister M. Pascaline as the endless details of planning gradually move toward clarity and reality. I am confident you will continue to pray for God's blessing on this new center of life and love within our congregation.

A week later Mother Audrey drove down to Tulsa to see the "Forest" for herself. All that was left now was for the abstract to be cleared and the deed to the land to be transferred to the BSPA, which happened on August 3.

Meanwhile, on July 29, the Tulsa Sisters and Fr. Jim drove to Conception Abbey near the Clyde monastery in Missouri for the series of lectures presented by Fr. Bede Griffiths and Brother Amaldas. This was the longest stop on the lecture tour that Sister Pascaline had arranged on behalf of the NABEWD. In order to make the long trip from India to the USA, Fr. Bede had overcome his famous dislike of modern technology and boarded a jet to New York. Upon arriving in New York, he fell ill, and six of the scheduled 24 stops on the speaking tour had to be cancelled.

At Conception Abbey, Father Bede spoke on "Vedanta, the doctrine of man's union with God, while Brother Amaldas presented Yoga, the practical discipline of man's union with God."[16] Here, Fr. Bede also gave the Tulsa group a "large bronze statue of Nataraj for our Ashram, figure of Christ in Resurrection."

Father Bede and Brother Amaldas arrived in Tulsa on August 6, and it was Sr. Pascaline's joy to welcome them at the door of the house on 22nd Place much as Father Bede had welcomed her to Saccadanada three years earlier. It was, as Sr. Pascaline noted, another propitious date, the Feast of the Transfiguration.

With the signed deed in hand, the Sisters only needed the construction of a common space and some sleeping quarters to transform 40 acres of Osage County woods, rocky outcroppings, hills and ravines into the Osage Monastery Forest of Peace. On August 8, Srs. Pascaline, Priscilla, Christine, Monica and Father Jim took the two visitors from India out to their "Forest." The group that gathered there also included the Wilkinson family, who were excited to be met at the gate to the property by a deer.

---

16 NABEWD Bulletin #6, October, 1979.

STANDING: SR. MONICA, SR. PRISCILLA, FR. JIM, SR. CHRISTINA, FR. BEDE GRIFFITHS.
KNEELING: SR. PASCALINE, BR. AMALDAS.

The Sisters spread a sheet of clear plastic on the ground. As Sr. Pascaline would later report in the *Eastern Oklahoma Catholic* newspaper, "We prepared for the Eucharist by dropping a large painter's plastic over the heavy foliage. Everyone sat in wonder as Father Bede and Father Jim prepared for the Eucharist – and creeping things crept right under us, like a glass bottom boat view."

Here, Father Bede "blessed the four directions, calling down God's peace, love and protection on all who were at that moment entering into the ancient and sacred tradition of forest dwellers, as well as on all who would visit in the future." Then, Bede and Father Jim together, using the forest floor itself as their altar, celebrated the very first Eucharist in the Forest of Peace.

The scripture was the text where the scouts went out to survey the land and came back reporting 'giants.' In his homily, Father Bede said there are giants today, giant forces of good and of evil, and so he prayed that the evil forces would never harm any who are here or come here.

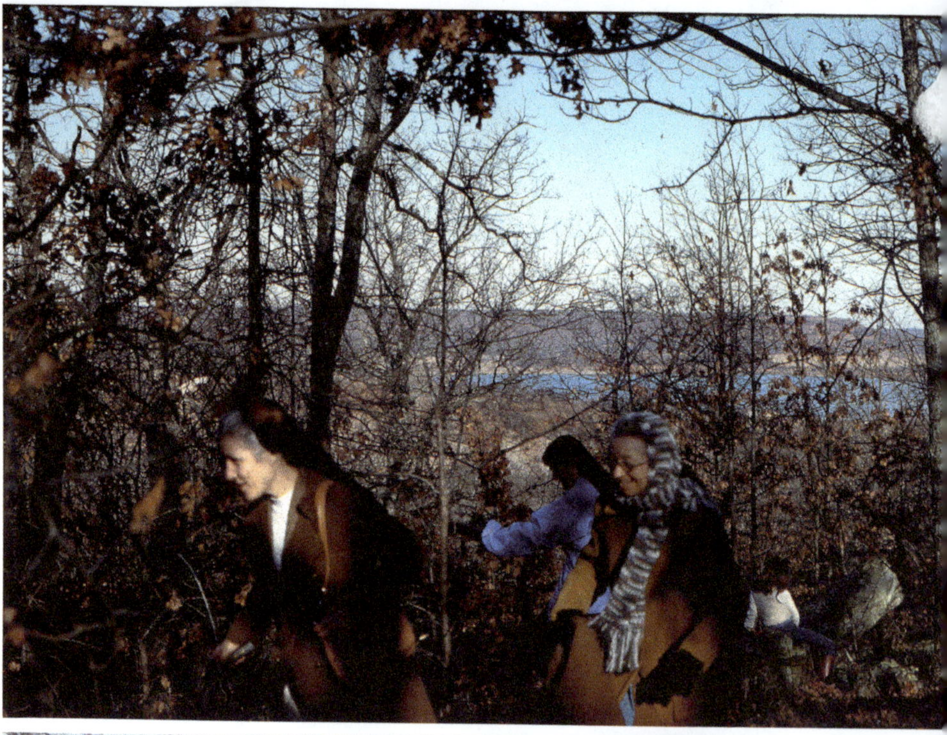

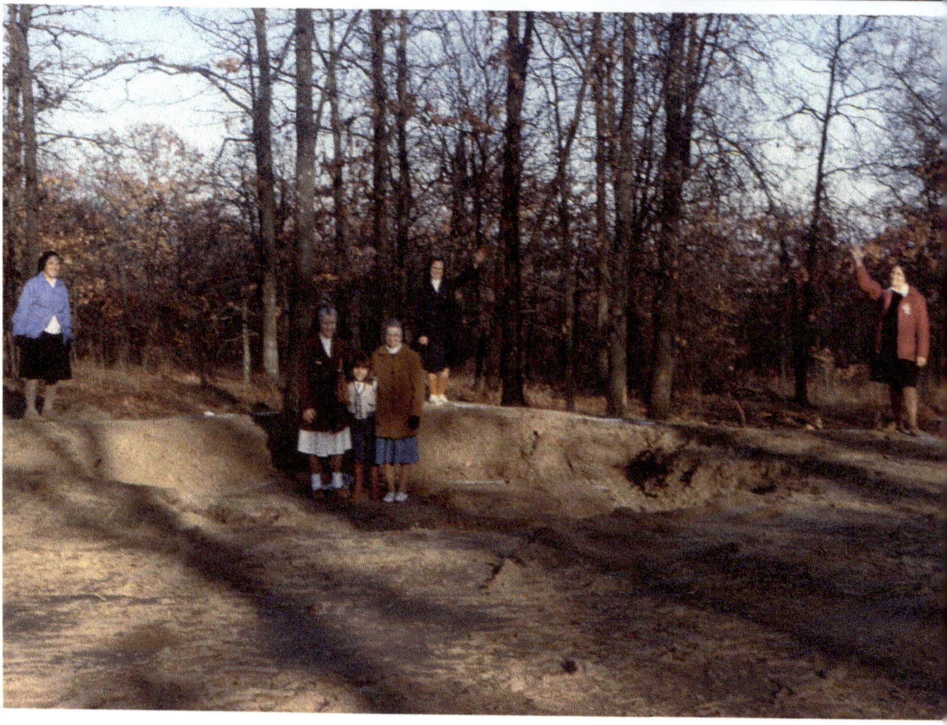

OSAGE FOREST
1979 & 1980

"Buildings greatly determine the character of a whole place."
—Letter to Prioresses Council and Mother Audrey from Srs.
Pascaline, Priscilla, Monica and Christine

By the time their purchase of the property had been finalized, the Sisters and their chaplain were reconsidering the original plan to move prefabricated buildings onto their land. On August 10 they took an architect to the Forest to look over the property and discuss ideas for building on it. The architect, Jack Butz, was a friend of Ruth Wilkinson, the real estate lady who had sold the land to the BSPAs. The following Tuesday, Butz showed them drawings he had made for the buildings, "gratis." They liked what they saw.

Sister Pascaline, anxious that construction get well underway during the fall, before a repeat of the previous winter's ice and snow could delay things, got busy getting price estimates for the first buildings. Bob Sellers, the builder for the nearby Shell Creek West residential development, had given them a bid for the proposed main building, constructed from the ground up according to Butz's design, that wasn't too much more than what the metal prefab buildings would have cost. The next day, in a four-hour meeting with Sellers, the Sisters convinced him to shave five percent off of his original bid, and they were "sold."

On Labor Day weekend the Sisters and their chaplain held a "special prayer day in our Forest. We staked off the common house and 4 cabins."

Two days later, Father Jim "shared deeply with us regarding our needs for special consideration in our building, atmosphere, etc." The group vision that emerged was unlike the typical Catholic monastic houses and convents, but not exactly like an ashram, either. In addition to the main house with its kitchen, refectory and chapel, the prospective forest dwellers had decided on separate hermitage cabins, scattered through the woods, where each would sleep and pray in solitude.

The Tulsa group would need approval from the BSPA Council for monies to build the monastery buildings, so a letter was drafted, addressed to the Prioresses' Council and Mother Audrey, explaining in detail what the group wanted and making a formal request. The hand-typed "letterhead" read: "Forest of Peace—O+M—Osage Monastery, Sand Springs, OK." This was the first appearance in the written record of the O+M or Osage Monastery name. Dated September 24, 1979, the letter read in part:

Request: in virtue of the great importance physical surroundings play in a life and lifestyle, we beg to build now a common house and to provide one-room structures conducive to contemplative prayer and its atmosphere, clustered but not doubled-up into plexes. This would keep the overall outlay [low] at this time and would avoid having "concrete plexes" which, once erected, will stand forever. We and others believe protection-wise there would be little difference between rooms touching and having one-room structures relatively close. But it would make a great difference in regard to prayer to be some distance from "touching" the next one's room.

The letter also asked that the cabins have indoor toilets and sinks, but no hot water or showers, explaining, "We want an opportunity to live poorly, frugally, the authentic and liberating witness of the Gospel." It isn't clear whether this was a desire shared wholeheartedly by all the group, or if it was mostly Sr. Pascaline's. (When the community's cabins were built, the only one without a shower would be Sr. Pascaline's.)

Enclosed with the letter were "floor plans, elevations, prices and specifications."

Bob Sellers is highly recommended by Mrs. Ruth Wilkinson, who sold us the forest. Bob is between buildings at the moment and in virtue of beginning ours immediately is not taking another. Mr. Paul Hoey and Don Piscopo of the Piscopo Construction Company were here last evening and have agreed to be our Construction managers, and together with the architect, Jack Butz, promised to oversee the work, going out every Sunday until it is completed. They will also help us line up individual fixtures, flooring, driveway, etc. needed to be agreed upon before commencing the building. Attached is also a list of monies collected or promised toward the buildings and land, all channeled to date to St. Louis. Thank you again for your trips, your tips, your trust, your love and concern. With trustful love in Him and in you, we wait,

Hopefully in His Heart,
Sr. Pascaline   Sr. Priscilla
Sr. Monica   Sr. Christine

Having completed this request letter to the BSPA Prioress General, the O+M group placed it on the altar in their little sunroom chapel on 22nd Place while they celebrated Eucharist on September 25, then mailed it to St. Louis.

As they neared the Feast of St. Michael, 1979, and thus the first anniversary of the group's arrival in Tulsa, they counted among their blessings the friends they had made in their new diocese, beginning with their "Trappist chaplain" Father Jim. In addition to the donations and promises of donations for buildings in the Forest of Peace, donations of services, and the free rent from the Benedictines of St. Joseph's for the 22nd Place house, there was the enthusiasm and generosity of the Bishop and of the real estate people and others that had become close friends and donors.

Support also came from retreatants. Most recently, Franciscan nun Sister Marie Therese, a Sioux, had come for a vision quest and spent a day out in the Forest alone as part of her retreat on September 27. She was, as Sr. Pascaline wrote in a letter to Bishop Beltran, "our first retreatant in the Forest. She prayed the moving prayer of Black Elk and then remained quiet in prayer for hours without food or water. The lessons of the Forest were profound."

Sr. Pascaline's talks about contemplative prayer to Catholic groups in town and articles in the *Eastern Oklahoma Catholic* newspaper had been greeted with enthusiasm and more requests for retreats, this time by laypeople. The A.I.M. salary had been well earned as the group had published five Bulletins, coordinated events, participated in the Merton conference at Columbia University, and organized Father Bede's North American tour. Bede's arrival just in time to bless the new property seemed to be a sign that all was unfolding just as it was meant to be. The group had by now adjusted to the little house in Tulsa, and they had worked hard at forming community with each other, not just in living and worshipping together, but by taking time to share in depth with each other, speaking heart-to-heart.

On September 29, 1979, Sr. Pascaline opened the pages of a new chronicle book for the Osage Monastery with the words: "Sat. 9/29 Feast of St. Michael — 1st Anniversary! A litany of gratitude was prepared spontaneously during Day Hours."

On October 1, M. Audrey sent the O+M request letter out to the BSPA Prioresses, along with her own letter explaining:

Sister M. Pascaline has continued to work toward the erection of buildings before the winter sets in and we have tried to be of some assistance in helping her objectify her aims.

At this point we will need to make a decision concerning an expenditure of major proportions. The extended council has a decisive vote in any building erected for the needs of the entire congregation.

The pressure of time comes, of course, because winter is also coming, a season which is not conducive to outside construction work.

The Prioresses would not be rushed, however. They voted to wait and let Sr. Pascaline make her request in person during their regular session in late October.

The next afternoon Sr. Pascaline had an appointment with Bishop Beltran, who gave her a handwritten note promising "to gift us with the Chaplain's Cabin." He was happy to see the actual work beginning and said he had so desired to do more but because of the renovations next door to the Chancery, he is caught short but will do more, and he knows people will help."

At the Prioresses Council meeting in Clyde, Sr. Pascaline presented a progress report on the O+M and made her formal request for approval to build. The prioresses voted on Saturday morning, October 27, and permission was granted to begin construction on "one common house, one duplex and four individual cabins with showers."¹⁷ Permission had also been given for accepting live-ins, both men and women, at the mutual discernment of the group. Incorporation procedures were to take place immediately.

After the session, Sr. Pascaline phoned Tulsa with the good news. "All were overjoyed."

In the days following the Prioresses' approval, progress sped forward.

On Monday morning Sr. Pascaline "spent hours in the K.C. basement sorting more of the boxes for Tulsa." These were items saved from the Mundelein BSPA house that had been closed the year before. That afternoon, she and Sister Benita, who was coming for a retreat, drove to Tulsa, arriving about 8 PM. Over a supper of hot soup and dessert they rejoiced with all the others that they would now begin to build.

On Wednesday, November 7, "Benita came out of retreat at noon just as the K.C. car arrived with Lillian and Bertilla, who all accompanied us out to the Forest to see the dozer knock down the first trees to clear a way for the chapel and ashram and the cluster of cabins." The group made sure that the clearing for the chapel was made near the spot on the Forest floor where Bede and Father Jim had celebrated the first Eucharist. "The weather was cold and wet, but we all stayed 'til 4:45 'til the bulldozer was finished and started for home where Bertilla's homemade pies were awaiting us."¹⁸

---

17   Discussing the request, the Prioresses were "open and affirming but wanted buildings to be re-salable and practical, so leaned toward showers in the cabins," Sr. Pascaline reported.

18   All facts and quotes in this section are from Sr. Pascaline's handwritten "O+M Chronicle Book 1979-1980," which is held in the BSPA archive in Clyde, Missouri.

The November 13 entry in the chronicle book reported that "Bob Sellers and Jack Butz met with Ruth to firm up our building plans. Bob now needs to do an elevation of the Chapel so Jack can take it and complete it. Also, we have been advised to have Bob bonded. It will be difficult for him to arrange this and will delay things somewhat."

Somewhat indeed! It would be after Christmas by the time the bond was issued. The concrete foundations for the buildings would not be poured until January 17, 1980, on the spots that had been bulldozed November 7.

On November 15, Srs. Pascaline and Marie went to the Forest and found Hubert Miller directing the bulldozer on the new road. "Bob Sellers and wife then went over final details of the contract with us and hopes all will be ready to go on Monday when Jack Butz, architect, will be finished with the final elevation."

All was *not* ready to go that Monday. Two more weeks went by and Thanksgiving came and went. November became December, and still no bond and no construction.

In the meantime, the Sisters prayed and worshipped and worked and waited. Each morning they walked to Cascia Hall, a nearby Augustinian monastery and high school, for Eucharist, then home again to work. They acquired a 1980 bulk mail permit. They got a topographical map of Sand Springs from the Corps of Engineers. They wrote letters asking for funds for the A.I.M. E-W board meeting and Symposium planned for November 1980, "which were placed before the tabernacle before being mailed out." Sr. Pascaline was also fundraising for the Forest, and, as word spread, a few large and small donations arrived.

On December 4, Sr. Pascaline reported, "We became a corporation today:" Benedictine Convent of Perpetual Adoration in Oklahoma, Inc. With the Advent season came planning for Christmas and the annual North American Board for East-West Dialogue meeting, scheduled for December 27–29 in St. Louis, which the BSPAs were again hosting.

The bonding process was slow and Sr. Pascaline "went to see Dick Allred of MidContinent" to get it moving. Bob Sellers, no doubt wanting to get cement poured while the weather was good, moved ahead with construction the week before Christmas, pouring the piers "to prepare for the slabs!" on December 19.

On Christmas Eve:

> Bob Sellers said he was putting in the grade beams this morning for our new buildings. He will try to move his accountant to get the necessary figures to MidContinent for the performance bond today. ... About 9 PM the Hoey family knocked on the door & sang Christmas carols for a few minutes. We invited them in, but they kept their coats on, all 10 of them, and kept singing. They gave us a large box of groceries with sugar, flour, canned goods Jell-O and nuts! Some of us were preparing for 10 PM Eucharist, so it took awhile to get everyone together before we departed. We drove to Madalene for a moving "midnight" liturgy with their exquisite choir directed by Sister Andrea OSB with trumpets and all. After

returning home we enjoyed hot chocolate, Sr. Monica's sister's fruitcake and opened packages from friends and our prior. "The goodness and kindness of God our Savior has appeared."

On the day after Christmas:

Last-minute preparations for East-West board meeting. Dick Allred assured us at 4:15 PM that the performance bond will be issued – we need to send him a copy of the contract and plans and he will have Bob sign an indemnity agreement. Another Christmas gift from Christ's heart!

The long-sought performance bond secured at last, Sr. Pascaline left for the East-West Board's annual meeting with a happy heart on Thursday, December 27, taking a Greyhound bus from Tulsa to St. Louis.

On New Year's Eve, Sister Judith accompanied Sr. Pascaline on her 10½ hour Greyhound bus ride back to Tulsa. Elva met them at the bus station and shared vespers and supper with the Tulsa Sisters. Sr. Pascaline wrote in the chronicle book, for the last day of the 1970s — a decade that had been momentous for her — "Later when all rose for midnight hour of prayer, Mary Vance, Elva and Sister Raphael joined us with bells and then the arati and bhajan: 'Son of David have mercy on me.' Then silence."

Sr. Pascaline's chronicle entries tell the story of the rich and busy life of the little community as they celebrated, prayed, worshipped, worked, planned and built the Osage Monastery in the first months of 1980.

New Year's was a day for the Sisters to renew their vows, and for these Sisters in particular, it was a day to look forward to life in their own Forest of Peace. It had also been declared World Peace Day. Sister Priscilla recalled that in "novitiate and training and that, you didn't have anything to do with the outside world or anything. We didn't know about the Viet Nam War ... nothing that was going on." That had changed for all the Sisters, and now the Tulsa group's involvement with A.I.M. had made them especially aware of and concerned about world affairs. Sr. Pascaline noted in the chronicle book that on this World Peace Day, "The Russians have over 50,000 troops invading Afghanistan while Iran continues to hold our American hostages."

On New Year's Day "Elva and Carrie joined us for a ride out to our property where Sr. Jude and Elva took pictures of the building forms, foundations and rocks and trees." The next day, Don Piscapo took Sr. Pascaline out to the Forest where Bob Sellers was overseeing construction. They viewed the work that had been done so far, had a "lengthy session with Bob," then gave him the signed contracts and the first down payment, and at last received from Bob the performance bond that had been requested by the BSPAs.

Donations of items for the new monastery came from friends in the Tulsa diocese. One family "offered many useful things from their garage (a bathtub! Electric breaker boxes, wire and plumbing pieces, which Bob says he can use)."

January 15 a picnic lunch in the Forest found the builder "hammering long and hard on the forms for the [chapel] pit! We hiked to the two canyons, picked up the bill for the performance bond, then headed home."

Two days later, the slab concrete poured at last, Pascaline wrote in the chronicle:

> We buried a St. Benedict medal in the chapel cement & sang "Holy Father Benedict, leader & our guide, … praying that God will be glorified by all who work, live and visit this Forest of Peace – an unbelievable blessing during this year of the 1500th anniversary of St. Benedict's birth when so much violence and turmoil reigns everywhere.[19]

On a frigid February 1, Bob Sellers reported that the framers began carpentry work on the main house. That same week, the Sisters collected more materials people had donated, including several hundred dollars' worth of insulation, "which we loaded into our Ford pickup then drove to Bob Sellers' barn to unload and see the Forest & framing."

Early February's cold weather slowed work in the Forest somewhat, but the Sisters had plenty to do indoors in Tulsa, with work on the NABEWD Bulletin, due out that month. For each issue they compiled, edited or wrote articles, typed up a rough draft, mailed it to Abbot Armand for approval, then retyped everything with corrections for duplication at a Tulsa copy service. Once copied, the hundreds of pages had to be assembled, folded, addressed, zip-code sorted and mailed out using the group's bulk mail permit. It was a job that required "all hands on deck" for several days at a time. The next issue would be due out in May, just as the community was moving out to the Forest and preparing a large dedication celebration.

During a reception at St. Joseph's Convent on February 10, Bishop Beltran told the Sisters that June 8, Corpus Christi Sunday, had been marked in his books for a year as the dedication day for O+M, and his "whole summer gravitates around it. Whatever time we choose for services will be fine — the whole day is ours!" They quickly began planning the liturgy for the dedication ceremonies and praying for the construction to be completed by the first week in June.

The O+M community made regular visits to the Forest through February, March and April, enjoying the progress as the framing rose, roofs went on "slated in a nice light color," showers and a bathtub went in. On March 3, Sr. Christine visited the KC priory and returned "ladened with love and good things from Kansas City." Two days later "we all went searching for furniture at an unfinished furniture warehouse, but prices were beyond us, so we ended up at Goodwill and Pink Elephant." At a farmers' co-op they found "some old doors Maurice wanted to make into beds."

When Sr. Lioba visited on March 7 they drove her out to see the Forest.

---

19 The anniversary of St. Benedict's birth in 480 AD was celebrated in special observances by Benedictines and Catholics throughout 1980. The fact that the Osage Monastery would be built and dedicated in the year of the Benedictine sesquimillennium seemed especially auspicious to Sr. Pascaline and her Benedictine Sisters.

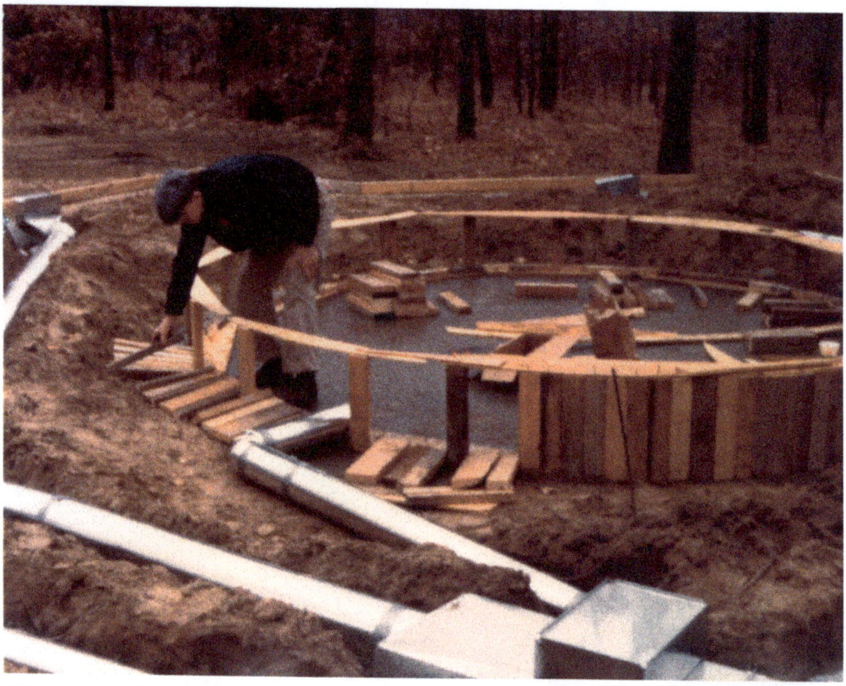

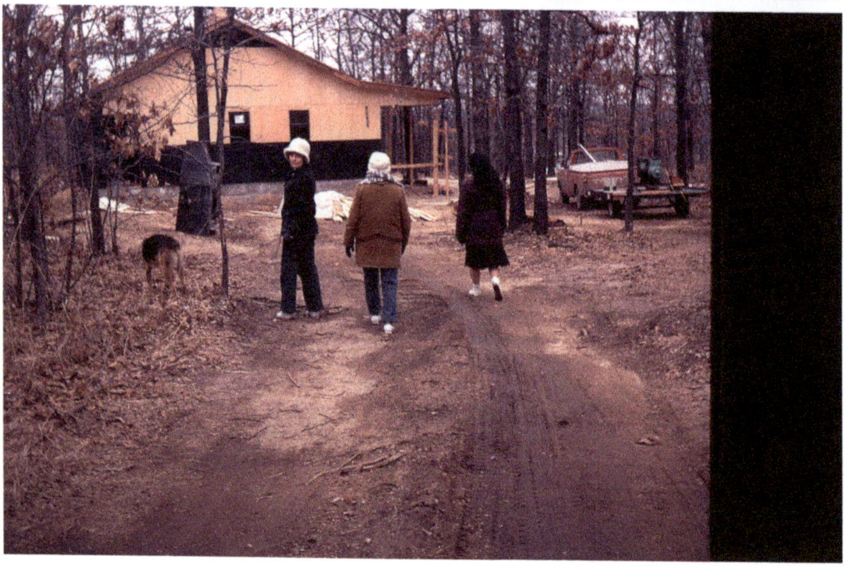

"Bob Sellers took the opportunity to ask us about electrical outlets and chapel appurtenances. The sides are now on the small cabins! Ed Gibson was supervising the sewage trenches." Bob Sellers called early the next Monday regarding the septic tank system, "asking us to go speak with the county health department. Srs. Pascaline and Christine did go to speak with Mr. Roy Wilson."

On a muddy March Sunday, they packed a picnic lunch and headed out to the Forest. Insulators were at work in the chapel trying to ready the building for the sheet-rockers, due the next morning. Bishop Beltran, whom they'd invited to come out and view the construction, arrived about 3:45 PM, "scurried up and down both canyons with us, blessed the buildings and enjoyed a piece of Sr. Christine's homemade pecan pie before departing with our rough draft of plans for Dedication Day."

On March 19, Sr. Pascaline wrote M. Audrey a long letter with her progress report for the past month, her tenth report since beginning the "small group living / ashram" project two years before. She reported the visit from the Bishop, adding, "This was his first time since the clearing of the trees and he just can't believe the transformation."

> He is eager to plan for the dedication and didn't insist but thought the best time for the priests to come would be afternoon so we have now decided on 2 PM for the Eucharist, followed by procession through the woods and benediction outside and inside. ... We are all so happy that all of the Council will be here and are planning on the evening meal with the Bishop and all of you and us, if he will stay. Am not sure who will cook it yet, but we have lots to figure out in the next weeks. PLEASE WOULD YOU BE FIRST READER AT THE MASS THAT DAY?
>
> It was great having Sr. Helen here. The two years have seemed so long and yet so short until she can be with us. She fit in so beautifully and seemed very happy with her few days in our midst.[20]
>
> A gorgeous Easter, M. Audrey, and do keep us in your best prayers. You are always in ours.

One+Heart

As spring brought nice weather, the Sisters visited the Forest almost daily, often accompanied by friends.

FRIDAY, MARCH 21, 1980
We all helped pack a picnic lunch after Praise and left for the Forest for an outdoor Eucharist! Rockers were putting stones in place and cement mixers were grinding so we went on the south side of the cabins to spread the same plastic used for

---

20 Sr. Helen Barrow had wanted to move to Tulsa when the group formed in late September 1978 but had two years left in her commitment as Kansas City Sub-prioress. She visited Tulsa for a short retreat in March 1980 and would soon move and become a long-term member of the O+M community.

FOREST COMMUNITY WITH "SUSIE VAN"

the first Eucharist. Ruth W. brought Carrie, Kimie and Kelly. And Mary Vance brought Juanita West, an Osage. Srs. Priscilla and Monica built a small altar of rocks to place the bread, wine and chalice on. The children rang small bells all during the Gloria and Father Jim sang the Our Father while the warm sun turned us all shades of red. Juanita was very touched and offered to dance for us on our Dedication Day! Sr. Christine's homemade cracked wheat sandwiches stole the hearts of everyone.

FRIDAY, MARCH 28, 1980

After dinner of "soybean crunch" we picked Sister David, SCL up at Greyhound on our way out to the Forest of Peace in "Susie Van." The buildings are all ready for the trim carpenter but there is no electricity so he couldn't proceed!

Holy week brought rain. For the Sisters, work on the East-West symposium to be held the following November, hospitality for guests, and efforts to keep construction moving forward in the Forest fitted in around the traditional Holy Week observances. Sr. Pascaline couldn't very well do the construction work herself, but she was not shy about making in-person visits at the offices of utility companies and others whose delays threatened to slow things down. On March 31 she visited the Sand Springs offices of the electric company "to expedite the electric installation! Mr. Heller was exceedingly good and promised to do what he can."

TUESDAY, APRIL 1, 1980

Eucharist at Cascia. Sister Ann CSJ and Sr. Pascaline drove to the Forest to view the four colors of paint. The painter will begin tomorrow with "saddle brown." This was predicted to be the last day of the world by a preacher in Texas. And here we are!

© SCOTT THOMPSON

On Easter Sunday the Sisters rose before dawn to drive to the Forest for a private Easter sunrise service. "The streets of Tulsa were empty as we watched the rising sun play on the clouds till we arrived at the Forest." When they turned into the grounds, "A wide, lovely rainbow welcomed us – the sign of God's covenant of peace forever!"

Forty days previously, they had "buried the alleluia" as was their custom, not to sing or speak it again during Lent. On Ash Wednesday, there had been no Forest chapel with its circular meditation pit – or "Sundance Circle." Now the chapel was under roof, and, although the floor had not yet been covered with wooden flooring, they held their first Easter celebration here, sitting on the bare cement. "Our incense, fire and bells added festive atmosphere to our alleluias – the first in the Sundance Circle."

That spring was full of activity, but time was set aside for the kind of contemplative studies for which they had all joined the Forest community. Father Jim regularly led studies of the writings of Teresa of Avila and John of the Cross in the living room of the Tulsa house. On the Saturday after Easter, "Sr. Pascaline and Bob Sellers met in the Forest of Peace to negotiate with Mr. Donald Skaggs, trim carpenter, about woodwork. Bob built the first fire in the fireplace to keep us warm."

Picnics in the Forest, sitting around the unfinished chapel pit or outside on nice days, became a regular thing. On Wednesday, April 16, "Denise and Sr. Pascaline took sandwiches to the Forest, measured rooms, floorspace, windows, then went to visit Mr. Skaggs who was building his own home! He will be happy to put in some bureaus, cabinets etc."

On, Saturday, April 19, they all picnicked in the Forest and hiked "down and up the two canyons, then concluded with the Day Hour in the chapel pit. Each took time on a rock for private prayer before heading home for a 5 PM Eucharist at Christ the King."

On Sunday, Sr. Pascaline sat down to write another report to M. Audrey and her council:

Dear M. Audrey, Sr. Miriam and Council,

Only six weeks from today is dedication!!!!!

Thanks so much for sending Rachel and Denise and for all they did to track down appliances while here.

The electric company is beginning to move, but very slowly. Enclosed is a copy of the easement, which needs to be signed by the owners. ... I'm happy for the drawing they did on the plot as we can use it as a basic map of the property. They still won't promise when they will have the electric connected but they are beginning. The trim carpenter wouldn't start without the electric as he says all his equipment takes high-powered motors, air compressor hammers, etc. I guess we can't suggest a more simple way!

OSAGE CHIEF SYLVESTER TINKER AND HIS WIFE ALICE

Gas company has finally agreed to redo their original agreement with the developers and extend their lines out in our direction at the same price they agreed to do it at about four years ago. This is a great achievement and we are grateful. They say they can't begin for 30 days, which will be about mid-May!! Pray!

Road: Hubert Miller, one of the developers who does the roadwork, says they still have to put some fill (rock) on top of where they brought in and packed down dirt and then that has to soak with rain, etc. I told him my community is getting anxious since it's so close to the opening and the road is muddy. According to the contract they would have it completed within 30 days of the signing of our original contract. He says he will see to it.

[Osage] Chief Tinker and his wife Alice came to see us on Friday. We've been trying to make an appointment, but it turned out nicely this way. They stayed for dinner. His sense of humor is delightful. He will carry gifts in the offertory procession. The Chief placed his hands on the tabernacle, on the cross and then on his forehead, his heart and then turned to me, put his hands on my head, on my shoulders and then stooped and touched my feet, then looked me right in the eyes! I didn't know whether to return the blessing or just drink in the one he seemed to be giving. We had him pray the table prayer and it was beautiful.

He mentioned when he arrived that we ought to be in Pawhuska. I'm glad we are settling where we are. He told us how he gave an Indian blanket to Pope Paul VI and told him he would have to relax in order to keep it on him. He said the Pope laughed out loud![21]

---

21 Sylvester Tinker, Chief of the Osage and a Catholic, had an audience with the Pope while on a European tour in the 1970s.

> Storage, St. Patrick's, Sand Springs: After Srs. Lioba and Joy arrived with our Ford pickup ladened with roll-aways and dishes from Mundelein from our K.C. basement, we drove on out to Father McGoldrick's parish where he was awaiting us with a man and lady who all helped us unload our things in the former convent basement. Father was a former Trappist from Snowmass and is a humorous but hard worker! He offered any help they can give us for Corpus Christi, 4 beds for visiting priests if needed, altar boys, vestments, chairs, trucks for moving, etc. All we need to do is let him know! He is so organized, he's like Josephine Marie!! God is soooo good.
>
> Tulsa is dancing for joy in its best Easter outfit ever. The redbuds and dogwood are glorious, and the lawns and parks are bursting with glory.
>
> Bell: the large black bell given us by Mrs. Ruth Wilkinson is being hung this week. Bob is ready to pour concrete for the front porch of the main house and will put beams all around the base of it. Next to this on the East side the bell will have its own little square with some beams standing so that it can be hung from them.
>
> Entrance design: we went to the architect to pick up his suggestion for the main entrance, but he had forgotten to bring it to work. He will have it Monday so we are eager to see what it will be. He was going to put two tepees on it but we assured him we don't intend to give the impression that we are 100% Native American in our thrust but we are surely open to our neighbors, the Osages!
>
> Rachel, Denise, Lioba and Joy all have been in and out the past two weeks and we are deeply grateful to you and to them for all the love and help given. Be sure you and all your needs are remembered by us audibly daily. And know that we surely depend on your prayers and love.
>
> *One+Heart*, Sr. Pascaline
>
> P.S. Sr. Helen's transfer — of course we are grateful and happy![22]

In the eighteen months since moving to Tulsa, Sr. Pascaline's typewriter had been in constant use, typing up letters, reports, grant requests, newsletters, Bulletins, NABEWD minutes, and Sr. Pascaline's editorials, articles and speeches on East-West monasticism. On Monday, April 14, Sr. Pascaline had pounded out a last-minute guest editorial for a Benedictine publication and mailed it just before midnight. The following Sunday's April report letter to M. Audrey and the council gave the Tulsa typewriter another workout, and soon Bulletin #7 would need to be produced. By now, not surprisingly, the machine was in need of repair. Sr. Pascaline's chronicle book—handwritten—shows the typewriter going for the first of several repairs that Wednesday, while Sr. Pascaline and the future O+M ashramites focused on prayers and progress in the Forest.

---

[22] The exclamation point here was dotted with a tiny heart. This letter is "4:80 report" in the Clyde archive.

As April was coming to a close, the Forest of Peace still had no electricity, but "The electric company put up poles today!" Sr. Pascaline reported on April 29. Apparently, Mr. Skaggs had been persuaded to start trim carpentry work "a more simple way," without benefit of his power tools. Much progress was being made, with help and encouragement from BSPA Sisters, friends, and the Sand Springs parish.

The Sisters had moved into the furnished rectory in Tulsa with little besides Priscilla's sewing machine, a typewriter and the clothes on their backs. Now they would be furnishing four cabins, a duplex, and a common house with kitchen, laundry room, bathrooms, refectory, sitting area and chapel.

In addition to the items from the Mundelein monastery that had closed, (carried to Tulsa in several pickup loads) the community — resourceful and creative — shopped for furnishings at garage sales and second-hand stores. They scavenged materials to make pillows and curtains, hand-fashioned chapel appurtenances, created artworks and received much help in all this from friends and neighbors. As items were collected, they were stored at St. Patrick's Church until the Forest buildings were ready. The Sisters collected paint and flooring samples, then voted on their choices.

As things came together in the Forest, excitement grew.

WEDNESDAY, MAY 7, 1980

Charlene Warnken accompanied us to the Forest of Peace after Eucharist. She took a whole roll of film and will do a story [in the *Eastern Oklahoma Catholic*] for our dedication. The electric company was finishing up with its wiring and the road was all graveled. Mr. Skaggs was finished and Bob Sellers was sweeping. We negotiated for the entrance sign. It is too large to leave as is. Bob says the light fixture proposed by Mr. Fusche will not pass electrical inspection, so we'll need to look further.

The problem of finding — or creating — a light fixture for the chapel ceiling was not an easily solved detail, nor was it an unimportant one. The Chapel was far from the usual Catholic place of worship. Nor was it a metal building as had been planned for the Pawhuska property. It is a room, circular in feeling, with little ornamentation except a wall of windows jutting out to reveal a spectacular view of the woods; bringing the peace of the forest indoors. The room is designed for people to sit on the floor — or *in* the floor, since it is dominated by a "sundance circle," a circular pit that is sunken into the earth and beautifully finished in wood. The altar that would soon stand in the center of the circle would be a simple burled stump of a tree, two feet tall, finished to match the floor.

The Sisters searched lighting fixtures shops in vain for a fixture that would give light to this room at night, be in keeping with the simple and natural design of the chapel/ashram, and pass an electrical inspection. After looking at hundreds of chandeliers, they had turned to Mr. Fuche to make a lighting fixture for them, but his design had turned out to be impractical. And time was short.

This chapel light choice was emblematic of a host of concerns in early May, as time grew ever shorter. "One + month + from dedication!" wrote Sr. Pascaline in the O+M chronicle book on May 8. By the end of this month, the entire place would have to be furnished somehow, and equipped well enough for the "ashramites" — Srs. Pascaline, Priscilla, Christine, Monica, and Father Jim — to move there.

Add to all this the NABEWD work that would need to be done. The May Bulletin was due out — an endeavor that would require everybody's help for several days. Then, too, arrangements for the move from Tulsa (and Bristow) to the Forest had to be made, detailed plans for open house celebrations for the O+M dedication on June 8 had to be finished and implemented, and during the week of May 29-June 2, in the midst of the move and less than a week before the dedication, Sr. Pascaline would be leaving to attend the Prioresses' Council meeting in St. Louis where she would formally propose the construction of more cabins in the Forest.

It was a lot, and as she looked at the month ahead, Sr. Pascaline might have been feeling a bit more stress than she had bargained for when she chose for herself a cloistered life of adoration and prayer. But this was also a fulfilling and exciting time, and her chronicle entries remained upbeat.

MAY 15, 1980 ENTRY IN PASCALINE'S CHRONICLE BOOK

FRIDAY, MAY 9, 1980
Carrie Wilkinson came for First Holy Communion preparations and stayed till 8:30. We were wood-burning a sign for the Forest when Mary and Elva surprised us for night prayers, roses for all!

SATURDAY, MAY 10, 1980
Many phone calls to Mr. Wallace and Mr. W.K. Warren brought us hope in Howard Davis for our chapel light. He will come by Monday for our design and then will make it at Mr. Warren's expense! Bulletin process was in earnest today. Completed in rough form by 9 PM! Ready to be mailed to Father Armand in Canada for proofing.

With the Bulletin roughed out, the focus shifted toward the upcoming Dedication Day in the Forest of Peace. After supper on a hot, "quiet" Mothers' Day, the Sisters all began the process of addressing and mailing out invitations. Never mind that the flooring was not yet in place, the plumbing incomplete, the electricity and phones not yet connected, the entrance sign not yet made, the trim carpentry unfinished; there was as yet no altar in the chapel, no flooring on the chapel floor, no light fixture overhead, and a thunderstorm that night was to bring almost constant rain, adding mud to the construction mess in all the buildings. Despite all that, the Sisters and Fr. Jim were moving to the Forest and the chronicle shows how, one after the other — somewhat miraculously — the details fell into place.

MONDAY, MAY 12, 1980
Rain! Pastor Wayne met Paul Halloway at his office and went to look at some floor coverings in a warehouse and then brought two rolls to be delivered from Oklahoma City on Wednesday. We were able to use our tax-exempt number. After lunch Mr. Wallace came and drove Srs. Christine and Pascaline to the Forest to meet with Mr. Howard Davis and carpenter from the W.K. Warren crew[23] and Steve Olsen, architect. They collaborated in designing a suitable light for the chapel so all can read around the pit and over the altar. Anselma and Sr. Priscilla worked on our invitations. Letter was left at Sellers' today to deliver to our new postman for change of address.

TUESDAY, MAY 13, 1980
New keys were made today for our front door. Father Jim came for Eucharist and was overjoyed at the prospect of our moving in, possibly next week. He will close up the rectory and come help us. He has a man making an altar from a tree stump in Muskogee. We all worked on invitations today.

On the afternoon of May 15 at 1:30, in a heavy rain, electric power went on for the first time in the Forest. Pascaline's chronicle recorded her "Alleluia!"

---

23 This "crew" was involved in construction at St. Francis Hospital in Tulsa, underwritten by the W.K. Warren Foundation.

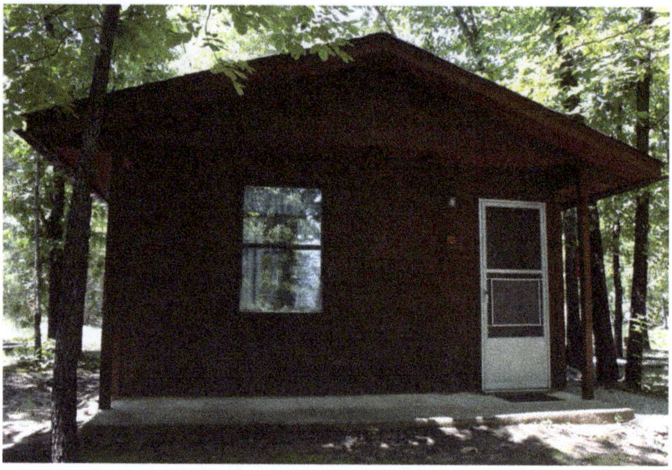

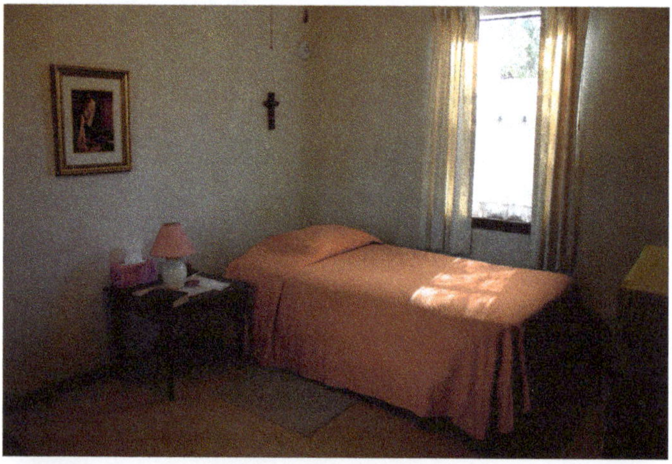

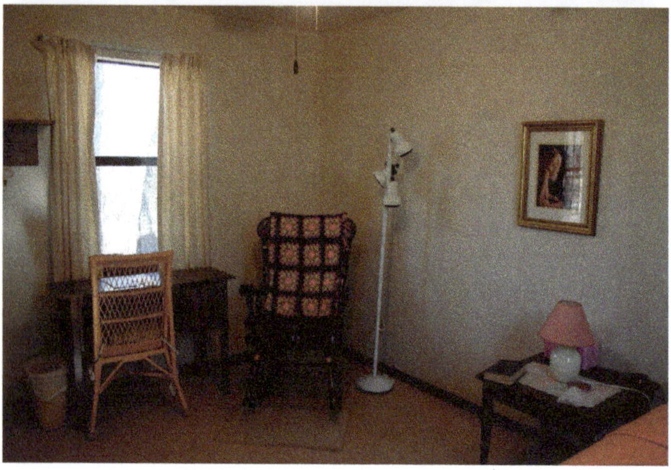

FRIDAY MAY 16, 1980

More rain. Srs. Priscilla, Christine and Pascaline went to the phone company this PM to arrange for service in the Forest, then drove out to the property to sweep up the cabins and clean out all the paper and boxes left from the electrician. All light fixtures are now in place. Margot had a package for us from our Sisters in Tucson — three more beautiful afghans ! for our new cabins.

As they cleaned up the cabins, the Sisters burned what they could of the construction trash and piled the rest in the back of the pickup truck, taking it to the dump – or to the dumpster at Monte Casino. Rain and mud challenged them, but never halted their efforts.

WEDNESDAY, MAY 21, 1980

Father Jim came for Mass and another class on St. John of the Cross — on the depth of God touching the depth of the soul! We found our first mail in our new box today: a reply to our dedication invitation – from the Archbishop of Oklahoma City saying he couldn't come but will remember us in prayer. We obtained gas and carpet samples in the AM. After 3 PM several went to the Forest even though it was drizzling. The cabin floors are finished, the chapel pit is yet to be covered. The kitchen area is done and a man was laying the fireplace Brigantine rolls. Hubert Miller was out on his tractor digging the waterpipe holes.

BSPA Sisters came and went, helping the "Tulsa Four" however they could, and enjoying an occasional prayer day alone in one of the cabins or "Eucharist on the rocks" with the Community and Fr. Jim.

Much work remained, but by May 24, the cabins had been finished, ready for one final cleaning and then the move-in, a process that would take place in stages, over the next two weeks as the Dedication drew near.

SATURDAY, MAY 24, 1980

Moving day! All went to the Forest early to clean and prepare for the belongings coming from Sand Springs. Father McGoldrick got four trucks to help us move our storage: Rollaway beds, trunks etc. to the cabins. He again offered to help in any way he can. We cleaned up and locked up afterwards.

The next day — the Feast of St. Bede and Pentecost Sunday — Father Jim met the Sisters in the Forest for the first Mass ever to be celebrated in the chapel. Sr. Pascaline wrote:

> In the evening of the first day of the week — Jesus came and said, 'Peace be to you!' Father prayed for special blessings through the Spirit of Love on all our undertakings. Sr. Priscilla prepared a picnic meal indoors. The temperature was 93° so we were happy to be inside for this 'feast of fire.' We returned home tired and happy, singing Vespers at 8:45 PM.

This first chapel mass was followed two nights later by the Sisters' first night in their new home.

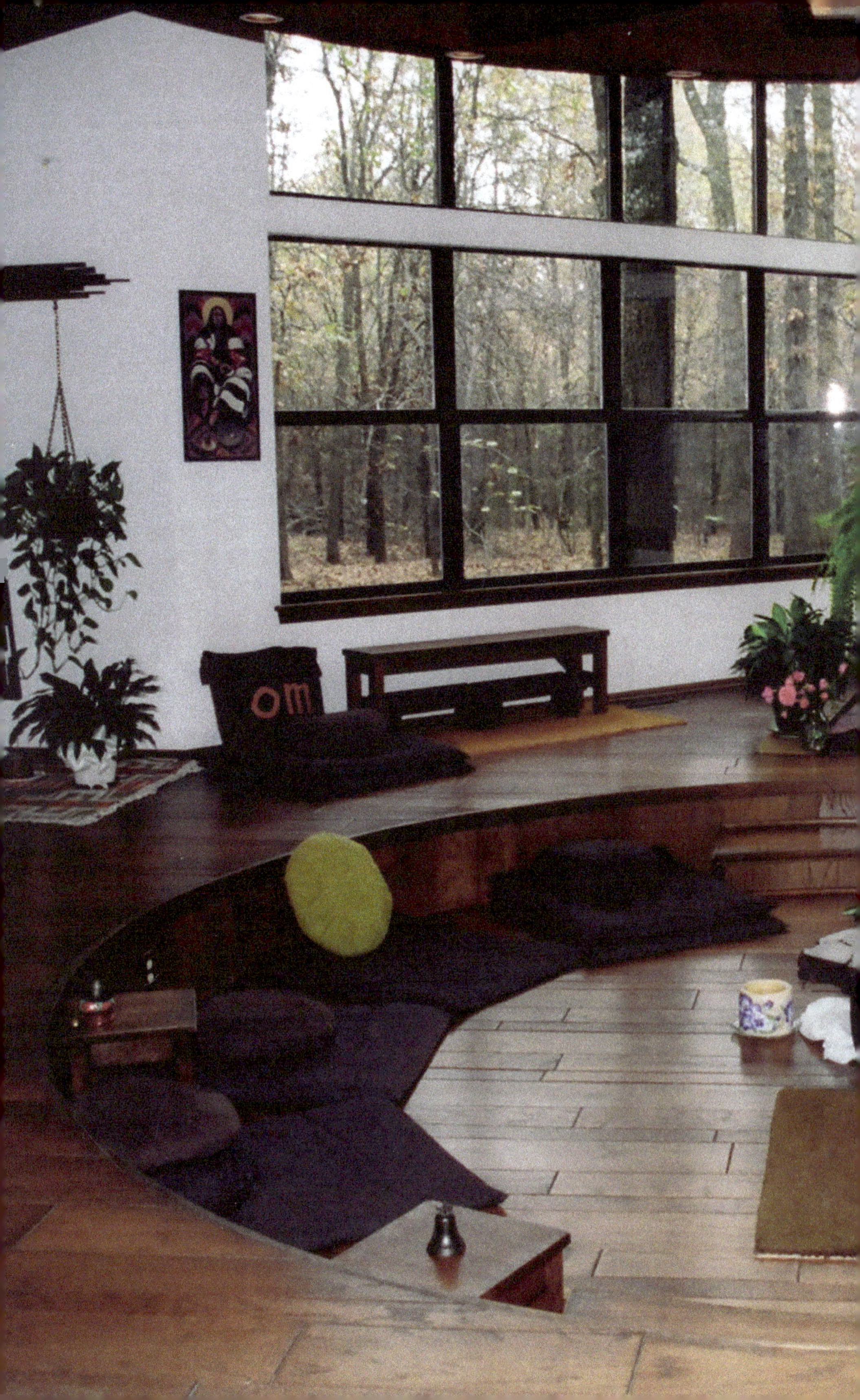
om

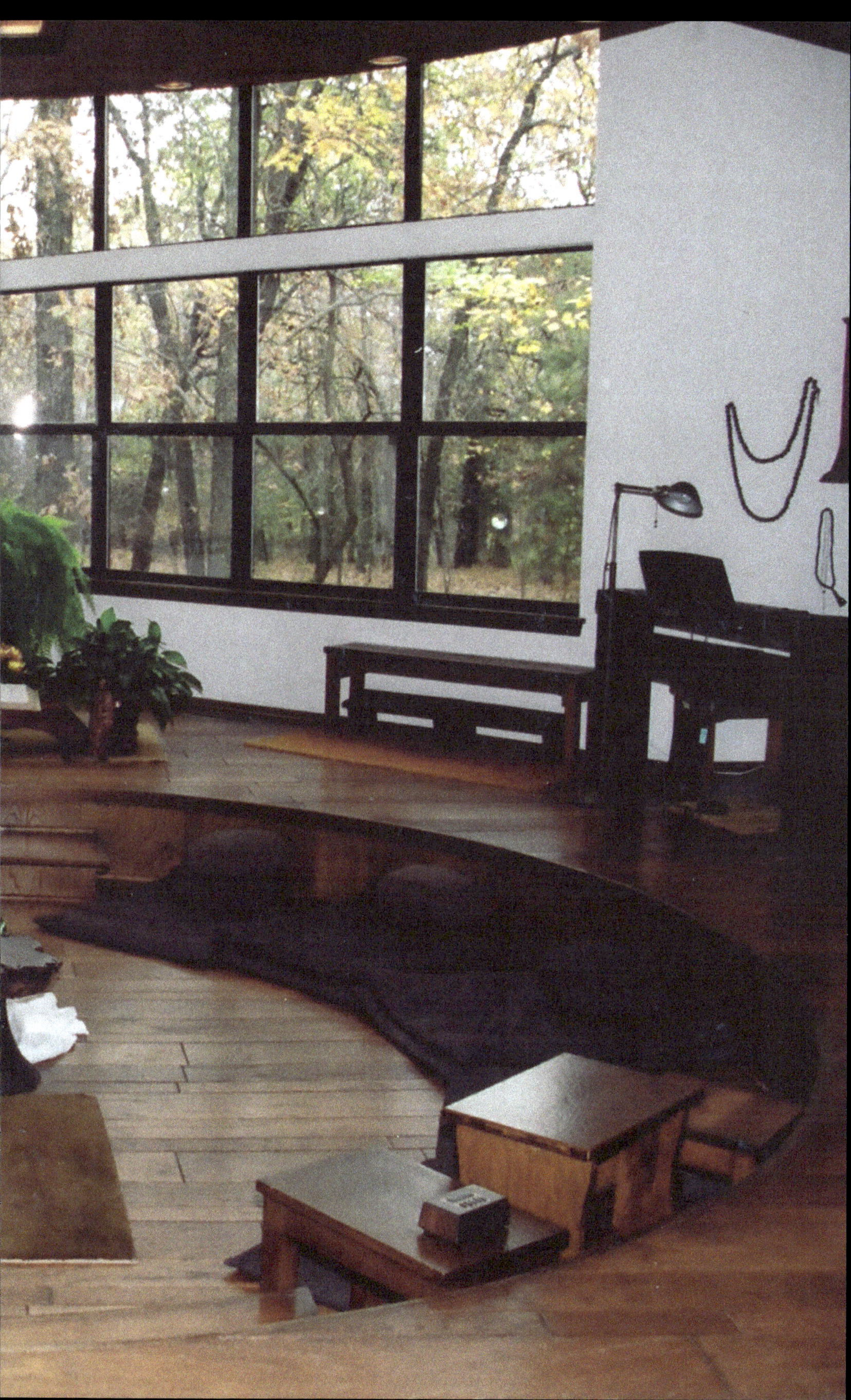

TUESDAY, MAY 27, 1980

Banking and shopping, car washing, and packing filled the AM. About 3:30 we all started out after Father Jim's Eucharist to spend our first night in the Forest. Nandie [the puppy] entered the pickup reluctantly but was happy to be with us. No Bulletin came from Canada in either mailbox.[24] Bob Sellers brought us water before we had our picnic supper indoors. Mr. and Mrs. Bob Garrett from St. Patrick's in Sand Springs came out to make our arrangements for Dedication Sunday. Nadine will help serve. After vespers in chapel each one retired to her cabin. Nandie slept on Sr. Priscilla's porch. Whippoorwills sang us to sleep.

WEDNESDAY, MAY 28, 1980

Praises and adoration for the second time in the chapel began our day, after which all drove back to Tulsa for Eucharist and breakfast. Sr. Dawn flew in around 2 PM to accompany Sr. Pascaline to the PC meeting in St. Louis! We brought her out straight from the airport to the Forest.

Sometime during this Wednesday morning or early afternoon, Sr. Pascaline typed up her report on the O+M for the Prioresses' Council meeting, listing all the details of the construction work, the move, donations and plans for the dedication, which was now just eleven days away. She reported more gifts to the Forest from Catholics in the Tulsa diocese. "Mr. W.K. Warren ... is donating the light fixture in chapel, also the sign at the entrance. People are beginning to recognize a Presence."

With her "Progress Report and Request" in hand, Sr. Pascaline, accompanied by Sister Dawn, left the next day for the drive to St. Louis. In her absence, work continued on construction and plans for Dedication Day, now just over a week away. On Friday, May 30, "Plumbing and carpentry still need completion. Mary G. brought some drapes and clothing in the evening."

The next day:

Father McGoldrick phoned regarding the food shower the people are having for us in his parish. At St. Louis today Sr. Pascaline presented the Tulsa progress report and submitted the request for eight cabins for the community side of the forest.[25] Mother Audrey decided the Council would vote on this on Tuesday of next week.

Sr. Pascaline, having presented her report, only stayed long enough to attend a Benedictine Sesquimillennium celebration on Sunday with Cardinal Basil Hume and "all four Benedictine communities" in St. Louis, then boarded a bus for an all-night trip back to Tulsa. The Council had not yet voted on the proposed new cabins, but she no doubt felt the need to be "home" to finish all that was still unfinished — the "May" Bulletin, the move-in, the chapel and other construction,

---

24   They were waiting on Abbot Armand's corrections to the rough draft of the May Bulletin.

25   Once these new cabins were constructed, the Forest Dwellers would move there and leave the original cabins for guests.

© MARY JANE MATTHEWS

© MARY JANE MATTHEWS

© MARY JANE MATTHEWS

© MARY JANE MATTHEWS

© 2015 ROSEMARY DELUCCA ALPERT

and the preparations for the dedication, now just six days away. She must have been exhausted, but that didn't keep her from writing in the chronicle book each day. There was a lot to chronicle.

MONDAY, JUNE 2, 1980

Sr. David and Sr. Christine came with the pickup to meet Sr. Pascaline at the Greyhound at 8. The bus arrived at 9:20 AM! Sr. David went shopping later and made a trip to the Forest with Bob Sellers's last building payment and the check for the fence. The E-W Bulletin was begun today, even though the rough draft has not yet been returned from Canada.

TUESDAY, JUNE 3, 1980

We made a late trip to the property to get another load out, to meet Jack Morgan at his home to pick up some fire extinguishers and to meet Bob Garretson and Randy who brought us a nice black loveseat and lots of groceries from the parish. As we left to return to the city about 8:45 PM, three deer were on the gravel drive and another larger one on the dead-end road! "He comes leaping…" The Bulletin was taken to Brookside around 4 PM.

WEDNESDAY, JUNE 4, 1980

Eucharist at Cascia. Another truckload was prepared for the Forest – Sr. David, Sr. Priscilla, and Sr. Christine took it out about 2 PM. Bulletin was retrieved about 4:30 so we began in earnest and went until 10:30 collating and folding to be ready for our last "move" tomorrow. Mary Vance came about 8:30 and helped fold awhile. Armand wrote — on the bus May 29 en route to his overseas plane— corrections for the Bulletin. A little too late but none that were essential. Father Jim phoned to plan for the move tomorrow. No call from the Prioress's Council?

In fact, BSPA Prioresses back in St. Louis had voted on Monday, June 2, to approve the construction of the eight additional one-room cabins in the Forest. Sr. Pascaline, busy as she was and rarely near a telephone, apparently hadn't gotten the word yet.

THURSDAY, JUNE 5, 1980

Two truckloads today. Sr. Christine stayed in the Forest while the rest prepared the second load. We arrived about 5 PM tired and hungry. Father Jim had stopped off to buy some supper, which all enjoyed. The O+M sign at the gate is perfect!

FRIDAY, JUNE 6, 1980

Father Jim, Sr. David and Sr. Priscilla returned to 22nd Place for another truckload and to prepare rooms for our Council. The first car of our sisters arrived from St. Louis about 4:30. Kathryn, Sr. Dawn, Matthias and Jude in our Tulsa Chevy. They were overawed at the place. Mr. Warren's crew arrived early to begin hoisting the wagon wheel light fixture. They also hoisted the cross and tabernacle for us.

The "wagon wheel" light was so large it had to be "brought into the building in pieces," Sr. Pascaline would later recall. The long-searched-for chapel fixture indeed resembles a giant wagon wheel and is a dominant feature of the O+M chapel. It hangs over the circular pit, centered above the polished "tree-of-life" altar. The chandelier augments natural daylight from the wall of windows and provides nighttime lighting in the chapel. Not until after they got it hung did the Catholic ashramites realize that it also resembled the medicine wheel of both Buddhist and Native American cosmologies, with its "spokes" radiating out to the four cardinal and four ordinal directions.

SATURDAY, JUNE 7, 1980

All pitched in to purchase needed supplies, clean the chapel floor and rearrange newly arriving furniture. M. Audrey, Sr. Mariam and all arrived around four and began helping everywhere. (Srs. Kristia, Helen, Kathleen, Margaret and Ramona). Mrs. Sellers obtained tables for us for the Sunday night supper and had her boys deliver them. Ruth Slickman arrived about 4 PM with our Sunday supper already prepared. We enjoyed the meal Bonnie Curtain prepared, which Sister David picked up this morning. Father Jim drove her in and brought back three large rockers and a rustic clock for our longhouse![26] After supper we rang a bell and began opening some of the packages which had been sent. We sang first Vespers of Corpus Christi around eight, soon after the Kansas City car arrived with Bridget, Sr. Trini, and Sr. Paul Marie (from Hogan). The Sand Springs parishioners brought the outdoor altar and chairs.

As the O+M community bedded down in their new home Saturday night, all was ready for Dedication Day in the Forest of Peace. The years of prayer and exploration,

---

26   Sr. Pascaline had not yet settled on what to call the building that contains the chapel, common area, laundry and kitchen. Here "longhouse" seems to mean the main building. "The main house" or "common house" is what it is often called.

discussion, planning and work had culminated in this joyful beginning in a uniquely holy place. The following day, Sunday, June 8, 1980, would be chronicled in Sr. Pascaline's neat and economical handwriting as "an awesome day."

DEDICATION DAY

SUNDAY, JUNE 8, 1980 — FEAST OF CORPUS CHRISTI[27]

It cooled off some 20° with no rain during the night, making for a perfectly beautiful Corpus Christi Sunday. Mother Audrey and all at 22nd Place, plus all staying at Bob and Barbara Sellers' home up the road, arrived in time for feast day Praises and brunch.

Sisters David and Jude did the liturgy preparation and it was moving with our full harmony, sung under the "cosmic wheel of life" in the Sundance Circle. Bob Sellers came to make the path through the woods for procession and mark off areas for parking. Bishop Beltran arrived about 1:30 PM and asked to have the large newly posted bell rung as he leaves the building vested, and again at the offertory.

About 250 people gathered outside the eastern peak of the chapel for this dedication Eucharist. About six priests concelebrated with the Bishop. His homily was one of amazement that the property was only discovered one year ago and already these lovely buildings are here! God is great in his works.

Carrie Wilkinson and Geralen Hoey received their first Holy Communion with their respective families, then received a lighted vigil glass at the end, from the altar. Chief Tinker carried the gifts. Mary Vance (surrounded by her family) and Bob Sellers were readers. The procession wound its way deep into the Forest where benediction was given then again back at the main altar. The Blessed Sacrament was exposed in the monstrance in the center of the pit until sundown. A moment of Eucharistic glory!

After everyone enjoyed the treat of Coca-Cola offered by Joe Ramey, the manager, and the cookies donated by the Piscopos, people began departing while Ruth Slickman began preparing her dinner for the Bishop and Mother Audrey — 25 in all.

Billy Newsham, Sr. Pascaline's nephew, showed up for the Mass and stayed the night en route to Denver. Laryngitis set in so Sr. Pascaline was all but silenced!

It was an awesome day in every way. "No phone service" added to the awesomeness! Jude made a lovely rustic sign "Forest of Peace" for the road with an arrow. The St. Louis car departed as they had to get an early start in the morning. Others were headed for the West Coast for discernment processes in our priories regarding new prioresses.

This was the day the Lord had made from beginning to end!

---

27 Corpus Christi is a moveable feast, celebrated the Sunday following Trinity Sunday. The earliest possible date falls on 24 May (as in 1818 and 2285), the latest on 27 June (as in 1943 and 2038). Anniversaries of the Forest have been celebrated on Corpus Christi Sunday in some years and on June 8 in others.

Dedication Day

Feast of Corpus Christi

This was the day the Lord had made from beginning to end!

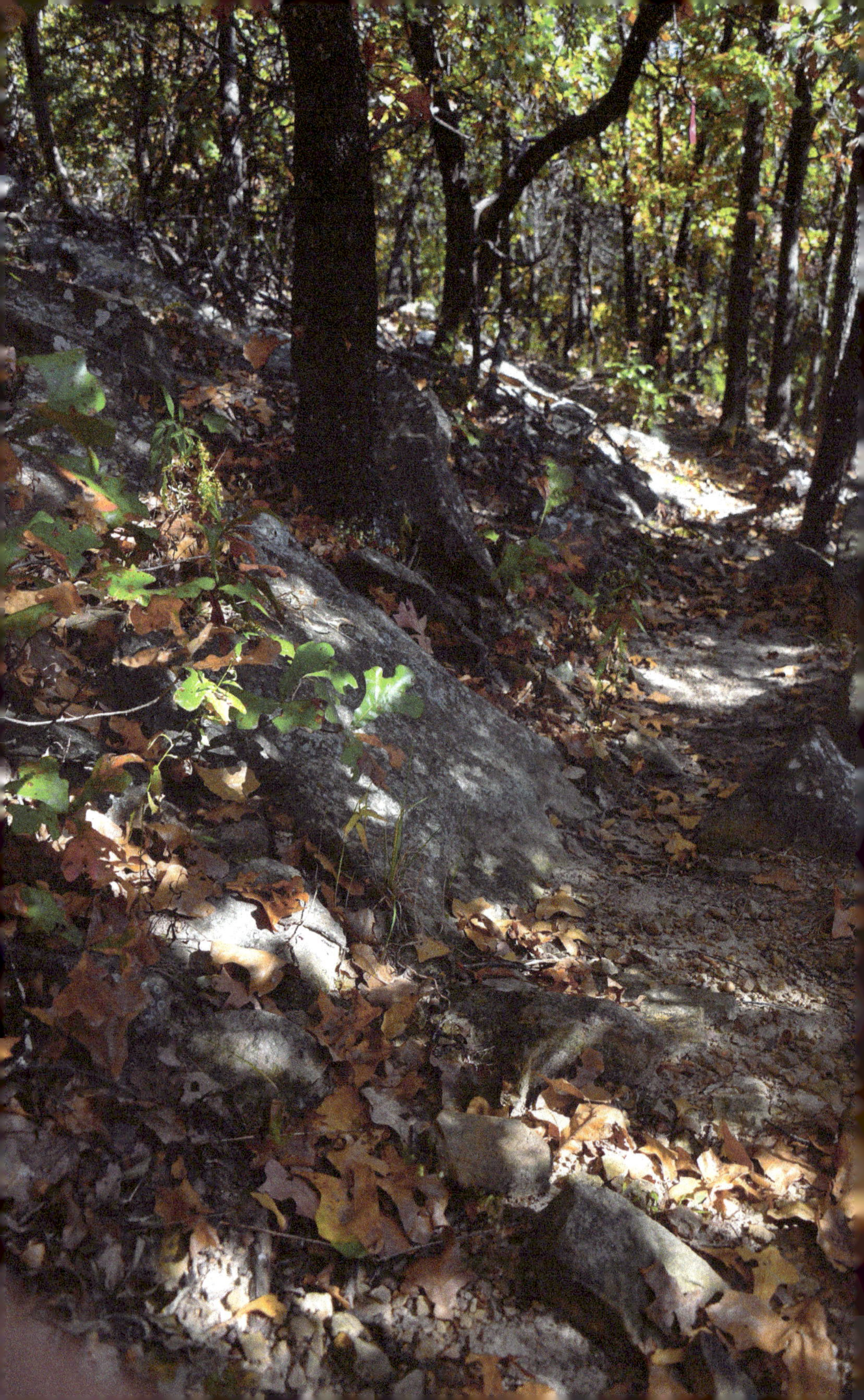

OSAGE + MONASTERY
1980

We have been called, chosen, by Jesus to go out and to bear fruit, fruit that will remain.

— M. Audrey, BSPA Prioress General
in her Corpus Christi message
to the BSPA Congregation, 1980

During the days following the dedication, visitors came and went from the Forest of Peace constantly, as Sr. Pascaline tried to recuperate and regain her voice. Mother Audrey, who had been on hand for the Forest celebration, wrote Sr. Pascaline after her return home to offer "congratulations again on all that you have accomplished in so short a time at Osage Monastery. As someone said, it seems to have always been situated in the forest. May it be the site of countless contacts with the Lord of the forest."

"It is the voiced joy of all to be without a phone this week," Sr. Pascaline wrote in the chronicle on Friday night following the dedication. The week was spent juggling visitors with errands and cleaning out the vacated house on 22nd Place.

Everyone, including Father Jim, helped with chores, cleaning up mud from the porches, painting benches and cleaning out cabinets to make more order. "Bob finished the new frames on our common house doors — too short for standard screen doors. More rain during the night!"

This would be the last rain for many weeks. As the wet spring of 1980 gave way to summer, the solstice ushered in a heatwave that would set records in northeastern Oklahoma, severely testing the O+M ashramites' determination to "enjoy poverty" in unairconditioned buildings those first weeks in the Forest.

In spite of the heat, gifts and visitors continued to pour in through the rest of the summer. The Sisters welcomed guests with Benedictine hospitality and worshipped together in a blend of Eastern and Western styles. News about the monastic ashram quickly spread beyond the Catholic community. One Monday in June. "Srs. Christine and Pascaline went grocery shopping in Sand Springs and hurried home for daytime prayer to find Channel 6 Eyewitness News waiting to film an interview — Rex Daughtery and cameraman plus a parishioner sent from St. Patrick's to show them the way." That evening the community watched the 5:00 news with "great respect," as "A hideaway behind Sand Springs to get away from it all" led up to the announcer quoting, "There's a monk hidden in every man and woman." Soon the reporters and cameramen were returning with their families to share prayers, refreshments and community celebrations.

© SCOTT THOMPSON

It was the last Friday in June before the peace of the Forest would be interrupted by a ringing telephone. Sr. Pascaline, who had driven into Tulsa to get an international plane ticket for a NABEWD speaker, was actually the first caller to phone the Forest of Peace. The next Sunday, "Jim Joseph, our telephone man, brought half his family from St. Monica's Parish."

Retreatants arrived to occupy the cabins, but so also did unwelcome creatures, no doubt seeking shelter from the heat. "Kris continues to find scorpions, snakes and tarantulas," Sr. Pascaline wrote in the chronicle for July 1. "The heat is intense! Jesus asleep in the boat."

The following day's entry began, "Jesus dispelled the demons today." It's hard to know exactly what Sr. Pascaline was referring to here. Prayer, no doubt, but perhaps also chemical pest control. Ten days later she would record, "Father Jim sprayed more of the houses for scorpions." From the point of view of the scorpions, snakes and tarantulas, their homes beneath the foliage and rocks on the forest floor had been destroyed by bulldozers. Once the intense summer heat came, they found convenient new homes in the relative cool of the new cabins.

More bulldozers and new cabins would come soon. On July 2, the chronicle records: "Bob and Mr. Paul Hoey had their final session on the building today. Mariam agreed to mail the final payment for the chapel, main building and first cabins and a contract for the remaining cabins is being drawn up." Once the contract was signed, construction on the new cabins went forward steadily during the long stretch of hot, dry weather. The extra space was needed as visitors and requests for retreats came in increasing numbers.

It was hot work, but a good time for learning pottery as temperatures exceeded 105° the last week in July. Sister Michael, Father Jim and Sr. Christine shaped pots and put them out to dry. Two days later, on Sr. Monica's birthday, the Forest dwellers celebrated with a special meal, and after vespers fired the pots, not in a kiln but in an outdoor pit full of dried cow dung:

> The potters began their primitive firing about 7:45 PM, just like the American Indians over the pit filled with cow chips and covered with teepee-like brushwood. White smoke billowed up for a bit, then a beautiful blaze, then it all simmered down and had dirt and sand heaped over it for several hours. One pot exploded but no one knew whose it was. Darkness descended and Sister Michael returned after night prayer until the fire was completely out.

The next day, "The potters all uncovered their treasures and placed them in the sun. Sr. Christine used her vigil light pot for Eucharist! Sr. Priscilla's bowl lost its bottom, Father Jim's lamp base cracked, but all other pieces were perfect."

By August 20, the new cabins had been framed. "A good storm blew up during supper, bringing a fair rain. Cabins have siding on 2½ now. Mr. Jim Bartlett will do the roofing on Friday and until finished he is staying overnight." Mr. Bartlett's

© SCOTT THOMPSON

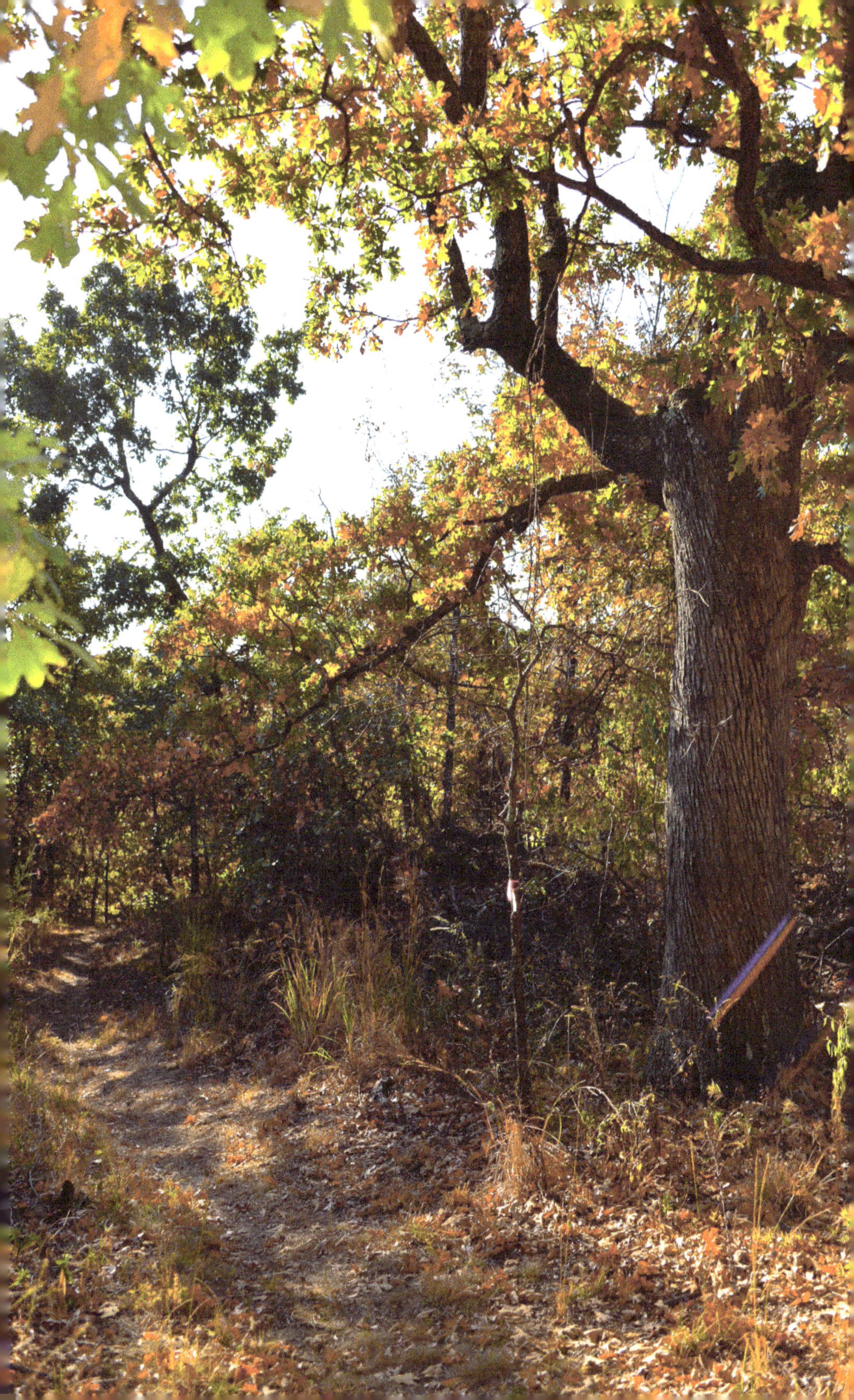

MIDDLE: GITANO
BELOW: GITANO AND ANGEL

MIDDLE: GITANO AND NANDI
BELOW: BARBARA BILDERBACK AND FRIENDLY DOG

dedication to the task of putting roofs on the cabins was doubly impressive because he was donating his labor. Sister Monica, meanwhile, was hard at work building a bed frame for herself, from an old door.

Sister Helen had finally completed her sub-prioress term in Kansas City; she arrived on the Greyhound bus to take up residence at the Osage Monastery. On the day of her arrival, "Father Vincent Gabriel OSB from Bangalore phoned from Kansas City. He will visit us on September 4."

With sleeping space in high demand and more Forest dwellers on the way, everyone pitched in to work on the new cabins. "Father Jim took us all painting today instead of having the usual lesson about John of the Cross," Pascaline chronicled on August 28. "We got one more cabin finished." Two days later:

> After Eucharist all went painting with Sister Christine holding down the house. She had two long distance calls! Our Kansas City car arrived after 7 PM with Srs. Benita, Leocadia, Lioba, Rachel, Virginia Anne and Father Michael from Africa. Where did they sleep? Father Mike in Father Jim's cabin (Father Jim left for Bristow), Sr. Leocadia with Sr. Monica (who just built her new bed), and Srs. Benita and Virginia Anne in Sr. Priscilla's, Sr. Rachel in Sr. Pascaline's and the rest — at the common house on church benches and planks.

Through September, the construction work continued, with the Sisters and Father Jim pitching in to do whatever they could. Sheet rock went up; inside painting followed. On September 26, the plumbers lit the pilot lights of the gas heaters in the common house and cabins for the first time. Cooler weather was finally here after the long, hot summer. Soon there would be the need for heating in the cabins. The next day, the plumbers finished work in the new cabins and pilot lights were lit there, as well.

By the Feast of St. Michael, September 29, the second anniversary of the little community's move to the Tulsa diocese, the initial construction was virtually complete in the Osage Monastery Forest of Peace. "Many intentions of gratitude were offered for the past two years," Sr. Pascaline wrote in the chronicle.

With the new cabins ready, the community members would move into them and the Osage Monastery could now go into full swing as a retreat center. Sr. Pascaline wrote in the chronicle on October 1, "Srs. Rachel and Pascaline slept in their new cabins for the first time." The next evening at Vespers, the O+M community dedicated them with a ceremony in a clearing near the three cabins furthest from the chapel. Paula Sullivan, a laywoman and staff writer for the *Eastern Oklahoma Catholic,* had arrived that morning for a short prayer retreat. She had been the Tulsan Catholic most vocal in urging the BSPAs to make retreat space for lay Catholics at Osage Monastery.

As she recalled 25 years later:
> I called the Forest of Peace and Sister Monica answered. I asked if I could make

a weekend retreat. Sister Monica said, "I'm sorry but we have only one cabin for retreatants and we are filled up for the next year." I complained, "I bet it's booked up with nuns and priests." She said that was true. I can hardly believe what flew out of my mouth next.

"Well if you're not going to open up to lay people, you might as well shut the place down. We have no place to go in this diocese." Three months later, on a cool October day, I received a call at the *Eastern Oklahoma Catholic*. Sister Monica said, "Paula, your cabin is ready. When would you like to come?"

When I arrived at the Monastery for my weekend retreat, Sister Pascaline greeted me at the door. She laughed heartily, "You're the one responsible for five new cabins."[28]

Fittingly, Paula joined the community for the dedication ceremony. As Sister Pascaline described the dedication:

... We combined the Vedic and Roman liturgy into a very meaningful hour using Panikkar's *Vedic Experience* for many of the readings and prayers. Psalms included:

126 "If the Lord does not build the house ..."

132 "How good it is for brothers to dwell together," using the antiphon from day hours "Lord of the Universe." Father Jim brought a blue bowl of holy water and an appropriate twig for the blessing, pouring the water to the north, east, south and west. Sr. Pascaline had the concluding prayer on love and unity from the *Vedic Experience,* page 857. The wind and sun were strong and supported the occasion!

The simplicity of the common house with its long front porch and circular "meditation room/chapel," the little one-room cabins scattered nearby through the trees, the winding trails that led between the cabins and into the woods, the deer for Nandi to chase, a perch Sr. Priscilla made for Shanti, the bell that rang to call the Forest dwellers to prayer: it was all in place and already gathering in the first of many people who would come. From that time to this, the people would arrive from all over the world to this little blackjack oak Forest of Peace for experiences of spiritual direction and East-meets-West ashramic monasticism with its sharing of chanting and silence; bread, wine and fire; shared laughter, ice cream and love.

Not surprisingly, perhaps, mechanical problems showed up with cooler weather in the Forest. That first autumn, breakdowns seemed to time themselves perfectly to weeks when Sr. Pascaline was away on extended trips. In late October she traveled to Kansas City for a Prioresses Council meeting. Immediately: "Our first major

---

28 From "Stories of the Forest" pamphlet published in honor of Sister Pascaline when she left O+M in September, 2009. Held in the archive at the Osage Forest of Peace. Paula Sullivan would take regular overnight retreats at O+M during which she began writing her life story, developing this experience into the My Story Workshop for spiritual autobiography and her book, *The Mystery of My Story*, Paulist Press, 1991.

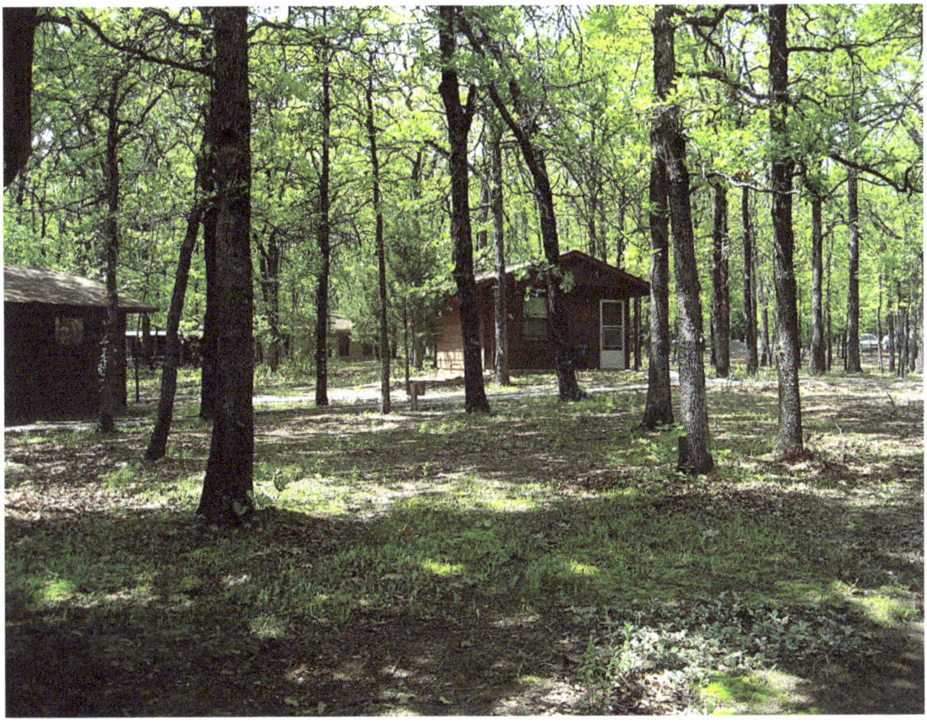

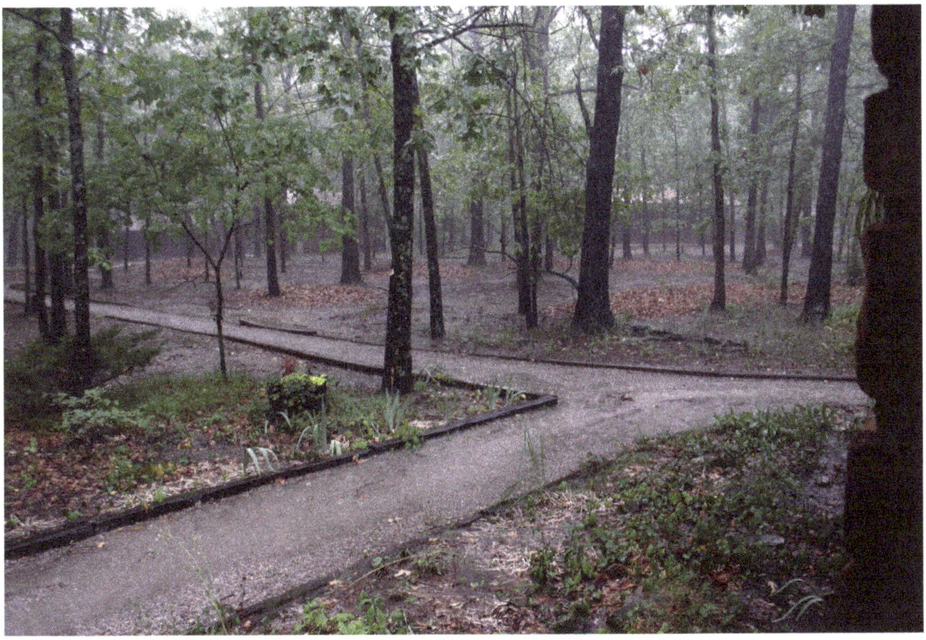

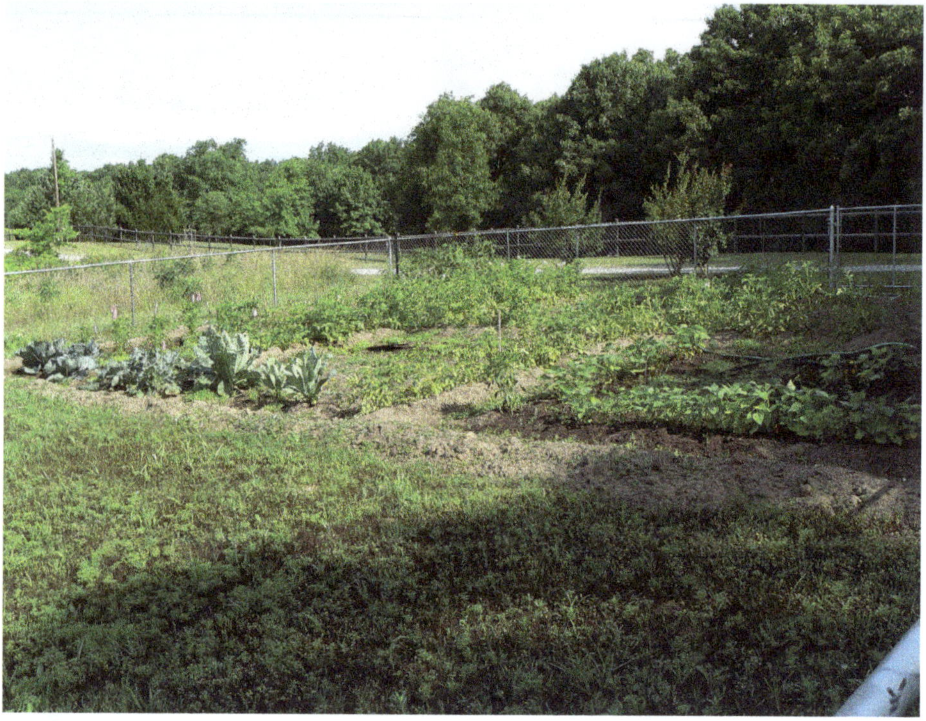

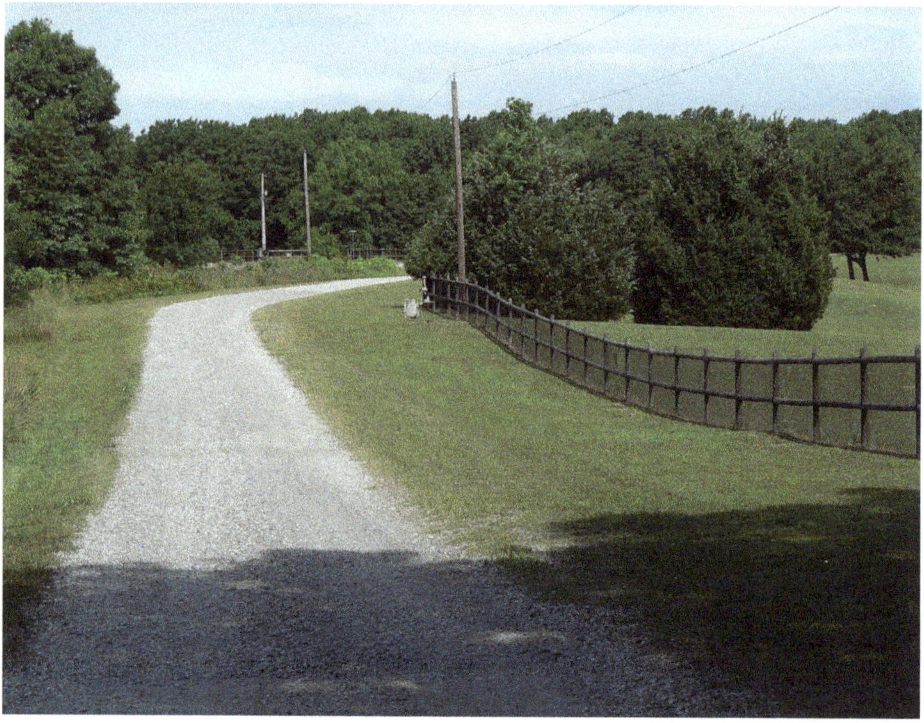

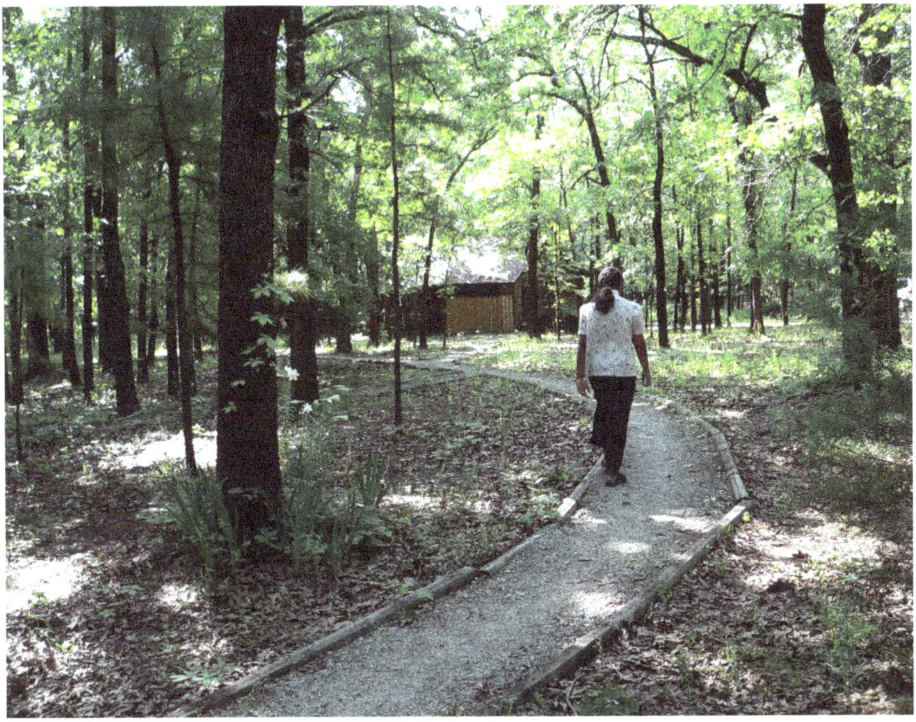

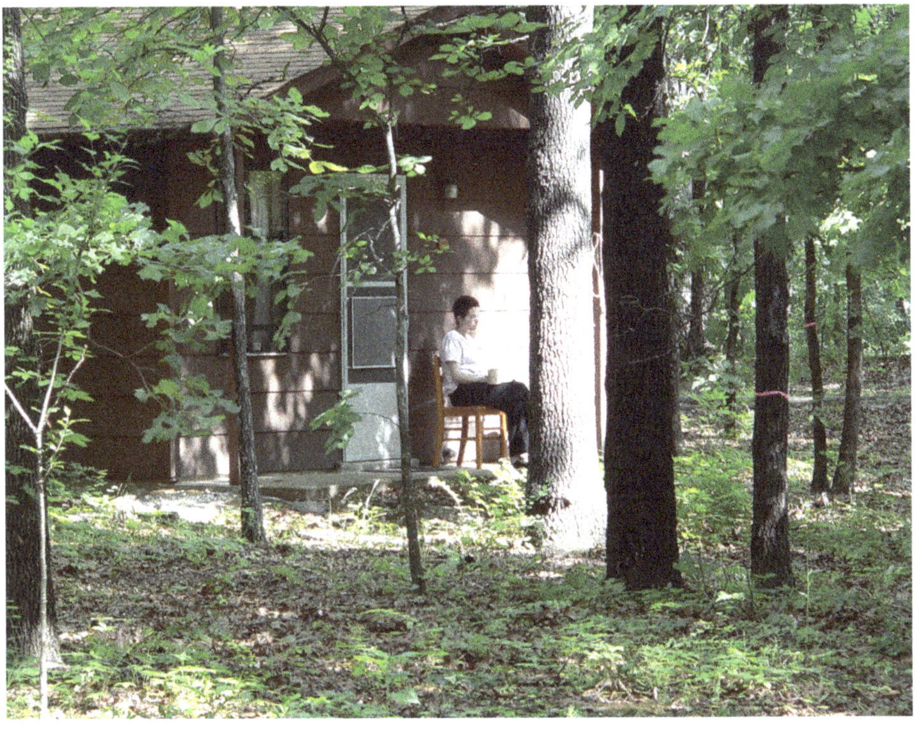

catastrophe — a leak in the underground water system. Bob Sellers called the plumber in to dig up part of the road." The water was off for four hours the next day, and the day after that, October 30, "First frost! Plumbers returned to check on road fill and heating units, which keep going off."

Meanwhile, Sr. Pascaline was busy with the BSPA council meeting in Kansas City: "Policies requested from O+M at the Prioresses Council were considered by the extended Council today, including 'Term of office for Superior' will be reviewed at Chapter. For the present Sr. Pascaline is to be appointed without a term." The next morning, Sr. Pascaline headed back to O+M.

Within days, Sr. Pascaline, Fr. Jim, Srs. Priscilla, Rachel and Helen left for the east coast for the long-planned NABEWD East-West symposium in Mt. Holyoke, Massachusettes. The Sisters were driving, a journey that would take three days. No sooner had they set out than cold weather came to the Forest, and the new heaters were not up to their job. When Sr. Pascaline phoned home to the O+M, she learned that a gas repairman had shown up to repair them.

The next day, "The Chases took Srs. Christine and Monica to church and when they returned they were unable to find Shanti." The dove seemed to have gone looking for Sr. Priscilla, and was never to be seen again.

MONDAY, NOVEMBER 17, 1980

[In Mt. Holyoke] the North American Board for East-West Dialogue began its fourth annual meeting at 9 AM and had Eucharist at 11 in a small side chapel. Sr. Pascaline was reelected [Executive] Secretary [for another 3 years], and an official charter of purpose was composed and agreed on. The entire board drove to Harvard (a 2-hour drive) in Ed Bednar's station wagon to hear Father Panikkar[29] and Michael von Brück speak. As we started home to Holyoke a severe snowstorm overtook us. Father Jim, Srs. Rachel and Helen had gone ahead to Boston for the day and were also at Harvard to hear Panikkar. It also snowed in Sand Springs, Oklahoma, today at 5:30 AM. Gas repairman came again for Hermitage furnaces.

TUESDAY, NOVEMBER 18, 1980

Many details about the symposium were considered by the board. Father Panikkar joined us for supper with Michael [von Brück] to plan the Eucharistic liturgies! Others began arriving for the symposium by mid- afternoon, eventually some 77 persons, including Odette Baumer from Switzerland, and the Abhishiktananda Society. Power went off all around Osage Monastery today!

The chronicle doesn't record how the power was restored or who was in charge of things back at the O+M. Instead, it is replete with details of the Mt. Holyoke Symposium, in which Sister Pascaline was deeply involved. As was reported weeks after the symposium in the NABEWD Bulletin, Fr. Panikkar's lectures were presented to "more than 80 participants … a superb admixture of monks, nuns, scientists,

---

29 Fr. Raimundo Panikkar's keynote discussions of "the monk in our modern day," would be the genesis of his 1984 book, *Blessed Simplicity: The Monk as a Universal Archetype*.

scholars, professors, contemplatives, psychoanalysts, therapists, artists, masters and disciples, seekers and the sought." His thesis might stand, also, as a simple statement of purpose for the Osage Monastery:

> The monastic dimension is one constituent which every human being has and must cultivate in one way or another. The monk is the one who before all else aspires to be whole, one, unified, integrated, centered. This monastic dimension is the primordial religious dimension, previous to all divisions, previous to and different even from the way it is lived by individual monks.

The next day, Sr. Pascaline reported, "Fr. Panikkar began on 'The Monk In Modernity' today. The morning meditation was all gestures, mandalas. Color."

Meanwhile at the O+M, "Plumber came!"

The Holyoke symposium was a mixture not only of Eastern and Western celebratory experiences, but also of head and heart energies, with an intensity of both that seemed heightened by the very act of bringing East and West together in such a way. This was the sort of spiritual revival that had been the impetus for Sr. Pascaline and her BSPA Sisters to establish O+M, and long after this symposium ended and the attendees returned to their homes, O+M would be a welcoming center for this new head-and-heart-opening spiritual experience for visitors from all over the world. In fact, three of the presenters from the Holyoke Symposium took advantage of this trip to the USA to visit the Osage Monastery. The Swiss Sister Odette Baumer joined the "Sand Springs" Sisters, as they squeezed into the car and headed back to Oklahoma. The Spirit seemed to be moving through all of it.

The trip back to O+M took three long days of driving, with stops in Washington, D.C., Indianapolis and St. Louis along the way. The weather was challenging at times. Finally, late on the night before Thanksgiving:

> We pulled in at Osage Monastery about 10 PM where Sr. Monica, Sr. Christine and Nandie were awaiting us with the smell of freshly cooked turkey all ready for Thanksgiving. Odette was overwhelmed at what she saw and so happy to be at last out of the car. The days of "confinement" with her were a real gift as she shared so much about Abhishiktananda and Oshida and many others.

The next day the new dining table was ready for Thanksgiving dinner. Abbot Cornelius Tholens, fresh from the Mt. Holyoke conference, flew to Oklahoma to share O+M's own particular style of Eucharist with the community and neighbors from up the road.

> Abbot Tholens of Amsterdam arrived about 9:30 AM. Father Jim met him and brought him in time for our Eucharist at 11. Ruth Slickman's corn on the cob and summer squash, together with a bouquet of sage and tobacco, graced the altar as Father Jim prayed from the Vedas for God's blessing on all the fruits of the earth. Chases joined us and Jimmy [a neighbor boy] prayed that Shanti [the missing

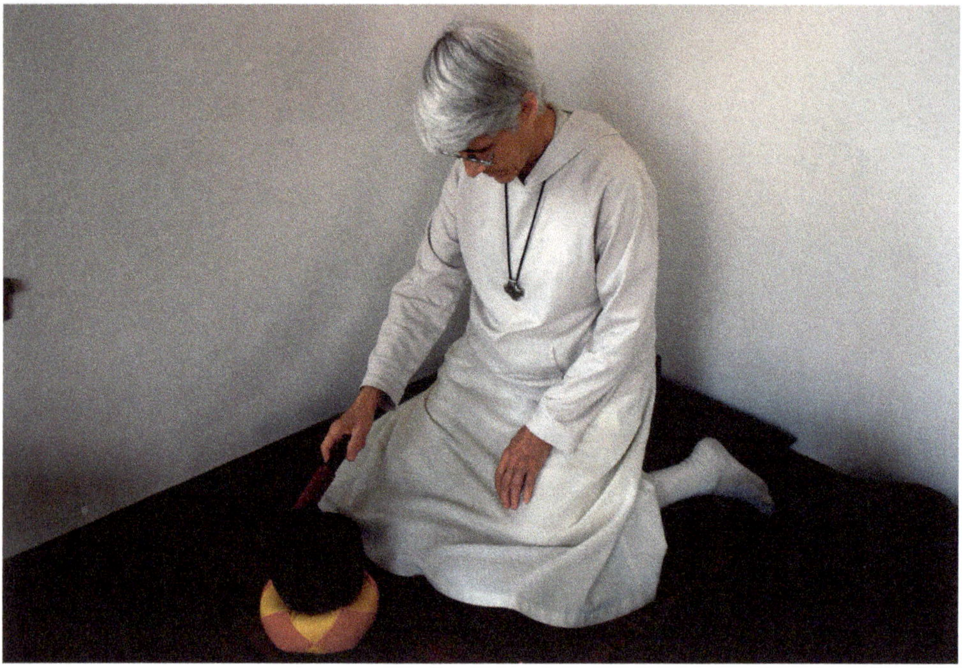

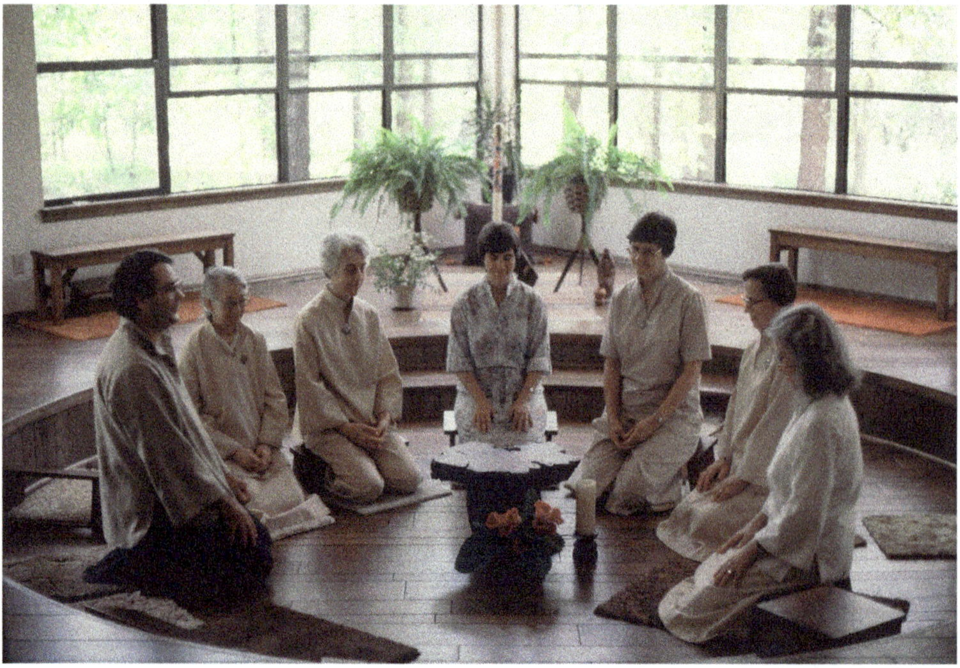

dove] would be safe and okay. Rachel prepared our turkey dinner for 2 PM with pumpkin pie and all the trimmings. Odette and Abbot Tholens shared with us in the evening as Father Jim told of his acquaintance with Thomas Merton.

The Abbot stayed through the weekend, offering Eucharist with Hindu symbols and Bhajans as part of a new liturgy. Then, on Sunday, he flew home. The Forest of Peace, he would later say, was "a wonderful new monastic realization."

The next week, with the Forest back to its core group, the Sisters met to share about their goals and priorities.

Sister Christine, who had helped to begin the Forest community and build the ashram/monastery "shared her desire to return to the larger community. She feels she has shared much of herself and is looking to her later years. She will be 69 on her next birthday," Sr. Pascaline chronicled.

That week, on Thursday, the sisters "cleared the morning in order to share on our goal number one — that top priority be given contemplative prayer and its atmosphere."

Most of the sharing centered around the need for friendship — Reguin says: the Christian experience of God began when Jesus said to his apostles: "I no longer call you servants but ... you are friends ... because I have made known to you all that my Father has taught me." John 15:14–15. It was a time of deep, humble honesty and confession. Another session after supper ended with the kiss of peace and night prayer. We combined this effort with our discernment for Srs. Rachel and Helen who have been with us for three months. All were unanimous in appreciating their presence and wanting them to stay on.

SATURDAY, DECEMBER 6, 1980

After Eucharist Paula and Maggie Sullivan joined us to prepare for tomorrow's first Holy Communion. David Johnstone asked to say a word to the community at the conclusion of his retreat. He said each one had gifted him: Sister Priscilla, "weakness made strong by the Lord"; Sr. Christine, lover of the earth and God's good things; Sr. Helen, so helpful; Sr. Pascaline, peaceful; Sr. Monica —her smile; Jim, "insights" and Rachel — he choked up as his retreat had meant so much, he stuttered how beautiful she had been to him — and he will return.

One of the key ministries of the O+M community was a ministry of spiritual direction. The first people coming for direction were mostly Catholic Sisters, then Catholic laypeople, and, very soon the Sisters and Father Jim were giving spiritual direction to non-Catholics and Catholics alike. The Forest itself would be for many a spiritual director of sorts, but this would not happen by accident. It required that the Forest Dwellers continue to prayerfully compare the reality they were creating to the goals for their community.

MONDAY, DECEMBER 8, 1980 — MARY'S DAY!
Community goal sharing day from 8 until 11:40 AM. We pondered our second goal: small, monastic ashram community.

A few minutes after this discussion ended, however:

We had 17 for dinner cooked by Sr. Priscilla. Paul Hoey came to see about our final payment for Bob Sellers on the new cabins. We came up with a list for Bob of things to be completed or repaired before final payment.

The momentous year 1980 was fulfilled with a round of activities to celebrate the first Christmas in the dwellings and chapel that had been mere blueprints the year before. Sitting around a warm fire, the Sisters addressed Christmas cards Sr. Denise had created for them. The card showed trees on the front with the wording 'All the trees of the forest rejoice.' Inside, it simply read, 'For the Lord is here' and 'Osage Monastery, Sand Springs, Oklahoma.'

M. Audrey visited and the community invited the builder, Bob Sellers, and his family to dinner with the Prioress General to thank him and celebrate the completion of their new home, and gave the builder his final payment.

On a mid-December Sunday evening, "Jerry Chase's parents came in time for Vespers, and brought our last seven benches for the dining room tables, made by Chuck Chase. They are spending the night in the Hermitage as a surprise gift from Jerry."

Christmas season was in full swing now — the first Christmas at the Osage Monastery. Friends and neighbors all wanted to participate in the celebrations with the Sisters and Father Jim, who was still splitting his time between O+M and his Bristow parish. In the days leading up to Christmas, people came up Monastery Road in waves, bearing gifts and greetings.

Wednesday, December 17 was typical. Two women from nearby Mannford surprised them by bringing a Christmas tree with all its trimmings.

They had the tree cut from their 240 acres on Keystone Lake and wanted to decorate it themselves. Many packages arrived by mail for Christmas today. Mrs. Pat Butz (the architect's wife) dropped in around 3 PM with a huge turkey and everything to go with it for Christmas, including pancakes for Sr. Monica. Bob Garrett arrived just before supper to repair our Chevy truck and then took coffee and fruit with us. He helped raise the tree before he left. After supper everyone helped assemble the tree at the front window. Kathleen, Marg and all were helping when Ferus Nuong arrived with his three-year-old sister and another Christmas tree!

THAT FRIDAY,

Our car from Kansas City arrived about 4:45 ladened with food and gifts for us for Christmas: Srs. David, Lioba, Mercy, Joan Anderson and Reparata came for the weekend. Free night saw some retiring early and others visiting by the fireside.

ABOVE: FINISHED TABLE AND BENCHES (FOREGROUND) AND KITCHEN (BACKGROUND)
BELOW: SR. PASCALINE, FR. JIM, SR. HELEN AND GUESTS

© MARY JANE MATTHEWS

On Sunday morning, a full moon welcomed each from her hermitage this morning en route to adoration and praises. Our Kansas City sisters brought supplies for brunch, then all together prepared pancakes and bacon for us.

It isn't clear how many of the Forest Dwellers were vegetarians at this point, but their new neighbors would make sure any non-vegetarians would not have to do without meat this first Christmas. On December 23, "Mr. Morgan phoned that he had a turkey for us for Christmas, so Rachel and Sr. Priscilla went for it and while they were out Ed Gibson came with a large ham. Jack also had eight fire extinguishers for us, plus a box of homemade fudge and divinity and a supply of grapefruit from the Eustices." Meanwhile, "Sr. Monica spent the day staining and last-coating our new dining room benches (16) made by Mr. Chase before he left for Mexico. We drew names today for a Christmas gift for one another, but kept drawing our own names until finally we traded openly!"

On Christmas Eve Fr. Jim and Sr. Rachel decorated the chapel and front porch with luminaria. They ate supper in "silence with music" followed by "Vigils in candlelight and moonlight!" as a full moon rose and its light came streaming in through the chapel's wall of windows. Then "Hoeys (10 strong) came singing carols and bringing food for us around 8:15 PM." For the 9 p.m. "midnight Mass," guests were given bells to ring during the carol, 'Angels We Have Heard on High.'

> Each one present received a candle and carried it in procession to the small crib Father Jim borrowed from Bristow for under our tree. After the tree/crib blessing each one placed the lit candle into a basket of sand on the floor. Father Jim gave a meaningful homily on another 'census' year like in Mary and Joseph's day. He had to depart for Bristow promptly for midnight Mass there. After hot chocolate and cookies we had a candle extinguishing party.
>
> CHRISTMAS 1980 BIRTHDAY OF JESUS CHRIST
>
> Nandie was on the road to meet the first risers at 5:30 AM since it was very cold and he was feeling nippy. The turkey was readied and into the oven by 5:45 and preparations for dinner were underway. Sr. Helen sang a new Bhajan for adoration about Christ's birth. Brunch followed praises with Christmas festive music. Father Jim returned from Bristow about 12:20 just as his brother Joe and family arrived. It was fitting to have a little child, a son, before our eyes and ears during the "third Mass" of Christmas! After hot chocolate and cookies the guests left and dinner was served by 2:15 PM. Before washing the dishes we moved to the other side of the fireplace to open gifts from each other and from benefactors and friends. During the 5 PM news some did dishes while Rachel and Sr. Priscilla wrapped Christmas presents for Father Jim's family, after which he departed for Kathryn's. We sat down at 5:30 to share and then sang vespers for Christmas at 6:45.

As 1980 drew to a close, the work of the NABEWD Bulletin and the problems of a changing world were on Sr. Pascaline's mind.

© MARY JANE MATTHEWS

LAST DAY OF THE YEAR!

The "star of Bethlehem" was supposed to be seen after 250 years but no one could find the phenomenon. Many and bright stars were to be seen, though! Rachel cooked another turkey rice dish from the new monastic cookbook. After vespers we had supper in "solitude" with music – a pick-up meal. Mrs. Jerry Chase, who just returned home from a family vacation in Mexico, came to share our New Year's Eve holy hour from 8 to 9. We began with compline, then knelt in adoration until 9 PM when the Marian anthem rang out to greet Mary, mother of God, whose solemnity this is. This is day number 424 in captivity.[30] Crime in the USA has risen more than 50% in four years. The NABEWD Bulletin was worked on in the rough again today — only five pages readied. Srs. Monica and Helen made this a hermit day within their retreat.

The year 1980 had brought fulfillment and with it much work, but the BSPA's original vision for a retreat center/small group living arrangement had manifested as much more than they could have imagined, already drawing retreatants and visitors from all over the world and abundantly fulfilling the mission for which it had been called into being. Of course, new buildings and other features would be added year by year, as needs arose and "lovers of the Forest" came to appreciate its special charism.[31]

Sr. Pascaline summed up the year in the 1980 chronicle book with these words:

> For all that has been, yes;
> for all that is, Yes;
> for all that will be, YES Christ!

---

30 This refers to the Iran hostage crisis in which 52 America diplomats were held captive for 444 days after a group of Iranian college students took over the American Embassy in Tehran.

31 In June of 1994, the BSPAs would purchase three more acres adjoining the original 40 acres of O+M. Seventy benefactors had given donations toward the purchase earlier, but the price was too high. Charles Heath bequeathed his house to O+M, which was eventually exchanged for the new three acres." Document from the personal papers of Sr. Pascaline Coff, dated 1978–1996.

© SCOTT THOMPSON

Osage Forest of Peace

1980–2022

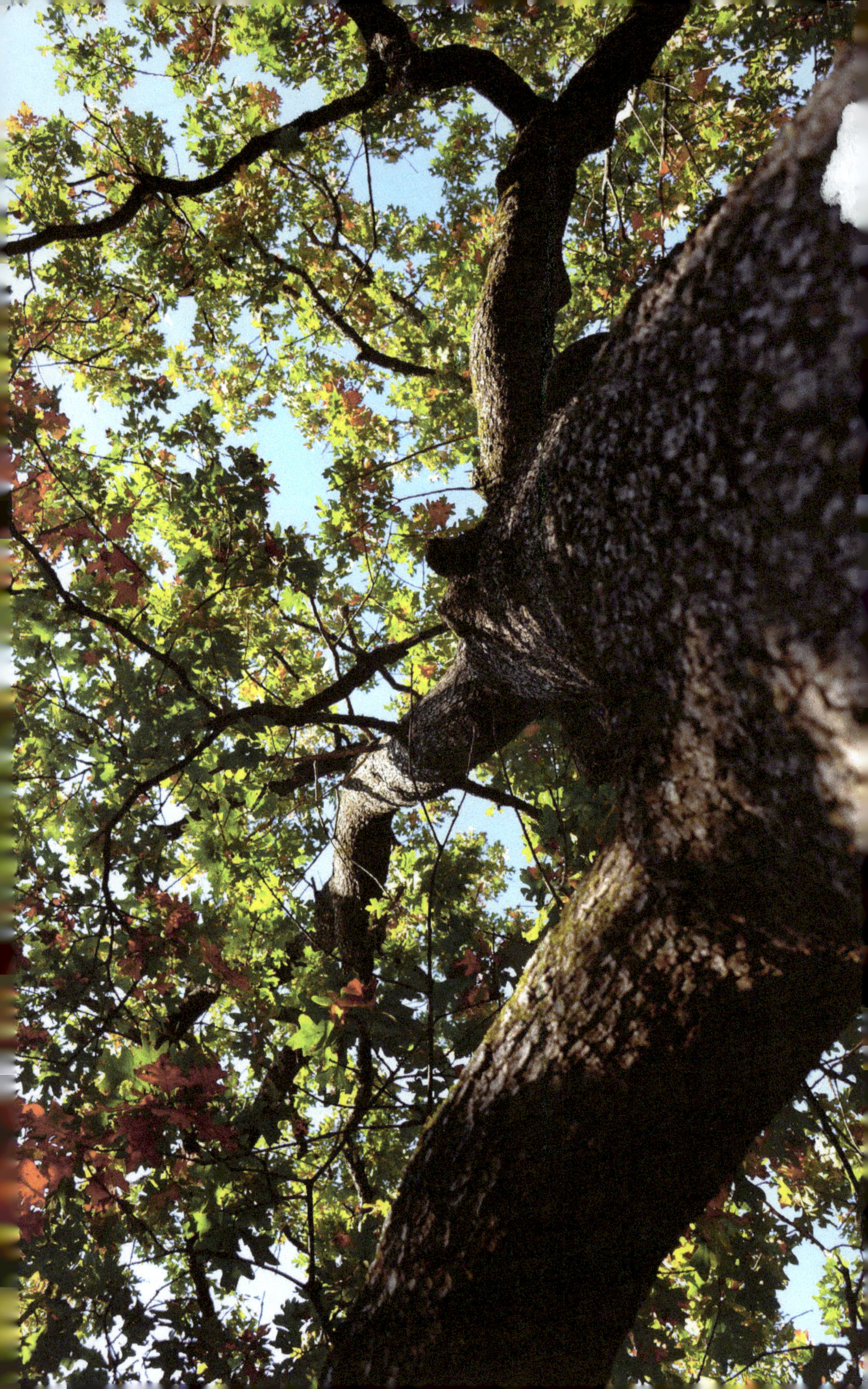

FOREST DWELLERS
1980–2008

Stand still. The forest knows
Where you are. You must let it find you.[32]

From "Lost" by David Wagoner

A new integral consciousness was arising during the late Twentieth Century and early Twenty-first in a world lost in rational materialism and dualistic thought. It was a vibrant, unitive consciousness, and the Osage Monastery was a center for that arising. In this Forest of Peace, the Spirit was nurtured, intensified and disseminated in a synthesis like that by which the trees were drinking sunlight, leafing, seeding, and purifying the air.

Certainly the O+M's nurturing power owed much to the BSPA Congregation of Sisters, daily engaged in Benedictine *ora et labora,* contemplation of the Divine and conscious service with willing hands. They organized and published the interchange between the mystical luminaries of this awakening. Fr. Bede Griffiths, Fr. Raimundo Panikkar, Fr. Armand Veilleux, Abbot Cornelius Tholens, Fr. Jean LeClercq, Fr. David Stendl-Rast, Fr. Thomas Keating, Fr. Bruno Barnhart and many others; most of them came to the Forest once or several times over the years, to be inspired and to teach.

From this little collection of cabins in rural Oklahoma, Sr. Pascaline, herself a luminary, studied, wrote, published, organized, traveled and taught. As Executive Secretary of the NABEWD she inspired H.H. the Dalai Lama to dispatch groups of Tibetan monks and nuns from his home in India to Catholic monasteries throughout the USA, including, of course, O+M.

She and her handful of Sisters welcomed and fed all these world-travelled visitors. There were never more than five or six BSPA Sisters at the Osage Monastery at any one time, although temporary members who were not BSPAs sometimes lived there as well.[33]

---

32 *From Traveling Light: Collected and New Poems.* Copyright 1999 by David Wagoner. Used with permission of the University of Illinois Press.

33 Except when traveling or recuperating from surgery, Sister Pascaline was there the entire time it was a BSPA monastery — and eighteen months beyond. Of the other founding Sisters, Sr. Priscilla left in 2007 at age 91, just six months before the BSPAs sold the O+M. Sister Monica was at Osage from the beginning until about 2000. Some 20 other Sisters lived the Osage "ashram" experience for a few years at a time. In her 1996 "Brief History" Sr. Pascaline summarized: "Sr. Trini left in March of '79; Sr. Christine in January of '81; Sr. Helen came in August of '80, [and was there until 1999, much of that time as a hermit]; Rachel in Sept. '80, left 12/3/81; Lioba came in May of '82; Daniel came in October of '85, left May '86; Sister Maureen came in February '87, left June '94; SM Bede came in July '90, left Feb. '95; Sister Josetta came November of '92 and Sister M. Regina came Feb. '95." In 2015, Sister Pascaline recalled, "Others who joined and remained for greater lengths included:

© MARY JANE MATTHEWS

Perhaps the first luminary to visit the finished O+M was in mid-October, 1980. A young Lutheran pastor from behind the Iron Curtain — Michael von Brück of East Germany. He had just completed his second doctorate with a study comparing Advaita (the Hindu experience of God) with the Christian experience of the Trinity. In mid-October 1980, von Brück was on his way to Massachusettes to speak at the East-West Monastic Symposium in Mt. Holyoke.[34] First, however, he would spend some time in the peace of the newly completed Osage Monastery.

The Sisters took full advantage of von Brück's visit to host two open-house gatherings at which he spoke on Eastern Spirituality. "About 15+ attended each session while 10 stayed for buffet dinner." Such events would be a regular feature of life in the Osage Forest, a feature for which the O+M would become well known.[35]

In addition to the BSPAs and luminaries who became part of life at O+M, numerous Protestant ministers and lay-people visited, attended programs and occupied the guest cabins for prayer retreats. The chronicle for August 1, 1986, is typical, recording that "Soo Noh, Korean, a Pentecostal minister, began a 3-week prayer/fast retreat and Betsy Moan, a Quaker, arrived to begin a one-month prayer experience."[36]

Greta Reed, a Philosophy professor and later Presbyterian minister who retreated there several times, recalls her experience of the spirit-infused daily life at O+M:

... Sr. Benita Luetkemeyer, Sr. Lucia Anne Le, Sr. Bede Luetkemeyer, Sr. Josetta Grant, Sr. Maureen Truland, Sr. Regina Arnold."

Sr. Pascaline reported in 1996: "Our first temporary member, Joan Cole, came in June of 1982. Ruth Slickman, Brook Reed, Kay Warren, Judy Walter, Daniel Pittman, Sue Gardner, Eleanor Forfang, Frances Meehan, Teresa Matyniak, John Mallon, Nancy Wakeham and Dung Le have all been temporary members of O+M."

34   *See* page 96.

35   Von Brück returned in November of 1985, speaking at the University of Tulsa, then giving an "Introduction to Meditation" at the Monastery. He was by then living in India and earlier that year had hosted an important conference: "Emerging Consciousness for a New Humankind" at his Gurukul Lutheran College in Madras. The Dalai Lama inaugurated the conference and Bede Griffiths was among the speakers.

36   In 1996 looking back over sixteen years at O+M, Sr. Pascaline reported that: Community retreat directors have been: Harold Grant '81; Dennis Rackley, Carthusian 7/82; Father Shigeto Oshida 9/83; Father Willigis Jager OSB 6/25/87; Sr. Ludwigis Fabian 6/25/88; Ruben Habito '91, '92, '93, '94, '95, '96. Hundreds have come to the Forest for retreats and direction since 1980.

© MARY JANE MATTHEWS

Before dawn each day, one of the Sisters would sound the large metal gong hanging by the front entrance to the main house — several long, loud bursts, followed by softer, cascading tones. The gong signaled time for the first of the day's two one-hour-long contemplative prayer sittings — with a midway break for a meditative walk around the circumference — held in silence, except for an opening and closing chant.

… With only candles to light our way, we filed quietly into the chapel, finding cushions, or a Buddhist prayer bench, or a straight-back chair along outer walls and windows. Depending on the season, the darkness of night would slowly give way to dawn, and, if we were lucky, a sunrise might break forth, visible through the east-facing windows looking out across the long expanse of valley below. That in itself was prayer.

Silence would be held until daily Mass at eight, Tuesday through Saturday mornings. The priest in residence —Fr. Jim — presided. In keeping with Sister Pascaline's vision, he offered the simplest of homilies — not more than a few interpretive, reflective sentences, presented after he had read the Gospel lesson for the day. Then he allowed for silence, inviting all those present to share their own responses.…

I had no idea we were practicing *lectio divina*, a sacred reading of Scripture, part of a long tradition in Western Christianity, especially in Benedictine practice.[37]

Reed recalls the long dining table that stretches the length of the common house from the kitchen to the chapel doors:

---

37 Greta Reed, *Sacred Enticement*, Chapter 20, published in paperback and ebook, 2015. Used by permission of the author.

© MARY JANE MATTHEWS

At that table any number of guests, from all over the ... world, might be seated with the Sisters for the main midday meal. Before the blessing, each would be asked to say only their first name. After all had gone to the counter to serve themselves and were seated on their individual bench-like stools, the conversations would begin. Never had I experienced such table talk as we had there: no one pontificating, no one striving to enhance their status ... Instead, words flowed compassionately, easily, as if graced.

One day I found myself seated next to an elderly man who introduced himself simply as Jean (with the French pronunciation). Innocently, I asked him where he was from and what brought him here. Very slowly, reluctantly, and only because I was curious and kept probing, did I discover he was the world-renowned Roman Catholic scholar Jean LeClercq.

Reed writes, "Little did I know that this was Benedictine tradition in practice," nor did she realize that the Rule of Benedict was the origin of "the very democratic practice of having everyone — guests and Sisters — clear the table and do dishes together. Think of it — washing dishes beside the renowned Jean LeClercq!"

Greta Reed returned to the Forest of Peace years later as a Presbyterian minister, newly graduated from seminary, and spent the summer of 1991 at Osage on a Taylor fellowship for meditators. Sister Pascaline was away most of that summer as the Rev. Reed struggled to be still and discern where Spirit was taking her, post-seminary. Reed recalls:

> One Saturday night, soon upon [Sr. Pascaline's] return, she discovered me preparing the communal supper with my Sony Walkman on — I always hated to miss Prairie Home Companion. With a look of horror, and treating me perhaps more as a novice than a summer intern, she let me know how very uncontemplative — and unacceptable— this was.
>
> I did not appreciate being reprimanded. But I quickly understood. All summer I had been getting away with this, and now the prioress had returned. It was her job to see that the vision and mission of the monastery be sustained. Benedictine practice placed at its core not only the blessedness of work, but also the consequent demand that we attend fully to the one thing we are doing.[38]

Alongside its function as a place of Benedictine order and hospitality, Osage Monastery has been a hermitage.

Over the years, many have come to O+M specifically to live as hermits, meditating, praying, studying, sleeping and eating or fasting in solitude for varying lengths of time.

During her 19 years in the Forest, Sr. Helen Barrow spent seven years as a hermit, alone in her one-room cabin.

Before she become a hermit in 1987, Sr. Helen took a more active part in the full life of East-West monastic experience at Osage and found herself enriched by that.

---

38 *Sacred Enticement*, Chapter 34.

She told her Sisters:

> The greatest influence on my life of prayer has been in coming to O+M — the interreligious dialogue, actual contact with Tibetan Buddhist monks and nuns, Episcopal ministers, Jews and, most deeply, the encounters with Father Bede Griffiths. So much of that I have tried to make my own — while still remaining and becoming ever more deeply cognizant of my own Christian faith. The Christian Zen meditation of Japanese Father Shigeto Oshida attracted Sr. Helen when he visited O+M in 1983, and she spent the next year at Takamori, Oshida's hermitage in Japan, meditating with his monks "Zen style" in a small chapel twice a day and working in the rice fields as an ongoing meditative practice.

SISTER HELEN BARROW

Back home at O+M, she, like the other Sisters, took occasional hermitage retreats away from the work of hospitality and programming for the Monastery. In the summer of 1987, however, Helen "entered hermitage permanently after a full day's celebration with all." During the next years she only occasionally emerged from her hermitage, especially when Father Oshida was at O+M giving retreats. Most of the time she spent in silent solitude, meditation and *lectio divina*, often joining in the silent communion services, but emerging to speak and teach only now and then.

Two years after Sr. Helen entered permanent hermitage, the community sought permission from the BSPA Council to build two new buildings at O+M. On November 4, 1989, "Permission came from St. Louis to proceed with buildings: Hermitage and office/council room," and within two days bulldozers were at work clearing the way for the additional buildings. The Hermitage would become Sister Helen's new cabin, while the office/council room

FATHER SHIGETO OSHIDA

would provide a meeting space apart from the main house. It would be dedicated as "St. Bede's" on Father Bede Griffith's 83rd birthday, December 17.

While the noisy construction work was underway in November, however, Sister Helen emerged to give a seminar on Evagrian the Solitary, a fourth century "desert father" whose writings had at one point been declared heretical by the Church. A few days later, she led Satsang with a review of: *Prophecy & Politics: Militant Evangelists on the Road to Nuclear War*.

The disruption of construction in the Forest was thankfully short-lived. On December 11, scarcely a month after construction had begun, Sr. Helen moved into the new Hermitage, and slept for the first time in a bed specially built for her by Stephen Daney, who had also helped build the new Hermitage.

Others who visited or retreated at O+M in later years would remember Sr. Helen drifting silently up the trail to the Chapel through the predawn twilight to join in meditation with the group, never speaking, but conveying a joyful presence, the fruit of her practice in profound listening and silent prayer.

For all of the Forest dwellers, Mondays were usually set aside for hermit days — "Forest Days" — when one person would be "on duty" to greet visitors and answer the phone while the others would spend the day, each in solitary meditation in her own cabin, after a "Zen Eucharist" in silence in the chapel or outdoors in nice weather. During Lent, the entire Osage Monastery community took a "solitude week" during which they limited all contact with the outside world and spent their nights and days in their individual cabins — "No speaking, reading, writing; no phones or anyone on duty."

Most of the time, however, the BSPA Sisters welcomed neighbors from Oklahoma City, Tulsa and the surrounding communities to come out to the Forest to meet whatever monk, mystic, teacher, or luminary was visiting there.

Ruben Habito is a Philippine former Catholic priest who studied Zen meditation as a young man in Kamakura, Japan, under Yamada Kuan Roshi. When he arrived to lead a retreat at O+M in March, 1991, he had recently left the Jesuit order to found the Maria Kannon Zen Center in Dallas. He would return to the Forest to teach and lead Christian/Zen retreats every year in April or May. A retreatant who came to Osage to be part of these later wrote, "The time this summer and during Ruben's retreats there over the past few years has awakened the 'Forest of Peace' in me."

By November of 1990, with O+M having passed into its second decade, Father Jim Conner's Abbot at Gethsemani recalled him for a six-week retreat there to discern his future status. He had been living in the Tulsa diocese and serving as chaplain for the little community of BSPA sisters for 12 years by this time. On his 57th birthday, December 3, 1990, the Forest Dwellers received a letter from Father Jim with the news that he had decided to return to Gethsemani permanently at the beginning of Lent, mid-February, 1991. On February 18, he "departed after Eucharist about 10 AM amidst much weeping."

RUBEN HABITO

In her 1996 "Brief History" Sr. Pascaline would report that, following the departure of Father Jim, "Communion Service during the week has been the norm for the community unless blessed with a priest in retreat. Sundays were covered by Father Patrick Eastman followed by Father James McGlinchy."

Many years later, Father McGlinchy would remember the Sisters at Osage Monastery fondly:

I had tremendous regard for them. I spent a whole year as their chaplain and was out there frequently.

I was very happy to do it for them that year. And then I went there always for my devotion after that. They were very good people and taught me to pray.

I took Father John Vrana out there. John had left the priesthood for a few years, and then one day he wanted to come back, but the Bishop wanted him to go make a retreat. I drove him out to the Forest of Peace and introduced him to Sister Pascaline, and she told John he could come for a thirty-day retreat. By the end of his retreat Fr. John was walking on air. He couldn't get over it. Sr. Pascaline was a very good retreat master — spiritual director — and she would make you think about a lot of things. The Forest of Peace turned his life around, as it turned my life around. Some of the nicest things I've ever done as a priest happened out there.

FR. BRIAN PIERCE AND FR. JOHN VRANA

Fr. Vrana would later serve as chaplain at Sunday Mass in the Forest Chapel under the "wheel of life" chandelier. Michaela Lawson remembers one Sunday when Father had all but lost his voice, speaking with a croaky rasp. But he was willing to serve the Eucharist as best he could. The moment he began to speak the blessing of the bread and wine, his full, resonant voice boomed forth in the little chapel. Michaela, who provided music for services, remarks that one can often hear overtones and harmonies there which seem to be coming from the room itself.

James Campbell and Fr. Brian Pierce, Dominican friars who had recently established a mission in Honduras, visited O+M in June of 1993. Fr. Campbell "came in view of resident chaplaincy," Sr. Pascaline wrote in her report to the Prioresses' Council that month.

Fr. Jim Campbell had no doubt heard about O+M from Shigeto Oshida. Both Fr. Campbell and Oshida were World War II veterans, but the two had fought on opposite sides in the war. Fr. Campbell felt tremendous guilt for having helped bomb Japanese civilians during the war. He traveled to Japan to Oshida's Zendo, where he went to Oshida, intent on expressing his remorse. As Fr. Brian Pierce recounts the story:

> Jim had practiced his reconciliation spiel for months and months. "I made this trip in order to atone for my sin for having bombed your people during WWII."
>
> Fr. Oshida looked fiercely back at him and said, "And I was a member of the

anti-aircraft squad. I tried to shoot you down — and I'm sorry I missed!" The two of them roared with laughter, hugging each other. Jim told me later, "At that moment all my pain was gone. It was laughter that liberated me." The perfect Zen Master at work!

At the time of their first visit to O+M in 1993, Fr. Jim Campbell was in his late 50s and Fr. Brian was his young confrere, age 33. They had been sent to Honduras earlier that year to found a Dominican mission among the poor. Fr. Brian recounts that "Jim was not in Honduras a month when he was run over by a bus and his leg was crushed." He spent the next year and a half recuperating from the accident and rehabilitating his leg. During part of this time, he was on retreat at O+M.

Fr. Jim Campbell was a "wonderful man, wild man," Bob Doenges recalled. "He kept the Sisters off guard because he would say some of the craziest things in the Mass. He was just so original and so connected to Spirit. Sr. Pascaline always tried to control the priests, but she couldn't control Fr. Jim. He was very irreverent and very reverent at the same time."

While Fr. Campbell was at O+M, Fr. Brian made brief visits, short breaks in Father Brian's years of work among the poor of Honduras. At the time he had no notion of living in the Forest of Peace or being chaplain there. After years in the slums in Honduras, however, he "was just overwhelmed by the poverty work."

To recuperate, during the year of 1996 he lived as a hermit alone in a hut in the mountains of Honduras with no electricity, no running water, until his provincial in the United States arrived at the door of the hut. "He told me, 'Brian, I think you need to come back to the United States and find a place like this hut and just spend as much time there as you need.' I didn't know what to do or where to go, but I remembered the Osage Monastery."

He telephoned Sister Pascaline from Honduras and asked her if there was a cabin available. Sr. Pascaline said, "Oh my goodness! We've just lost our chaplain. Brian, if you would come here and only celebrate Mass every morning for us, you can be in complete silence all you want. You don't have to pay anything. Just come and live with us and celebrate Mass for us." Fr. Brian came to live at O+M in January of 1997. Already he was "very interested in Merton, the East, the Dalai Lama…"

> … but I knew nothing about Meister Eckhart, who was one of the greatest contemplatives of the Dominican order — my order. The whole year of 1997 we studied the three volumes of sermons of Meister Eckhart. The study group included the BSPA's here [at O+M], three Dominican Sisters working in Tulsa and me. The way we did it was, I took the three volumes and divided them into little pieces so that we could work on it piece by piece. We made copies for the eight of us and each week we would read three sermons of Eckhart. On Monday I would give out the copies and on Friday afternoon we would meet and each of us would share what we got out of those sermons.
>
> After Meister Eckhart, we spent six months studying Catherine of Sienna,

another of the greatest Dominican contemplatives. Then I went back to Honduras.

Fr. Brian returned to the Forest of Peace from time to time to lead meditation retreats and teach.

Sister Maurus Allen, who had traveled to India and spent the year 1976–77 with Sr. Pascaline at Fr. Bede's ashram, visited O+M several times and offered yoga lessons while there. In the summer of 1994, she spent several weeks on a retreat at Osage preparing for her Golden Jubilee as a Benedictine Sister and her 70th birthday. While there she shared stories about her experiences with Father Bede. The 4th of July that year "found Sister Maurus, Linda Straub, and a Hindu and Sikh couple at O+M eating vegetarian hot dogs," wrote Sister Pascaline in the chronicle.

One Protestant to visit repeatedly was the Rev. Thomas Letts, a Presbyterian pastor from California, and later Alaska. After he had been making regular retreats at Osage for over 20 years, "Rev. Tom" wrote the Prioress General and Sisters of the BSPA at Clyde to tell them how much the O+M and the Sisters there had meant to him. "What a truly unique and vital ministry you have fostered here. …It is hard for me to put into words the importance of such a place in our world today."

O+M's Benedictine attention to the activity of each hour made heart-centered Benedictine hospitality a palpable reality at O+M. In spring, 2000, Linda, a retreatant from Erie, Pennsylvania, recalled:

For the duration of my recent two-week sojourn at Osage Monastery … my name was listed on the community chalkboard. Hung on a narrow piece of wall separating the kitchen from the entryway, one half of this small chalkboard carried the day's horarium and the other half listed monastery guests who, along with the monastic community, would bring that schedule to life. And, no small matter, the names on the chalkboard determined just how many places were to be set for meals at the long wooden table.

Only once did I hear someone writing on the chalkboard, and never did I see anyone take eraser in hand. Yet, the particulars were always current. Hours came: we sat in quiet contemplation at this hour, we shared a meal at that one, we prayed vespers at another. And hours went. With its silent communication, the chalkboard facilitated our presence to each other.

Names also came and went. For several days I noticed when a name or two appeared and other ones were erased. Then … well into my second week … it occurred to me that in a few days my name, too, would be erased from the chalkboard. This voiceless community courier would no longer be speaking my name, assuring a place for me at the table, inviting me to be a part of those hours, of this community.

In this forest of peace I had heard my name clearly spoken by a loving God … and I wanted my name right out there where God — the Good, True, Beautiful, Holy and One (according to Aquinas and Sister Pascaline) —and everyone could see it.[39]

---

39 Linda [?], manuscript in the personal collection of Sr. Pascaline Coff.

© MARY JANE MATTHEWS

Every time visitors from another part of the world dined at Osage Monastery they would be asked to say the blessing in their own language at the long table where meals were shared. Later, they would be asked for the English translation. Over time, the Sisters gleaned a banquet of table prayers:

BEFORE MEALS

[Christian] Bless our hearts to hear, in the breaking of bread, the song of the universe. Amen.

[Native American] Great Spirit, we thank you for this gift of food; we thank you for the earth, our Mother, who holds and nourishes all the tender seeds; may our feet walk gently upon her; may our hands respect her; may we learn the lesson in every leaf and rock. May our strength restore her. Help us to walk the sacred path of life without difficulty, with our minds and hearts continually fixed on you. Amen.

[Hebrew] Blessed are you, O Lord, our G-d, Eternal King. Who feeds the whole world with your goodness, with grace, with loving kindness and with tender mercy. You give good to all flesh, for your loving kindness endures forever. Through your great goodness, food has never failed us. O may it not fail us forever, for your name's sake, since you nourish and sustain all living things, and do good to all, and provide food for all your creatures whom you have created. Amen.

AFTER MEALS

[Islamic] In the name of God and with blessings from God, all praise is due to God, Who has given us to eat and to drink and Who has made us to surrender. Amen.

[Hindu] May the Lord of Love protect us. May the Lord of Love nourish us. May we realize the Lord of Love. May we live with love for all; May we live with peace for all. OM Shanti! Shanti! Shanti!

[Christian] In the energy of this food of which we have partaken, may the Spirit take us by the hand and lead us deep into the center of our hearts. Amen.

ONE-HEART GRACE

As we make ready to eat this food, we remember with gratitude the people, animals, plants, insects, creatures of the sky and sea, air and water, fire and earth— all turning in the wheel of living and dying — whose joyful exertions, not separate from ours, provide our sustenance this day.

May we with the blessing of this food join our hearts to the One Heart of the world in awareness and love, and may we together with everyone, realize the path of awakening, and never stop making effort for the benefit of others.

Grace Before Meal by John O'Donahue

As we begin this meal with grace,
Let us become aware of the memory
Carried inside the food before us:
The quiver of the seed
Awakening in the earth,
Unfolding in a trust of roots
And slender stems of growth,
On its voyage toward harvest,
The kiss of rain and surge of sun:
The innocence of animal soul
That never spoke a word,
Nourished by the earth
To become today our food;
The work of strangers
Whose hands prepared it,
The privilege of wealth and health
That enable us to feast and celebrate.

OTHER BLESSINGS

♦ For food in a world where many walk in hunger;
For faith in a world where many walk in fear;
For friends in a world where many walk alone;
We give you thanks, O Lord of Love. Amen

♦ For this and all we are about to receive, make us truly grateful, Lord. Amen

♦ For good food and those who prepared it,
For good friends with whom to share it,
We thank you, Divine Giver of Life. Amen.

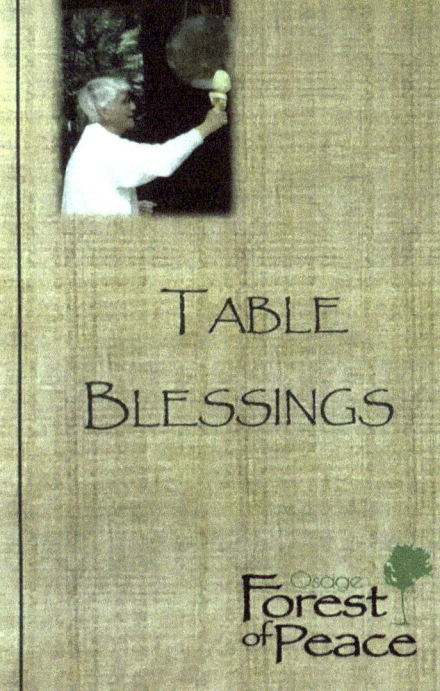

TABLE BLESSINGS

Osage Forest of Peace

COURTESY TULSA WORLD

TIBETANS
1981–1996

"THE TIBETANS ARE HERE!"
— Bro. Joe from St. Procopius Abbey

As the Secretariat of the North American Board for East-West Dialogue from its founding, the Osage Monastery attracted visitors from the East. Perhaps the most remarkable of these (in addition to Father Bede Griffiths) were the Tibetan Buddhist monks and nuns living in exile in India, who came to live and share with the O+M community as part of a series of seven interreligious monastic exchanges sponsored by the NABEWD in the 1980s and 1990s. The Tibetans spent months traveling in North America and visiting Benedictine monasteries. In return, Catholic monastics, including Sr. Pascaline, would visit the Tibetans in their Buddhist monasteries and schools in India.

These exchanges made a lasting contribution to interreligious understanding in both East and West. They were seeded in the summer of 1981 when Sr. Pascaline and Fr. Jim traveled to Boulder, Colorado, for a workshop at the Naropa Institute. While there, they and others from the NABEWD had a private audience with the most famous religious refugee in the world — H.H. the Dalai Lama. It was Sr. Pascaline's first audience with the Dalai Lama, but would not be the last. She met with him on four later occasions during her momentous years as Executive Secretary of the NABEWD.

During that first audience in Denver, Sr. Pascaline asked His Holiness if he might be open to the possibility of some of his Tibetan monks experiencing Western monastic life first-hand in North American monasteries.

> His Holiness beamed a delighted "yes, this is very important." But he was wise enough to foresee many problems in working out practical details. Abbot Lawrence Wagner, OSB of Assumption Abbey in Richardson, North Dakota, also a member of NABEWD, then cordially invited the Lama to choose a few of his monks who would best profit by the experience and warmly welcomed the monks to his monastery in North Dakota, as soon as this can be arranged.[40]

"Assistance with the hosting of Tibetan monks in six American monasteries" was placed at the top of the NABEWD agenda in the planning for 1982 at their fifth annual board meeting held at O+M the following December. The Osage Monastery was not one of the six monasteries that year, but an article in the October, 1982 Bulletin reported, "Plans for a similar tour of Western monasteries by three Tibetan Buddhist monks in 1983 are underway." Osage was on the itinerary this time; three Tibetans would visit O+M for a week in July, 1983.

---

40   NABEWD Bulletin, October, 1981.

PRESENTING GIFTS TO HIS HOLINESS DALAI LAMA, EAST-WEST CONFERENCE, NAROPA, COLORADO, 1981

The O+M community began preparing for the monks' arrival weeks in advance, with satsangs to educate the Forest Dwellers about Tibetan Buddhism. Meanwhile, it fell to the North American Board to help arrange travel around the USA for the visitors. Of course, Sr. Pascaline and the Sisters were in the middle of the arranging, which included fundraising. On the back page of the May, 1983 Bulletin, in a box with a heavy rule around it to make it stand out, appeared an appeal for financial help.

The night before the expected arrival of the monks, the Sisters "brainstormed ways to prepare for their week in our midst." One of the preparations that took place as the Buddhists were en route to Tulsa was the acquisition of gifts to give them from the O+M community. The Sisters decided on prayer beads, and one of them was sent to get beads while running other errands in town.

That evening, as the Chronicle records:

As we knelt to begin Vespers a voice called this from the back door: HELLO THIS IS BRO JOE FROM ST PROCOPIUS. THE TIBETANS ARE HERE! We rose to the occasion and went to the back door to greet them. Geshela placed a white silk scarf on Sr. Pascaline and through his interpreter said it symbolized purity, peace and friendship in their happiness to be here. After cold drinks they joined us for Vespers and a bite to eat. They retired early as did Bro Geo. and Joe. — Jesus and Buddha meet again!

Jesus and Buddha would no doubt get along well, but welcoming these Buddhists into their midst posed something of a challenge for Christian monastics like the BSPA Sisters who had chosen to spend their lives in Perpetual Adoration of the

Eucharist. Sr. Pascaline's chronicle entry for the following day (Friday, July 8) reveals her struggle with Catholic Eucharistic doctrine and the Benedictine value of hospitality that was, to her, an expression of the Savior's sacred heart:

> The Body and Blood of Jesus given to one, a believer seated elbow to elbow next to unbelievers to whom the Gift, this Life, cannot be offered! Are these maroon-robed monks loved less by Jesus? Are we "better" now than they who are so compassionate, sensitive to others, loving and truly humble? It causes pain in the heart to ponder this. They are in exile, they are at peace with the world. We are "receiving them as Christ." Is He in them, in us?

Here Sr. Pascaline is grappling with an issue that had dogged the inter-monastic movement from the beginning, the issue of intercommunion — that is, communion offered to persons other than Catholics during the celebration of the Eucharist. Explains Fabrice Blée in *The Third Desert: The Story of Monastic Interreligious Dialogue:*

> In the Catholic Church only baptized Catholics are allowed to take communion; apart from some specifically determined exceptional situations, Christians are not offered the Eucharist, even though the Catholic Church recognizes the baptism of Protestant and Orthodox Christians. Given this state of affairs intercommunion is extremely controversial. The practice raises all sorts of questions and creates a fear that it could destroy the sacramental system at the heart of the Catholic Church.

The issue had been raised after the Petersham Conference in 1977, when word got around that Abbot Tholens had served communion to a non-Christian who came forward to receive it. The rumor included the suspicion that this intercommunion had been planned into the program. This was not the case; it had been a matter of the non-Christian coming for communion unexpectedly and Abbot Tholens being unwilling to refuse him. The Abbot later explained, "My opinion about intercommunion is that we may not, as a matter of course, go against what the law lays down. But we are not robots, and when someone comes forward to receive communion in special circumstances—someone who feels 'in communion' with me—I will not refuse to give communion to such a person."[41]

This controversy might be said to be part of the DNA of East-West monastic exchange, because the exchange, with its outreach across the boundaries of religious systems, was in occasional tension with tradition on both sides. Sr. Pascaline, of course, was always aware of this tension, and worked hard to show that East-West exchange had been legitimized by Rome in Vatican II.

During that first day of the three Tibetans' visit in the Forest of Peace, there was a sense that history was being made as these Benedictine Sisters welcomed three Buddhist monks in maroon robes and shaved heads into their midst. The appearance of Geshe Lobsang Choephel (aged 50), Ven. Kalsang Dadul (29), and Ven. Losang Sonam Lodoe (28) in northeastern Oklahoma fascinated the local news media and drew crowds to the Forest as word spread.

---

41   Blée (2004, 2011): p. 103

FRIDAY, JULY 8, 1983

The Tibetans joined us for Adoration and Praises and joined in our hymns and psalms. Father Jim and Sr. Pascaline spent time with them after Eucharist until Grant and Dave from the Tulsa news[42] came to interview them. We left the monks free space in the afternoon, then gathered at the Crafthouse after supper to dialogue with them. Our first question lasted the whole session. (Satsang=husband & wife!) What does deity yoga mean? Meditation the manifestation of a deity (merging with). There are 32 deities — manifestations of the Buddha in a mandala = all One.

SATURDAY, JULY 9, 1983

How can these holy monks be brought to know that we love the Father? How are we manifesting Christ to them? About 10:45 the reporter, Grant Williams, returned and checked details about the article for tonight. At 3 PM the community and Marguerite gathered with our Buddhists for *choe do*. Geshe La asked us what the goal of Christianity is. And we probed together the similarities and differences in understanding hell, death, reincarnation, karma. Buddhists believe eventually everyone will be purified so that hell is not permanent!

During supper someone from Tulsa phoned after seeing the evening paper and the story about the monks. Sister Jocinta, Barbara, Clare, Bro. Peter, C.B. and a postulant came to see our slides and the monks. After showing our pictures of O+M and India, Geshe asked for a comparison of the way of life of Christian, Buddhist and Hindu from experience in India. Much dialogue ensued. A rich, full evening.

SUNDAY, JULY 10, 1983

Our three Buddhist brothers joined us for morning prayer.

Many came for Eucharist and enjoyed meeting the monks afterwards. Jim geared his homily on the Good Samaritan to the Tibetans.

We tried to take a walk about 3:30 but it was too hot and there was no shade on the path. Geshe put his robe on his head!

After supper many (35) came for the Tibetans' film showing the Chinese takeover in March, 1959. The discussion afterwards was helpful.

MONDAY, JULY 11, 1983 — FEAST OF ST. BENEDICT!

Adoration and Praises began at dawn with our Buddhist brothers, followed by a festive breakfast of caramel rolls and hard cooked eggs, which the monks enjoyed. At Eucharist Jim made the arati for St. Benedict at the beginning of Mass. Mary Helen from the Mannford paper came about 10:15 AM with her granddaughter and a friend and a photographer to speak with the monks. After dinner we exchanged gifts, the monks giving us some pamphlets on Tibet and Buddhism and we gave them *Blessed Simplicity* by Panikkar, *Marriage of East and West* by Bede

---

42   The *Tulsa Tribune*, an evening newspaper.

Griffiths, and *Contemplation* by Merton, plus some books on E-W dialogue. We also had them phone the Office of Tibet. At 2:30 several people, including Sister Theresa Korean joined us for a sharing that was very profound on vows, training, and obstructions to enlightenment. After supper many came again to see the film, "The Dalai Lama Taking the Geshe Exam."[43] Many plan to return on Thursday.

TUESDAY, JULY 12, 1983

The monks from Tibet joined us each AM for Adoration/Meditation and Praises. After Eucharist at 8 AM today all departed in 2 cars for Woolaroc Museum. As we arrived (11:30) a showing of the origins of our nation began, which was much enjoyed by our guests. We then toured the [American] Indian museum and enjoyed a picnic lunch near a white Indian bullock at the picnic tables.[44] We arrived at Chief Tinker's home about 3:10 PM and some newspaper reporters joined us as Chief Tinker showed his eagle feathers and told the plight of the American Indian. He greeted the Tibetans, fanned them with his feathers and put on his headpiece for photos with them. We brought Alice [Tinker] and the Chief some homemade bread and potato salad but did not stay for anything after the session. Charlene Warnkin from E.O.C. and her daughter and father and mother-in-law plus several from the Mannford paper were present. We stopped at Braums on the way home for American ice cream.

WEDNESDAY, JULY 13, 1983 — PEACE DAY!

Today we had sessions more privately with the monk guests from Tibet. We addressed questions about poverty, vows, celibacy, reincarnation, and Tibetan monastic life to them at table and during teatime. After supper [in a public session] the Tibetans showed slides of their present monasteries in India where they study and debate. Questions were good but one fundamentalist loudly called out to them, "Have you ever met the Lord Jesus, Lamb of God, King and Savior, who died and rose and sits enthroned at the right hand of God the Father?" They asked what the question was. The man repeated adding several more invocations. They consulted with Geshela then replied: "We have not met the Lord Jesus but we are among many of his followers whom we like very much." Everybody in the room applauded except the questioner who afterwards gave them a King James New Testament.

THURSDAY, JULY 15, 1983

Today being "Meditation Day" with the monks and laity, Father Jim offered a quiet Mass with no homily. About 10:30 people began coming. About 30 joined us for the sessions, bringing food to add to the light lunch available before, during the rest time and after the session. Geshela, Kelsang and Losang sat in the Eastern peak facing the doors. Bro. Keeling translated the free flowing lectures of Geshela,

---

43   Geshe ("virtuous friend") is a Tibetan Buddhist academic degree for monks.
44   Woolaroc, the Osage County ranch of oilman Frank Phillips, pastures a collection of herd animals from around the world, including the white bullocks native to India.

which were interspersed with periods of 10 and 2 minutes meditations for the group. He spoke of hindrances to enlightenment such as: attachments, laziness, pride, anger; and antidotes or remedies, through meditation practice, for each of these. Joanie taped the sessions and other periods of chants at table. All who came voiced appreciation for the sharing. At 7:30 we asked the monks to debate for us. Geshela and Losang did excellently well! A full and rich day ended about 9:15 PM.

FRIDAY, JULY 16, 1983

Our 3 Tibetan monk brothers joined us for Adoration-Meditation and Praises, then Sr. Priscilla fixed them scrambled eggs for the way. The Eucharistic texts included the Passover so Father Jim addressed the topic of liberation to us and to the visitors. After Mass we again exchanged gifts, the white scarf and a "stick." We gave them large handmade prayer beads for each (108) and a book of all their news clippings for the Dalai Lama, and Tibetan and American Indian cards. Many pictures with the community were taken, then tea and their trip to St. Louis where they will stay the night before proceeding to St. Louis Priory. Father Jim will then return on Saturday night to be here for Mass Sunday.

Two years later, one of the three Buddhist monks made a return visit to the Osage Monastery. "All Saints Day, 1985, brought Ven. Kalsang Dadul, Tibetan monk from the Dalai Lama's monastery in Dharamsala, India, back for a second visit to the N.A.B.E.W.D. Secretariate at Osage Monastery in Sand Springs, Oklahoma," Sr. Pascaline reported in the Bulletin.

He was accompanied by Ven. Lhakdor of the same School of Dialectics in India. Dialogue sessions on topics of compassion and prayer were scheduled daily. In the evenings friends of the monastery joined the monastics of Eastern and Western traditions for faith-sharings. During four days of their two-week visit, the Tibetan monks traveled to Kentucky to be hosted by the Cistercian monks at Gethsemani. When departing from Sand Springs the Tibetans said: "We shall be eternal friends." They were given a videotape of their last sessions to bring home to their fellow monks in India.

Then, in autumn, 1986, Sr. Pascaline was part of "Inter-monastic Exchange, Phase III" and visited the Tibetans at their School of Dialectics in Dharamsala. Her group of six American Catholic monastics also had an audience with the Dalai Lama there. She wrote detailed letters about her travels in India back home to the O+M community. One, quoted at length in the October Bulletin, gave an interesting picture of life at the Dharamsala school:

> It was quite a sight to find the 70 robed monks from the Dialectic School and 80 monks +30 robed novices from the Normgyal monastery (next door) all arranged on the lawn of the temple debating in small clusters, with a black cow browsing in their midst. We also attended group debates one evening, which looked like good assertion training as they vied with one another to be the questioner.

TOP: PASCALINE RECEIVING SCARF FROM DALAI LAMA, 1986, INDIA
BOTTOM: DZONGSAR INSTITUTE, NABEWD, DIR, INDIA, 1986

Yesterday we had a session with the Dialectic School. Father Gabriel Coless (St. Mary's Abbey, New Jersey) gave an introductory talk on Western monastic traditions, followed by Father Timothy Kelly (St. John's Abbey, Collegeville) on "The God of Christianity and Creation as Love." Kalsang attended as interpreter for those who couldn't understand English, though most of the Tibetan monks here do. Their questions were interesting and often humorous. In fact, humor is a real gift among the Tibetans. We were taken on a tour of the School and all through the Temple, turning prayer wheels and greeting colorfully dressed Tibetan villagers.

In the morning we visited the Tibetan Institute of Performing Arts where they had a cast of three perform different Tibetan dances for us — so much like our American Indian dances. We also visited Nyingma Tantric Monastery and the Abbot presented all six of us with scarves and served us tea in his temple.

The General Secretary of the Council for Religious Affairs for the Dalai Lama, Kalsang Yeshi, came to visit us yesterday. He is responsible for all the arrangements and they are very happy with our Monastic Hospitality program. We asked if he would be interested in sending their nuns for Phase IV; he said, 'yes' enthusiastically. So the NABEWD will need to consider that possibility at its coming meeting. We attended their morning prayer at 6:00 AM, which consists of ½ hour of prostrations (more than 100) and ½ hour of chanting. We are to have a private audience with the Dalai Lama on Sept. 19.

For the Bulletin, Sr. Pascaline wrote a long narrative account of the visit and had this to say about the meeting with the Dalai Lama:

Dharamsala, among many other things in North India, is a lovely Tibetan village surrounding the home-in-exile of the Dalai Lama. Red-cheeked peasants with bright and muted Tibetan clothing and prayer beads in hand were continuously circumambulating the mountain on which the temple and the palace of the Dalai Lama is located. Tibetan and American monastic participants of both Phases II and III united for a 35-minute interview and exchange with His Holiness the Dalai Lama on September 20th. After giving each one the traditional white scarf His Holiness shared deeply with the group. He expressed his pleasure over "this beginning of Tibetan and Christian inter-monastic exchange" and was eager for the American participants to experience the larger Tibetan monasteries and Colleges in South India, each having more than 1000 monks. He also voiced his hope that what had been begun "might continue and increase in the efforts at love and understanding among all religions as both an example and experience of peace and harmony in the world." He is open to the possibility of some of the Tibetan nuns visiting America with the next Phase of the Inter-monastic Hospitality Program.[45]

---

45 February, 1987 Bulletin, p. 2. The Dalai Lama also told the group about the plight of young monks, many of them refugees from Chinese persecution in Tibet, who had no means of support while they studied at the Buddhist Colleges. In a later issue it was reported that the O+M was sponsoring four of the Tibetan monks to study in India.

Thus it was that in June, 1988, three Buddhist monastics — two monks and a nun — visited the Osage Monastery as part of the monastic exchange, Phase IV. As Bernadette Pruitt reported in the *Tulsa World*:

> One has the trusting look of a child. Another has a mischievous twinkle in his eye. The third has a scholar's gaze.
>
> Acharya Ngawang Samten, Geshe Konchok Tsering and Tenzin Dunsang, two exiled Tibetan monks and a nun, are at peace with themselves in a very unpeaceful world.
>
> For the past three days, the monastics have been doing their contemplating in the Osage hills, where their saffron and claret robes are a world apart from the bass boats, Weedeaters and other forms of consumerism gone rural.[46]

In late January, 1989, Sr. Pascaline and Judy Walter were in India for a six-week sojourn at Father Bede's ashram and made a side-trip to visit Ngawang and Tenzin at the Tibetan Institute for Higher Studies in Saranath, India.

> Ven. Ngawang and Sister Tenzin were so good to us, taking us on a personal pilgrimage of the famous Deer Park where Buddha preached his first sermon and they explained some of the monastic ruins nearby, much like ours on Mt. Tabor or at Cluny. Ngawang's mother baked us a stack of Tibetan bread to take along on the next lap of our journey. Tenzin cooked us supper and invited us to dine with Ngawang and her Ven. Uncle who teaches at the Tibetan University. Still quite young, they are hoping Tenzin will begin studies at the Institute there next year since it is now open to women.

The following year, on July 31, 1990, Lekshi, a Tibetan nun, arrived at O+M for a short visit, dialogue, and "taped lectures on meditation."

In September and October 1992, Sr. Pascaline and three other monastics from the USA traveled back to the Tibetan monasteries-in-exile in India as part of Phase V of the Inter-monastic Exchange. She spoke to the Buddhist monks on the subject of "Christian Watchfulness," as emphasized by the Desert Fathers and Mothers of early Christianity, and began by introducing many of the core teachings of Jesus— "compassionate, limitless, non-violent love," — which were not unlike core Buddhist values. Sr. Pascaline wrote home to O+M every few days.

> We have had 2 great days of dialogue at Namgyal (Dalai L's Monastery) and the Dialectic School. … Kelsang sends love.
>
> We've just had another 2-hour exchange that was very lively, with another packed hall — monks sitting side-by-side on the flat floor, all ears.
>
> It is such a joy to be sharing who Jesus is with all those who have not really heard of Him. Their questions are enriching, even for us — at least the answers they bring forth. It is such an awesome responsibility as we share over and over how the first followers of Jesus were persecuted, then many went into the deserts

---

46   *Tulsa World,* June 16, 1988, p. D1.

ABOVE: SR. HELEN AND TIBETAN MONASTICS; BELOW: TIBETAN-CHRISTIAN MONASTIC EXCHANGE, PHASE IV, OSAGE MONASTERY, 1988 — SR. MONICA, SR. PRISCILLA, SR. HELEN, FR. JIM, SR. PASCALINE AND (SEATED) SR. MAUREEN WITH VISITORS.

and how much they loved to live intensely the teaching and life of especially loving God with one's whole heart, soul and mind and all beings as oneself![47]

One letter to O+M reported that on September 8, "We had a wonderful full hour with the Dalai Lama. He feels the differences in our religions must be clearly claimed and not lost as these make for the richness of the whole of humanity. He is very happy with the exchanges and hope they continue."

Sr. Pascaline would cross paths with the Dalai Lama again in September of 1993 at the Parliament of the World's Religions, held in Chicago to mark the centennial of the 1893 Parliament of the World's Religions. The ten-days-long meeting was historic, attended by over 6,000 people. She spoke on spirituality and healing in a presentation titled, "Life to the Full." The next day H.H. the Dalai Lama gave the keynote address.[48]

Tibetan Buddhist monks would return to the O+M during the week between Christmas 1994 and New Years 1995. As with earlier visits, the appearance of the Tibetans in the Forest of Peace was news in the Tulsa area, covered by the ABC television affiliate, KTUL. The monks gave teachings every night, attended by many, including a Lutheran bishop and a group of Vietnamese Buddhists from Tulsa. Sisters Helen and Pascaline took the Tibetans to Gilcrease Museum and to tour Christ the King, a Catholic church in Tulsa famous for its art deco architecture. The Tibetans showed a video, "Snow Jewel," and the next day visited Catholic Charities with Sister Bede and Sister Pascaline before the two Sisters drove them to St. Gregory's Abbey in Shawnee, Oklahoma, for the next leg of their trip.

Phase VII of the exchange program took Sister Pascaline, three other American monastics and two students into Tibet in June and July 1995.

Then, in the summer of 1996 Sr. Pascaline met the Dalai Lama for a fifth time at the first Gethsemani Encounter between Buddhist and Christian monastics. Father Jim Conner — by this time no longer chaplain at O+M but back in residence in his Trappist Abbey of Gethsemani in Kentucky — wrote an overview of the Encounter in the October 1996 Bulletin:

> The Buddhist-Christian Meeting on the theme of Meditation took place from July 22–27, 1996, at the Abbey of Gethsemani, the home of Thomas Merton. It was the Dalai Lama himself who requested this meeting after the experience of the World Parliament of Religions. He had specifically asked that it be held at the Abbey of Gethsemani because of his respect for Thomas Merton whom he had met very shortly before his death in 1968.

---

47   Letters written by Sr. Pascaline home to O+M and to Sister Monica dated September 6, September 22 and October 3, 1992, are held in the BSPA's Clyde archive.

48   Another Catholic nun in attendance was Sister Jane Comerford, who was greatly inspired by what she experienced at the Parliament. She would later serve for 3 years as the Director of the Osage Forest of Peace.

1996 GETHSEMANI ENCOUNTER

This conference had been organized by MID (the new name of the NABEWD). In his summary of the Encounter, Father Jim noted that "Abbot Timothy Kelly of Gethsemani first greeted the Dalai Lama in the name of the monastic community and then Father James Wiseman, OSB, Chair of the East-West Board, spoke of the meaning of the event. Sister Pascaline Coff, OSB, gave a survey of 'How We Got to this Point.'"

During the Gethsemani Encounter the Dalai Lama mentioned his admiration of "the work that Christians have done in the fields of education and health care," and that "he is urging Buddhist monastics to follow suit by spending a larger part of their time in work that directly benefits humanity."

By the time of the Encounter, though, Buddhist nuns had already responded to that call. On March 1, 1996, two Tibetan nuns had arrived at O+M to take a health care course, which Alice Kelly, Barbara Bilderback and Virginia Atwood, three O+M oblates, helped them to plan. For the next three months Srs. Desel and Dechen would live at O+M, taking English, learning CPR, disaster relief, and first aid while joining in the life of the community and enriching it in many ways. They cooked Tibetan dishes on occasion, shared about their own practices and beliefs, and attended an ordination of three Tulsa seminarians with the Sisters as well as numerous workshops taking place at O+M. They were there for Lent and Easter services, and even had a Bible lesson, given by Sr. Priscilla. During the nuns' visit, on April 15, "Abbot James brought two Tibetan monks for 10 days." Along with giving a satsang, all four Tibetans helped move and spread a load of gravel on the walking paths in the Forest.

When it finally came time for the two Buddhist nuns to depart at the end of May, there was a "farewell for the Tibetans with special blessings, gifts, sharing, and an oriental meal provided by Virginia and Dr. Atwood. As Desel and Dechen left, there were "very teary blessings. Sacrament of all that is good in their religion."

Sr. Pascaline's summation of the East-West Board exchanges during those years left no doubt as to their value to Catholic monastics like the BSPA Sisters at the Osage Monatery Forest of Peace:

> ... [They] have brought non-Christian monastics into the heart of our monasteries and we into theirs with a real face-to-face in-depth encounter. ... While dialogue was the eventual aim, hospitality was the immediate and necessarily first gentle channel through which much happened both for Christians and for the Tibetans. They have prayed with us — we have prayed with them — at the core of each others' monastic lives. We have mutually learned much, not only about beliefs but how the other lives what is believed. To have experienced their compassion and transparent, giftful presence is a deeper-than-ever lesson in Incarnate Love and in Who our God really is — the totally Other.
>
> Light from the East continually floods our Christian path.[49]

---

49 Sr. Pascaline Coff in "Eastern Influences on Benedictine Spirituality," paper given at the meeting of the American Benedictine Academy held at St. Gregory's Abbey, Shawnee, OK, August, 1988. Printed in Cistercian Studies from which it was offprinted as fasc. 2, 1989.

SR. PASCALINE IN THE OFFICE AT THE OSAGE MONASTERY

PUSHBACK
1989–1990

The difficult but essential process of awakening.
Sr. Pascaline Coff

Eleven days before Christmas, 1989, a "Letter to the Bishops of the Catholic Church on Some Aspects of Christian Meditation" was released to all Catholic Bishops worldwide by the Vatican's Sacred Congregation for the Doctrine of the Faith. The letter was signed by its Prefect, Cardinal Joseph Ratzinger, who would, fifteen years later, become Pope Benedict XVI. Sr. Pascaline received a phone call about it the next day, and on December 28 the letter was the subject of a satsang discussion at Osage Monastery.

Despite the letter's pastoral tone, it must have been hard to read it and not sense that everything O+M and the NABEWD stood for was being looked upon as dangerous, not just by the uninformed and backward few, but by the Vatican itself. While the letter did not condemn the Inter-monastic exchange outright, its overall tone toward all non-Catholic forms of prayer and meditation was negative. There were allusions to ancient heresies in the letter, with the implication that such might be reappearing. For instance, under the heading "Erroneous Ways of Praying," the letter said, "With the present diffusion of eastern methods of meditation in the Christian world and in ecclesial communities, we find ourselves faced with a pointed renewal of an attempt, which is not free from dangers and errors, to fuse Christian meditation with that which is non-Christian."

The Letter speaks of "the exaggerations and partiality of … [non-Christian meditation postures], which, however, are often recommended to people today who are not sufficiently prepared."[50] This long and detailed letter of warning was backed up by the Pope: "The Supreme Pontiff, John Paul II, in an audience granted to the undersigned Cardinal Prefect, gave his approval to this letter, drawn up in a plenary session of this Congregation, and ordered its publication." It was signed "Joseph Card. Ratzinger, Prefect."

Two months after the publication of "Ratzinger's Letter," Sr. Pascaline presented the prestigious Harvey Lecture Series at the Episcopal Seminary of the Southwest in Austin, Texas. In it, she mentioned the Ratzinger Letter and focused first on the ways in which it supported the kind of Eastern meditation practices used and taught at Shantivanam in India and at O+M.

> Some Catholic experts on Eastern meditation concluded that it [the Letter] was far more measured than early press notices indicated. Eastern approaches to prayer, the 7,000 word letter said, should not be rejected out of hand simply because they

---

50   www.vatican.va

1985 PARLIAMENT OF WORLD RELIGIONS

are not Christian, but it insisted that there be some fit between the nature of prayer and Christian beliefs about ultimate reality. ... Without these truths, the Vatican said, meditation, which should be a flight from the self, as we have been insisting, can degenerate into a form of self-absorption.

Father Thomas Keating, O.C.S.O., Chairman of our monastic East-West Dialogue Board, said of the document: "In my experience of talking with Eastern spiritual masters, they are just as cautious as this document is about mistaking psychological states that can be induced by meditation for some great enlightenment.

She then made her own statement about one inadequacy of the letter, one that went to the heart of the matter for her:

The document did, however, fail to address the absence of any intense experience of God's power that today is sending many Christians to Eastern religions.

I myself looked to the East for this very reason in 1976, not for God's power so much as for consciousness of his presence, for deeper levels of consciousness of divine love, and in view of what I found I am happy now to share with you some of these treasures of both East and West.

In the two Harvey Lectures, Sr. Pascaline addressed her audience personally about their role as people called to be "other Christs," who were "chosen to discover and uncover the lost 'fire' in Israel." She talked of their "radical identity" as "a unique image of divine love," and their "responsibility to awaken fully yourselves to who you are and to who God is so that you can be authentic sacraments of Christ's presence and therefore catalysts of awakening for others."

"So it is vital," she went on, "that you focus on and give priority to your own inner journey and the difficult but essential process of awakening. And this cannot be without grace and some form of regular, personal meditation leading deeper and deeper into the inner journey, which ... is itself the transformation process in us."

Sr. Pascaline went on to quote a number of early Christian patriarchs and writers on the subject of meditation and its importance. She didn't back off of her insistence that the meditation practices she and others adapted from Eastern spiritual traditions were important means to awakening the heart of Christ, who was "compassion incarnate" within one's own heart. She spoke about the compassion shown by the Dalai Lama, and quoted a teaching about compassion of Shantideva, the 8th Century A.D. Buddhist master from Nalanda University. Then she moved on to a consideration of meditation as a path to the compassionate heart of Jesus:

> While Christ never mentioned the word 'meditation' as such, he did leave us the perfect example of regularly going up into the hills to "be still and know" the Father. ... Notice the important rationale for meditation — for sitting still in order to know the Lord: defects are not removed except by the perfection of some kind of goodness. To pray is to accept Christ's compassion for us, to open ourselves to the divine goodness. ... We are all full of grace. We just must be still and let it ferment.

Later that year, Sr. Pascaline again commented on the Vatican letter. *The National Catholic Reporter* (May 11, 1990) quoted her as saying: "The Document is a good start, but it's far from being a complete treatise on Eastern and Western prayer." She regretted the absence of reference to Christian mystics and Eastern religions in the Letter's definition of authentic prayer. While the Letter did not reject out of hand Eastern forms of prayer, she explained, neither did it present them as worthy of attention from a spiritual point of view.

In the same *Catholic Reporter* issue with Sr. Pascaline's comment was one by Fr. Bede Griffiths. In a letter beneath the headline "Vatican Letter Disguises Wisdom of East Religions," Fr. Bede drew attention to several Christian movements in ages past that endorsed mystical prayer, then added, "This is not to say that Hindu, Buddhist, and Christian mystics all have the same experience. But it is to recognize an analogy between them and to look upon the Hindu and Buddhist experience as something of supreme significance, not to be lightly dismissed by a Christian as of no importance."

Years later, in a *National Catholic Reporter* interview, Thomas C. Fox asked Sr. Pascaline, "What gifts have other religious traditions brought to your life?"

She replied, "The deepest understanding of hospitality is welcoming the divine in the other person. That's always been my own stance with regard to others, whatever their religion might be." She went on to say:

> I spent a formative year among Hindus in India who believe strongly in the presence of God's spirit in everyone. They live it out in practice. ... Hindu scriptures are filled with wisdom. ... Anyone with contact with Buddhism is impressed with their particular gift, their efforts both to generate and practice compassion. ... Muslims give important lessons on fidelity to prayer. ... They practice surrender to the divine Word. When we have dialogued with Muslims in Tulsa, they describe their religion as a passionate desire to be right with God.
>
> Contact with the deepest wisdom from other religious traditions is a consolation to all of us who are dismayed at fundamentalism in our own religions and in others. In their depths all religions are filled with compassion and wisdom beyond rational understanding. It is a gift from the Spirit, as we know in our own tradition.[51]

From the beginning, Sister Pascaline and others involved in East-West Intermonastic Dialogue had been required to defend their use of Eastern meditation practices, but they had always been supported, at least in theory, by the Vatican, acting on the new interfaith openness that had been promulgated by Vatican II. The Ratzinger letter must have been especially troubling because it expressed fears that lay people "who are not sufficiently prepared" were being encouraged to meditate. In fact, as we have seen, the Osage Monastery developed as a place of prayer, contemplation, and meditation, open to all who came seeking such a place, whether Catholic monastics or not. The Benedictines' core value of hospitality perhaps dictated that this should be so. Lay Catholics in the Tulsa Diocese insisted that this new prayer center must have room for laity to come for meditation retreats, and, once the new cabins were built, they came.

While Catholic lay people entering into the practices developed in Eastern religions — the waving of the arati fire, the chanting of the Bhagavad Gita, the practice of Zen meditation, and even "Zen Communion" — might be frowned upon by the Congregation for the Doctrine of the Faith, the lay Catholics and others who braved such exposure to Eastern practices often felt their faith deepened and lives enriched.

In 2007, Sister Pascaline would write of the BSPAs and the Osage Monastery: "The sisters believe dialogue with other religions has always been important even though practiced by only a few, but now it is crucial for all. As a monastic ashram, from the start, O+M has had a simple life style, open to all religions, and has had intensive spiritual exercises — the three qualities of every authentic ashram."[52]

---

51 "Religious exploration, wisdom and truth," by Thomas C. Fox, *National Catholic Reporter*, September 21, 2007, p. 23.

52 Sr. Pascaline Coff. "Osage Monastery, Looking Back," in The Golden String: Bulletin of the Bede Griffiths Trust, Vol. 14 No. 2, p. 1.

© 2015 ROSEMARY DELUCCA ALPERT

FR. BEDE GRIFFITHS

FATHER BEDE
1979–1993

All creation and all humanity are taken up into this infinite, incomprehensible, inexpressible Being of God . . . This is Christian advaita.[53] *We are one with one another and one with Christ: we are one in this mystery of the Godhead.*

—Father Bede Griffiths,
The Cosmic Revelation

Fr. Bede Griffiths visited the Osage Forest of Peace four times in the final years of his life, beginning in 1979 when he came to bless the land on which it would one day stand. He called it "the most peaceful place I have ever known," and said, "This place has had a profound effect on me. It makes me feel the presence of God more intimately."[54]

Fr. Bede's visits were usually part of an inter-monastic dialogue tour in the USA, much of this travel orchestrated by Sister Pascaline. That was the case in the hot August of 1983, when he arrived for a few days' rest at the Osage Monastery before keynoting an East-West Seminar in Kansas City.

Sr. Pascaline recorded Bede's arrival, and the attention he and his companion, Bro. Joseph Rymondraj (Raymund), attracted when she and Sr. Lioba met them at their arrival gate in the Tulsa airport. "Father Bede was in Kavi[55] and Raymund in yellow so as they did their namaskars[56] everyone gazed at the colorful procession."

Standing in the main house at the Osage Monastery, "Father Bede took tea and a banana, but kept looking at the library books with great glee!" It was, of course, the first time he had seen the place with its buildings and walking trails. "He retired immediately but came up for dinner, then retired again. It is a deep joy to have him, but his frailness is a concern," Sr. Pascaline wrote in the chronicle on August 8, a day when the Oklahoma heat was well over 100 degrees. "He appreciated the special fan in his window. After Vespers (including arati) and supper, Father Bede retired."[57]

The Osage Monastery and its cabins were not air-conditioned, in part because Sister Pascaline had wanted to make this Forest of Peace as much as possible like

---

53   From Indian philosophy. Advaita is often translated as "non-dualism" though it literally means "non-secondness." *Internet Encyclopedia of Philosophy*.
54   Quoted in Sister Katherine Ann Smolik's "An Ashram: A Response to the Signs of the Times."
55   Saffron-colored robe
56   Traditional Indian greeting
57   The fan for Bede's cabin and another for the common house had been provided by Kathryn Grant two days earlier.

Father Bede's Shantivanam in South India. However, August in northeastern Oklahoma could rival any day in South India for heat, besides which Bede Griffiths often became ill when he traveled, and he was now 76.

Free to join in the various meditation and communion services or rest quietly in his cabin, he seemed to rebound somewhat. The day after his arrival at O+M, "Father Bede came for tea at 4 and returned again in time for news at 5:30. After supper Father Bede retired early and the rest enjoyed Satsang." The Chronicle book reports details of the visit:

WEDNESDAY, AUGUST 10, 1983

Father Devananda offered an Indian Eucharist for us. Father Bede was present so Sr. Pascaline had the joy of bringing him Communion. Also, the arati later in the day at Vespers. ... Bede is feeling stronger today! He had several conferences with Devananda, Judy, Martha, etc. After supper we showed the O+M slides with the script, plus some of the Tibetans debating and visiting the Indian Chief.[58]

THURSDAY, AUGUST 11, 1983

Father Bede offered Eucharist and gradually all fans were shut off so everyone could hear his words in between. Jeri and Paula came for Eucharist, also Greta with her flute! Eileen from *Mannford Eagle News* brought some vegetables for Father Bede. Father Joseph Propps came in time for Day Hours and dinner with Father Bede. At 4 PM Grant Williams of the Tulsa newspaper came again — to interview Father Bede. His photographer, Don, took 3–4 rolls of film (!) as he taped his interview. [In the evening] Father Bede retired to work on his conferences and rest, but is feeling stronger and stronger.

The next day after Eucharist, Sr. Helen, Lioba, Brook, Janice and Sr. Pascaline drove to Savior of the World Seminary in Kansas City to prepare for the conference on "Formation and Transformation through an Eastern Perspective," sponsored by AIM and the NABEWD. Father Bede, Brother Raymund and the rest of the O+M community plus Judy Walter, Jeri Chase and others, made the six-hour drive the next morning, leaving at 5:30. That night at 7 Father Bede opened the conference.

The air-conditioning and microphones went on the blink. Father Bede's talk on "The Necessity of the Church and the Monastic Order to Dialogue with Eastern Spirituality" was eloquent with no notes and great joy! All had put in a full day with vans and arrangements, our staff, Seminary personnel and participants. The tone of profound awe has been set. When Father Bede invited all to move closer it dispelled the formal setting and everyone circled around the stage.[59]

Father Bede attended the early gathering the next morning and spoke at 9 AM, again using "little or no notes." A new microphone had been secured "which helped in every way," Sr. Pascaline wrote.

---

58 Osage Chief Sylvester Tinker.

59 Sr. Pascaline also reported that "many of our BSPA Sisters from K.C. and St. Louis arrived" for the conference.

Eucharist was Indian-style with our O+M altar on the top step, Bro. Raymund in Bramachari yellow and Father Devananda in Kavi. An afternoon panel melded the speakers with the participants as Bro. David [Steindl-Rast] moderated a question-surfacing. Father Jim [Conner] had the evening conference on Thomas Merton and the East — the experience of God and nothingness.

A couple phoned from Tulsa after seeing Grant Williams's article and are driving in today.

By the third day of the Conference Sr. Pascaline could report that:

Father Bede's strength is returning more and more. While Father Jim offered Eucharist in the large Chapel with Bro. Raymund and Father Devananda flanking him, Father Bede sat in the front pews and gave the final blessing, also an individual blessing to each who stepped forward. ... Father Bede's question-and-answer period was superb. Many are asking to see Bede privately.

A meeting with the staff and board afterwards culminated in moving the altar to the Conference Room and rearranging the furniture. Father John Martin and Bro. David felt strongly we need to get people more involved! Many have praised the arrangements in spite of the faulty equipment throughout. A "flaw in the ointment" of his joy!

THE NEXT DAY, AUGUST 16, 1983

Father Bede's 4th talk, on tantra, was exquisite — the furthest he has gone in public. The message on the FEMININE was well received.

Many more heard about the conference in this area and joined us today.

The free period in the afternoon allowed many time for a swim. Some took Father Bede to the K.C. Art Museum, but the intense heat (107°) was wearying.

ON WEDNESDAY, AUGUST 17, 1983

Father Bede's 5th and final talk took us all across the threshold of the 21st Century — awesome, hopeful and exciting. It was on the convergence of mysticism and science. Some 150 persons were present ...

The fruit of this conference would later become a set of audio tapes published by Credence, "Riches from the East." Sr. Pascaline also reported that, "Dr. Robert Potter brought Bede his blood test results with good news, and refused to give any bill for his service."

Father Bede and the other speakers concluded the conference the next day with a panel discussion, after which "the audience gave a standing ovation to Father Bede and the speakers. And everyone began packing for the trip home. Some participants walked along the highway in the moonlight — looking like Halloween with all the orange and yellow garb."

After the seminar, Father Bede and Brother Raymund returned to O+M for three more days, celebrating "East Indian Masses" each morning, giving satsang teachings

ABOVE: FR. BEDE BLESSES THE CUP; BELOW: OSAGE CHIEF SYLVESTER TINKER BLESSES BR. RAYMUND, WITH EAGLE FEATHER FAN.

each evening. They also visited Gilcrease Museum before the two left to return to South India.

Sr. Pascaline's relationship with Fr. Bede continued through the years in letters written back and forth between South India and Sand Springs. Then, in December 1988, Sr. Pascaline returned to visit Father Bede's ashram where she spent six weeks, and celebrated his 82nd birthday in December and her own 62nd in January:

> It was a deep joy to be back at Shantivanam. For me these 6 weeks at Father Bede's ashram were again a profound experience of 'living lectio.' His homilies, twice daily, are like a fountain ever pouring forth very pure energizing waters. He has such penetrating insights into our scriptures and those of other religions and overflows with joy as he shares. One cannot help but love the Word and respond to it wholeheartedly. He is such an experience of ... mystical joy.

Judy Walter, a Maryknoll Sister and nurse who had looked after Bede's health during his seminar in Kansas City in 1983, travelled to India in 1988–89 with Sr. Pascaline. A missionary nurse in Bangladesh, Sr. Judy had regularly visited Bede's Shantivanam in South India, and Bede had introduced Judy to Sister Pascaline, believing they would enjoy knowing each other. They became close friends. Sr. Judy lived at O+M in 1984 and 1985 while she worked at a hospital in Tulsa. When Sr. Pascaline returned home to Oklahoma in 1989 after her six weeks at Bede's ashram, Sr. Judy returned to Bangladesh.

A year later, on January 25, 1990, Father Bede suffered a stroke, which almost killed him. Soon afterward, Sr. Judy visited Shantivanam and phoned Sr. Pascaline to share news of Bede's condition. The chronicle records that one month after Bede's stroke he was "cured by the Divine Mother." The details were recorded by Sr. Judy several years afterward:

> On January 25, 1990, Bede Griffiths suffered a first stroke in his hut at Shantivanam. One month to the day, in February, he was cured in a struggle with death and divine love. He later described this as an intense mystical experience.

Sr. Pascaline wrote that Father Bede spoke of his stroke as being "the awakening of his repressed feminine side which demanded attention and integration. His cure 30 days after the stroke he called an intense experience of the divine feminine, loved like never before. He wept and could not speak for days."

Bede himself reported:

> I was overwhelmed and deluged with love. The feminine in me opened up and a whole new vision opened. I saw love as the basic principle of the whole universe. I saw God in the earth, in trees, in mountains. It led me to the conviction that there is no absolute good or evil in this world. We have to let go of all concepts which divide the world into good and evil, right and wrong, and begin to see the complementarity of opposites which Cardinal Nicholas of Cusa called the *coincidentia oppositorum*, the "coincidence of opposites."[60]

---

60   Bede Griffiths speaking to an audience in Jaiharikal in May, 1991.

In her 1994 memoir, "Father Bede's Influence on My Life," Sr. Judy wrote:

> His attitude was one of surrender and observation, allowing the process to unfold without analysis or interference. I believe this was a deeply contemplative response to the process of final integration that was taking shape in the depths of his being. Father's openness and receptivity of this integration could only come from a lifetime experience of contemplative living.

By May, a few months after his stroke, Fr. Bede was back on the road for a speaking tour. His book *A New Vision of Reality: Western Science, Eastern Mysticism and Christian Faith* had been published and he traveled back to the USA "to be with some of his disciples and to assist an experiment with a small group who eventually hoped to form a lay contemplative community." He was still experiencing heart fibrillation, however, and on arrival in California he was very weak. Sr. Judy recounted, "Therefore, the other planned stops on the way were canceled and all involved were invited to join him in Harrison Hoblitzelle's chalet in the Vermont Mountains."

Sr. Pascaline was part of a small group that met him there.

> In 1990 several of us close to Father Bede (Russill and Asha Paul, Wayne Teasdale and myself) lived in a chalet … with Father Bede. Among other things, Russill recorded "An Experience of Shantivanam" with sacred chants, poetry, music, devotional songs, spiritual readings and commentaries by Father Bede and the group. Each morning all of us would gather in Father Bede's bedroom with his "milk with tea in it," and he would be radiant describing the experience he had had at 2 or 3 AM. It was always the Holy Trinity, the Son coming from the Father and the intense love between them being Itself the Holy Spirit with a fresh nuance each morning.
>
> [We] were there in semi-community, praying together, cooking and doing dishes. Father even sat on a chair near the sink in order to help dry dishes, while sharing some of his English humor with us all. We took turns at liturgy preparation, lighting oil lamps, incense and the camphor for the sacred arati — the Fire Blessing. We sang bhajans, read portions of the Scriptures from the East and West and Father Bede shared some of his favorite Tamil poetry. Faith sharing (satsang) after supper was always special, spontaneous and profound. His short homilies at Eucharist and at Vespers (Evening Prayer) were offered with that same radiant joy he manifested back in South India at Shantivanam. The Scriptures truly moved his heart and in turn each of ours.

Later Sr. Pascaline would write of Bede after his "Great Awakening": "As an octagenarian, with a twinkle in his eye and in his throat, he told me while walking on a country road in the mountains in Vermont, that on his Mass Card he put the words, 'Priest forever according to the Order of Melchesidech,' the universal priesthood."

She would recall that:

… his intuitive mind was vibrant with insights on the divine mysteries, while his heart often suffered from some new insight of discrepancy in the Bible, or with injustice. He was convinced that the Old Testament has to be re-read in the light of the life and teachings of Christ. Jesus' prayer to his Father "that they may be one as we are one," (John 17:21) consumed Father Bede's great heart.

After the stroke and the cure, Father Bede did a great amount of travel to foreign countries. He said he never lost this sense of the divine presence from that time on.

Ten days after returning to O+M after her sojourn with Bede and the small group in Vermont, Sr. Pascaline fell from the deck of St. Bede's, which had no railing at the time, and injured her hip. She had surgery in Tulsa the next day, and was in a rehabilitation center for the next two months, requiring arthroscopic knee surgery on February 8, 1991. Even after physical therapy, she needed a second hip surgery in May. For this she traveled to St. Louis, while, back in the Forest, Kevin and Theresa Matyniak completed work on a railing for the deck from which she had fallen — "their gift!" Sr. Pascaline was recuperating from this surgery a few weeks later at the BSPA house in St. Louis when her crutch slipped on a slick chapel floor and she tore the ligament in her knee. She had arthroscopic knee surgery again in St. Louis and was still there when Father Bede returned to the USA and the Osage Monastery on August 8, 1991.

Two nights after Bede's arrival, about 40 guests came to O+M for his lecture, and many returned the next morning for his Sunday service with Indian liturgy. His informal talk that Sunday showed that the idea of a lay community for prayer and spiritual growth was much on his mind, as he was preparing to speak on that subject at the John Main Seminar. He said:

> It's all in the air at present. We try to be present ourselves. How can this tradition now be open to people everywhere? The lay community seems to be the answer. These communities should be small, forming a loose network, each independent of the other, not highly organized, each developing their own style of life, but each focused on meditation, prayer, and contemplation; the contemplative life, trying to live in communion with God.[61]

Sr. Pascaline was greatly missed, and on Tuesday, Father Bede and his two traveling companions, Russill and Asha, drove to St. Louis to see her, returning to O+M on Saturday. The next day, "About 50 attended Sunday Eucharist offered by Father Bede with Russill singing and playing." On Monday, Russill, Asha and Bede in his saffron robes were driven to the airport in Tulsa in the O+M's new maroon 1990 Isuzu Trooper and took off for the John Main Seminar in New Harmony, Indiana.

The John Main Seminar and Bede's teaching there has been called "transformative."[62]

---

61 Father Bede Griffiths on Sunday, August 11, 1991. Partial transcription from audio tape held at Osage Forest of Peace. Don Chatfield graciously sent this excerpt to author on April 14, 2016.

62 WCCM.org, accessed on Oct. 12, 2015.

He chose to speak about John Main's thoughts on meditation and community, and developed it in his mystical understanding of Christ. Father Bede strongly urged the laity to form small groups for contemplative prayer. It was during this seminar that The World Community for Christian Meditation was formed.[63]

Bede continued to travel, giving roving lectures before going to England, Germany and Australia. While in Australia he met with His Holiness, the Dalai Lama, and the exchange was enriching for both. Afterwards Father Bede said, "I do believe he liked me!" That H.H. did indeed like and admire Bede is apparent in his book *Toward a True Kinship of Faiths,* published in 2000, in which the Dalai Lama quotes Bede extensively and refers to him as a friend.

Father Bede took the long way home, giving more lectures in Germany and England. Sr. Pascaline would later say, "His heart was fluttering but he was always energized by all that went through him."

The next summer, Father Bede's USA 1992 tour included a stop at the Osage Monastery where it seemed that his spirit was luminous, though his health was failing. The chronicle book records the visit, which was to be his last.

TUESDAY, JULY 7, 1992

Our guests, Father Bede, Asha, Russill Paul, landed from California at 11:15 PM, right on time and in good spirits. It was about 12:30 when the white van arrived back at O+M. After some tea, all retired. Father Bede came with his same small handbag, stuffed but neatly packed.

WEDNESDAY, JULY 8, 1992

Because travelers arrived late we gave them a late schedule for Eucharist — 11:30, but the community rose for 5:15 contemplative sitting as usual. After supper Father Bede joined us for Satsang, telling all about his travels and talks in Europe and Australia. John Douglas drove in from Dallas to be here with Father Bede.

THURSDAY, JULY 9, 1992

After supper the community enjoyed a free night. Sr. Pascaline showed the O+M slide show to Father Bede, Asha, Russill, John, Martha, Sisters Michael and Gemin, and Jordan.

FRIDAY, JULY 10, 1992

Father Bede took the Mass of the Sacred Heart and spoke on Christian Unity.

SATURDAY, JULY 11, 1992

(Feast of St. Benedict) Father Bede meditated on his cabin porch as we all meditated at 7 AM. He had been up much earlier meditating and had a little breakfast.

Father Bede came to Satsang to share his newest perspectives on St. Benedict and the priesthood and that the monks had only Communion Service (not Mass) before going to the refectory.

---

63   These lectures were published as *The New Creation in Christ*, by Darton, Longman, and Todd, Ltd. in England (1992) and Templegate Publishers in the United States (1994).

SUNDAY, JULY 12, 1992

Eucharist was special with Russill singing his Credo and Father Bede expounding on St. Paul's letter to the Colossians — Christ the center of all. It was a full chapel.

People began arriving for Father Bede's first Sunday public lecture. Some 71 people overflowed for his lecture on the Church and the Feminine.

MONDAY, JULY 13, 1992

Father Bede had heart fluctuation so asked if he could see a doctor.

TUESDAY, JULY 14, 1992

Doctor says Father Bede's heart enlarged and needs medication, and two [weeks?] complete rest.

WEDNESDAY, JULY 15, 1992

We began phoning to cancel all appointments and arrangements for Sunday lecture.

Father Bede apparently rested the next six days.

TUESDAY, JULY 21, 1992

At 3 PM Father Bede gave a great talk on the Church, eschatological and institutional. We taped the talk and question period.

THURSDAY, JULY 23, 1992

Father Bede awakened at midnight with his heart fibrillating. He was moved to sit and write (on O+M stationery) a total surrender of himself into God's hands and Mary, Mother of Jesus, wanting no further doctors or medicine. He was radiant when sharing this and said it gave him immediate deep peace.

FRIDAY, JULY 24, 1992

Several of us went to Father Bede's room at tea time to have a question and answer session. Asked about evil and poverty in the world, Father Bede said if we start with what to do it is overwhelming, but if we begin with prayer then we are shown what to do and we can only do what we can do, trusting God to do what we cannot.

SATURDAY, JULY 25, 1992

Father Bede awoke during the night with his heart fibrillating again. He was depressed and began to pray and reconfirm his total surrender — the fibrillation stopped. He truly believes that when we are in our mind, the body is in pain; when we pray and go beyond it, the body is no longer afflicted. He was so happy with this experience.

After supper Linda shared and narrated slides of Peru. Father Bede joined us for this.

SUNDAY, JULY 26, 1992

Many came for Eucharist. Father Bede's homily was powerful — the need to move beyond the law to unconditional love. About 30 were here at 7 PM for Father Bede's talk on transcending the self.

MONDAY, JULY 27, 1992

Father Bede completed his reflections on the three vows and religious life for Sr. Linda and asked us to pass it on. The problem is we are all self-centered and need to move beyond our self. The vows help us to do this.

TUESDAY, JULY 28, 1992

During Satsang the community had a Q&A session with Father Bede — good questions — profound answers.

THURSDAY, JULY 30, 1992

Russill "prayed" an hour of music for us at 7:30 PM … Fr. Bede joined us in chapel for the evening and night prayers.

FRIDAY, JULY 31, 1992

Father Bede wrote letter to NCR re. homosexual restrictions by the Church.[64]

After supper we had a last Satsang with Father Bede. He does get energized by his marvelous sharings — a font of wisdom and gentleness. We must never be overwhelmed by all the evil, as it is passing and isn't what it seems. Behind it all God is at work and we must trust.

SATURDAY, AUG. 1, 1992

Father Bede difficult night — new surrender in prayer.

SUNDAY, AUG. 2, 1992

Father Bede offered Eucharist; 7 PM conference on *Marriage of East and West*.

MONDAY, AUG. 3, 1992

Father Bede and Asha left for Vermont.

At the end of that month, Sr. Pascaline traveled to India with Sister Katherine Howard, Father Kevin and Brother Harold for Phase V of the NABEWD monastic exchange. The highlight of this trip was an hour-long audience with H.H. the Dalai Lama. In her letter "home" to the Sisters at O+M Sr. Pascaline quoted the Dalai Lama's comment about his meeting with Father Bede in Australia.

The D.L. mentioned an elderly monk in Australia who gave him new insight

---

[64] This was in response to a statement by the Vatican's Congregation for the Doctrine of the Faith on homosexuality, favoring laws that banned avowed homosexuals from public services, especially service in schools or the military. Bede's letter was ironic in tone, saying that the Church, to be consistent, should "be equally severe against all those who offend against public morality. …This could lead to a severe crisis and might force the church to attend to the saying of the Gospel, 'Let one who is without sin among you cast the first stone.'" — From a copy of Bede's letter in the *National Catholic Reporter* in Sr. Pascaline's personal archive.

into reincarnation. We said 'Bede Griffiths' & he gleefully said 'yes.' Then he spelled out how the creator puts life — soul — into a body and this forms an intimate relationship with God. Yes, he used that word and said this made him feel something very good inside and he very much appreciates receiving this teaching from Father Bede. This is the part of the dialogue I love. It fires even more that fire within that Jesus and his message was also invigorating! I'm trying to get him to put it into an article. Yes, I took notes.[65]

Sister Pascaline returned to the United States in October, 1992, just as Bede arrived back at his ashram in South India. An Australian film team was awaiting him at Shantivanam. Their documentary, "A Human Search" was completed just before Bede suffered another major stroke on December 20th — three days after his 86th Birthday. This was followed by a series of strokes in January, which, Sr. Pascaline would later write, "finally brought him to his Mahasamadhi on May 13, [1993] in his hut at Shantivanam in South India, surrounded with much tender loving care. Father Bede Griffiths was laid to rest nearby the temple, next to one of his first disciples, Father Amaldas, who, half Father's age, died some years before him."

The anniversary of Bede's death was observed at O+M with a Mahasamadhi celebration the next year and for years thereafter. The first such observance, on May 13, 1994, was recorded in the O+M history summary as "buffet supper followed by documentary on his life: 'The Human Search,' followed by 30 minutes of 'remembering' and then Vespers with readings from his works; Dr. Atwood & wife, Eleanor, Martha and Sister Maurus who had first-hand experiences with B.G. added much to the sharings." In later years, the Bede Mahasmahadhi included "a visit to a local Hindu temple, Vespers and a conference by a speaker."

Three years after Bede Griffith's death, Judson Trapnell, writing in the *American Benedictine Review*, gave a summary analysis of the effect Father Bede's life had on the culture of his time, writing:

> Through surrendering ever more thoroughly to the Spirit within, the individual may become a more concrete expression of the change being worked in a culture by the Spirit. Such persons not only express symbols that mediate cultural change, they themselves become living symbols who through their transparency allow the healing light of the Spirit to touch the culture. Here is the lasting witness of Griffiths' life: that true spiritual surrender brings transformation not only in the individual but also through that individual in the world.[66]

Certainly the Osage Monastery is one concrete expression of the cultural

---

65 Bede's explanation to the Dalai Lama on the topic of reincarnation is recounted in the Dalai Lama's book, *Toward a True Kinship of Faiths*: "He [Bede] said that belief in reincarnation would contradict the Christian understanding that this very life, one's particular life, is created by God. I was moved by the conviction and simplicity with which he said this. The power of this concept immediately struck me...."

66 "Bede Griffiths as a Culture Bearer: An Exploration of the Relationship Between Spiritual Transformation and Cultural Change," (Sept. 1996): 283.

© MARY JANE MATTHEWS

transformation that was and is taking place in the once firmly bounded worlds of religious faiths. In 1979 Sister Pascaline had returned from her year with Bede carrying a new fire in her heart and waving a literal arati fire in the marble and stained-glass chapels of the BSPA. Thus inspired, she and her sisters built the Osage Monastery and put structures in place to create the NABEWD / MID and extend its work of East-West dialogue into Western monasteries, retreat centers, churches, and universities.

In turn, it was through the NABEWD Bulletin published by the O+M community that Father Bede became even better known, his teachings more widely published and read. Their work to organize and facilitate inter-monastic dialogue events spread the new cultural awareness in both East and West. His Christian ashram in India attracted more and more people as years went by.

One important actor in Bede Griffiths' later life and after his death was a Dallas attorney who learned of Bede through O+M and Sister Pascaline. John Douglas had been strongly influenced as a high school student in the 1950s when he lived for a summer with Thomas Merton and the monks of Gethsemani, including Father Jim Conner. He recalls that he first visited O+M in 1985 to see Father Jim, "and that was my first contact with Osage, and with Sister Pascaline." Douglas and Sr. Pascaline had something in common: India. "I had lived in India for three years."

Through Sr. Pascaline I was introduced to some of Bede Griffiths' writing. I wrote a letter to him: "Dear Father Bede, I would like to come to India to visit you." He wrote back to me and said, "Dear John, you just stay where you are, because I'm coming to Osage Monastery and I'm going to be there for approximately a month." This was in the summer of 1992. I went to Osage that summer and spent two weeks with Bede. Then I went back home to Dallas. A few weeks later Russill Paul called and asked me if I would write a trust agreement for Bede Griffiths.

FR. BRUNO BARNHART

I went out to the Camaldolese Monastery in Big Sur, California, stayed with Bede for five days and drafted the trust agreement for the Bede Griffiths Trust. I drafted the trust, and it was simply a legal document at that point, sort of like a will. Then, in May of 1993, Bede died, and the trust came into effect. When it came into effect, the Bede Griffiths Trust was formally established.

The Trust still exists. It's played somewhat different roles at different times. Sr. Pascaline was one of about 11 Trustees and she was very active. Effectively, she acted as the main source of energy. She was the driving force behind the Trust until her retirement from the Osage Monastery.

There were other players along the way. One of the players who was fairly active was Father Bruno Barnhart. Father Bruno was a Camaldolese monk out at Big

Sur. He wrote the [Trust] newsletter [*The Golden String*] and kept it in existence for 8–10 years until he had monocular degeneration and he had to give up the newsletter.

The website was established approximately five years after Bede died. It was set up by Teresa Matyniak. The driving force behind the material on the website was Sr. Pascaline. The Osage Monastery was very much involved in the establishment of the Bede Griffiths Trust.[67]

One main thrust of the Trust was the establishment of a Bede Griffiths literary archive at Graduate Theological Union in Berkeley, California. "We did a fairly good job of collecting material from around the world and putting it all in the archives of the GTU."

During the last 15 years of his life, Bede wrote some 50 letters to Sr. Pascaline and, as we have seen, he visited the O+M repeatedly during those years. Each visit attracted larger and larger crowds to sit in his presence and hear him speak.

One afternoon in the summer before his death, over 70 people crowded St. Bede's at the Osage Monastery to hear him speak — so many that the audience overflowed onto the deck. The sliding glass doors that separated the 20' x 40' meeting space inside St. Bede's from the deck were opened and folding chairs lined up both outside and in. People filled all chairs and others leaned against the railing and sat on the deck and floors. When Bede Griffiths emerged out into the dappled sunlight that filtered through the jack-oak trees around the deck, he looked very much the Hindu sannyasi in his vibrant saffron robe, very much the ancient sage with his flowing white beard, his sunken chest and one boney, bared shoulder visible. He had the pallor of a man dying of cardiovascular disease, while at the same time he seemed lit from within, as if the blush of vitality were being replaced in his body by a white gold spiritual radiance.

When he began to speak, his voice was soft at first, then gathered strength. He had the accent of an Oxford don. He spoke, then answered questions from the audience, but it was his person — his unlikely mixture of erudite English monk and glowing sannyasi saint, here in the woods of Osage County, Oklahoma — that communicated more than any of the ideas he expressed.

On that day, Bede was a man back from the edge of death, a visionary who was living out his amazing visions and giving them to the world. As a champion for the contemplative life and the sharing of its fruits in every tradition and culture, he had become something of an Old Testament style pariah and prophet within Catholicism. He was obviously living on borrowed time, but still speaking out against the excesses of a growing fundamentalism in religious institutions worldwide, and especially in his beloved Church. Still, he radiated joy and love. The Forest dwellers at Osage Monastery, and all who had gathered there that day and in the days after, knew they sat in the presence of a human being who had been opened and expanded.

It was just as his doctor said: This was a man with an enlarged heart.

---

67 John Douglas interview with author via phone, February 26, 2016.

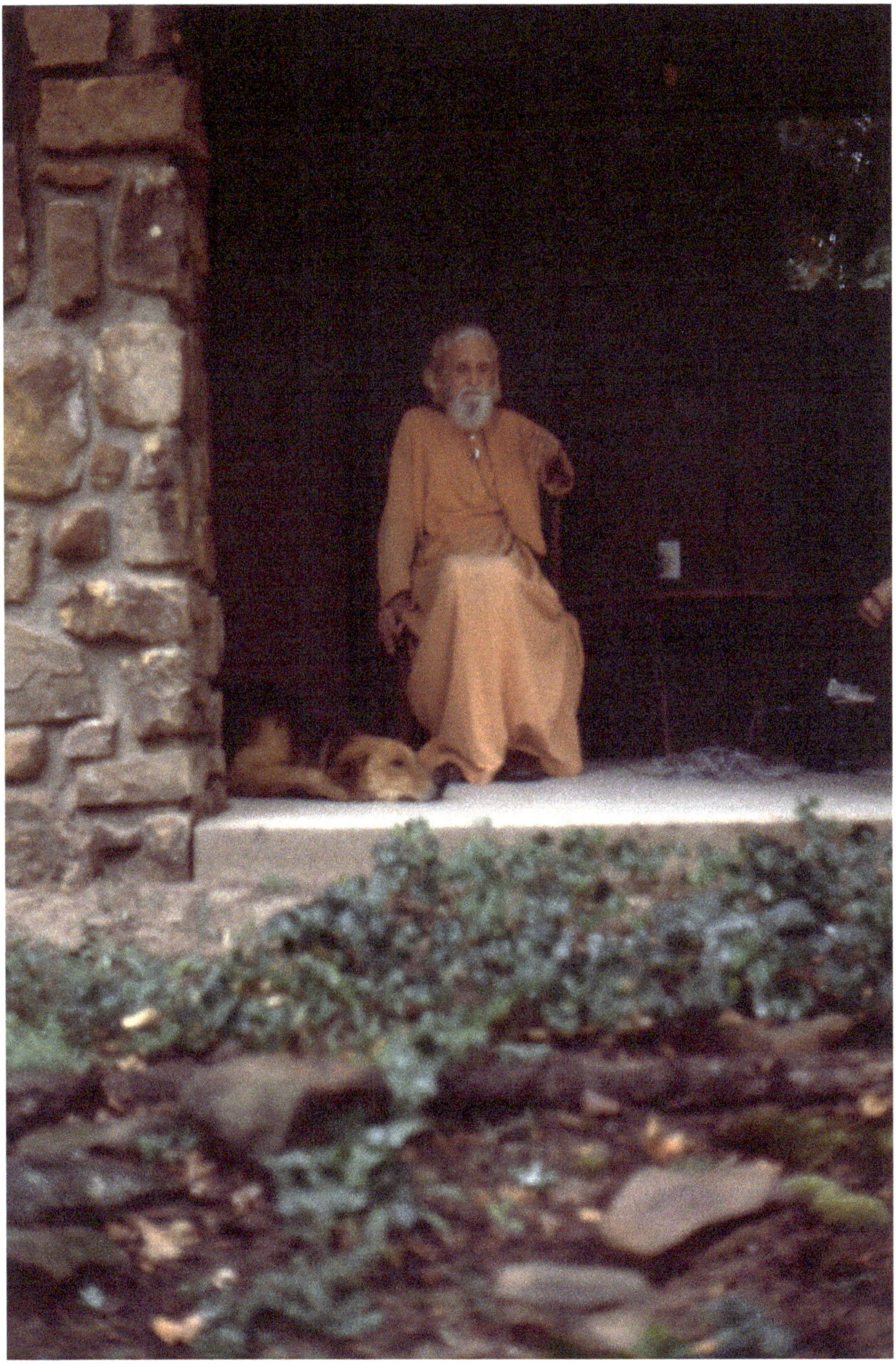

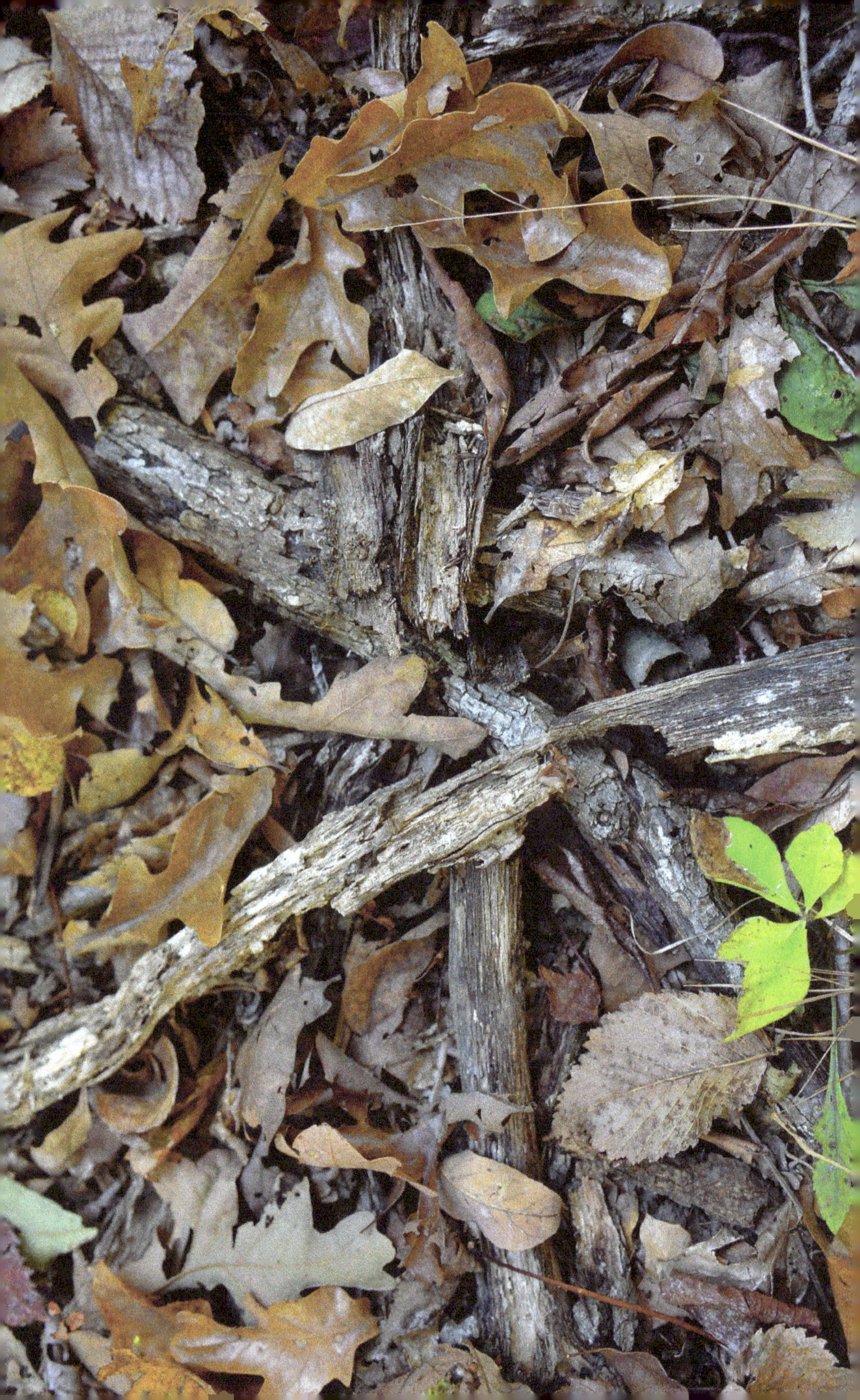

TRUSTEES
1991–2022

To die and so to grow...
—Johann Wolfgang von Goethe
"The Holy Longing"

Thirty years after Sr. Pascaline and her BSPA Sisters first moved to Tulsa to plant this Shantivanam of the West in American soil, there came the decision that they would be uprooted from the Forest. The BSPA Prioress's Council voted to close the Osage Monastery.

The story of how the Osage Forest of Peace survived the departure of the BSPA Sisters, like the story of the O+M itself, begins with Father Bede Griffiths.

Bob Doenges had never been to the Osage Monastery before he went there to hear Father Bede in the summer of 1991. Bob was a Tulsan and an automobile dealer when he and his wife, Liddy, heard about Bede.

"Liddy and I were at a dinner at a friend's house and Virginia Atwood was at the dinner. Virginia said, 'You know, the two of you ought to go out to the Osage Monastery because Father Bede Griffiths is going to be there. You'd be very interested in it because of your path.'"

"We'd lived in Japan in the 1960s when we were newly married, and I'd had an awakening to Zen Buddhism in Japan. I'd been drawn to exploring other paths and never dreamed that a place like O+M, open to all paths, existed thirty minutes from our home."

Bob and Liddy Doenges did go out to the Osage Monastery to meet and hear Father Bede. They felt an immediate connection to both the monk and the monastery. In fact, what they found there in the Forest of Peace changed their lives.

"After the meeting with Father Bede, we started going out to Osage on a regular basis. We'd been going to All Souls Unitarian [in Tulsa] for twenty years, and all of a sudden we felt much more drawn to the inter-spiritual aspects of Osage — all paths and all traditions in a contemplative setting."

"We got more and more involved. I started doing Zen sesshins there when Ruben Habito would come. We went almost every Sunday after we met Father Bede."

Liddy and Bob were at O+M for Father Bede's return in 1992 when he spoke on the subject of his visions regarding the feminine and the Holy Mother. Bob would later say that what drew them was Bede's person, his embodiment of something powerfully divine, more than anything he taught.

© SCOTT THOMPSON

They felt the same way about the BSPA Sisters, especially Sr. Pascaline, who became a spiritual advisor to both Liddy and Bob. By the fall after Fr. Bede's death, 1993, Liddy and Bob had decided to take RCIA[68] classes, to explore conversion to Catholicism. A few weeks after Easter, 1994, however, Liddy Doenges — bright, vibrant and in her early 50s — was diagnosed with inoperable brain cancer and given just three months to live.

Liddy began to organize her thoughts, and she called Father Greg Gier.

Father Gier, who was at the time the priest at Christ the King parish in Tulsa and instructed the RCIA course, brought Liddy into the Church on May 27, 1994.

The Church and the Osage Monastery provided important support for the Doenges family during that summer of Liddy's illness. On June 1, Sr. Pascaline recorded in the O+M chronicle that "Liddy came for spiritual direction, discerning treatment for many tumors." On June 19, "Liddy D now has seven tumors in her head, plus others elsewhere. She was freed from pain tonight through the intercession of St. Elizabeth."

Liddy was "anointed by Father Gier at home," Sr. Pascaline recorded on June 24.

On June 28, Asha and Russill Paul, musicians from India who had accompanied Bede Griffiths on his travels during his life, came to Osage on a two-month visit, stopping by the Doenges home in Tulsa to visit Liddy on their way out to the Forest of Peace. They brought Liddy an object that carried great spiritual significance for all of them — Father Bede's saffron robe.

On July 3, Sr. Pascaline recorded, "Liddy Doenges' last Eurcharist here. Russill and Asha night of Indian music, many came." Two days later, Sr. Pascaline "was called to Liddy's bedside," and on July 8, "Bob and the Doenges children came to prepare for Liddy's death."

The Japanese Dominican Father Oshida arrived on July 11 to lead a workshop at Osage. While he was there, Bob recalls, "Oshida woke up one morning and said to the Sisters, 'Take me to the mother with cancer.'" Sister Pascaline and Sister Helen drove him to Tulsa to see Liddy. Bob remembers the scene well:

> So here comes the van with the "Save Tibet" sticker on the front bumper, up into our drive, and here comes Sr. Pascaline with a smiling Japanese Dominican monk carrying a single rose, and here comes Sister Helen, who was a hermit at O+M, coming in behind to the front door to see Liddy and to pray for her. … It was the first time I ever heard Sr. Helen speak."

During the weeks Liddy had to prepare for her death, Father Gier recalls he visited her almost daily to serve her communion. Liddy told Father Gier during one of his visits to her home, "I want to know exactly what my funeral is going to be like." He recalls:

---

68   The Rite of Christian Initiation of Adults (RCIA) is a process developed by the Catholic Church for prospective converts to Catholicism who are above the age of infant baptism. Candidates are gradually introduced to aspects of Catholic beliefs and practices.

TOP: BOB DOENGES WITH SR. PASCALINE
BELOW: GROUP MEETING AT O+M

I went through every single part of the ritual with her. And she, in her morphine hand, wrote the whole thing down. She said that she wanted the Sisters from Osage to be the Eucharistic ministers, that they would be the perfect people to do that. That was all decided that day. When my whole explanation of the service was over, she took that little tablet she'd been writing on and she pressed it to her chest and she said, "Ahhh … This religion just speaks to my heart."

At 3:30 AM on Sunday, August 14, 1994, twelve weeks and two days after her first diagnosis, Liddy Doenges died. Sr. Pascaline recorded that Bob attended Mass at O+M later that morning, and "brought back Father Bede's sannyasi orange habit."

Bob Doenges continued to be involved at Osage Monastery after his wife's death, with Sr. Pascaline as his spiritual director. During the autumn after Liddy passed away he started RCIA with Father Gier as instructor and entered the Catholic Church on Easter, 1995.

In the winter and spring of 1996, "Liddy's Garden," a Zen garden, designed by Katherine Keefer, from Oakland, California, was created in the Forest, not far from St. Bede's retreat house. Plans included new trails to connect the cluster of buildings and cabins with the trails through the woods. Teresa Matyniak oversaw that work. With the help of friends from Tulsa and retreatants from around the world, the garden and new trails further took shape in the Forest of Peace.

Tibetan Buddhist nuns and monks who were visiting O+M helped Katherine spread gravel in the Garden and on the walking paths. Meanwhile Dung, a Vietnamese BSPA novice, chiseled a stone birdbath for the Garden.

By the end of May, work was complete, and Liddy's mother, aged 80, came with Bob to see the garden that had been created in her daughter's memory.

In the years following his wife's death, Bob's grief deepened into serious depression. His slow recovery, he would later say, was an experience of death, birth, and renewal.

> "And so long as you haven't experienced this: to die and so to grow, you are only a troubled guest on the dark earth."[69] Looking back, the experience of Liddy's death and my depression became a great gift.

Over the next decade, as he recovered, Bob Doenges grew more involved with the Osage Monastery Forest of Peace:

> Osage serves so well because it helps with that interior journey, which is also a journey into the vertical aspect of life. The vertical aspect has to be integrated with the horizontal — the day-to-day business of life. At Osage we can bring in Hinduism and Buddhism and Christianity and all spiritual paths to help with our integration. It helps us become better Christians. Fr. Bede would say that all the different religions were like fingers on a hand. "They all point to the center, and that center is God."

---

69   Here Doenges quotes a favorite poem, Robert Bly's translation of Goethe's "The Holy Longing."

PASCALINE HOLDING SAM KEEN'S
PEACH SEED MONKEY

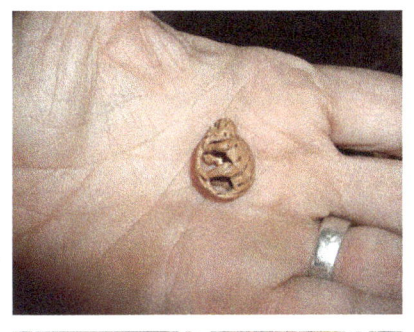

I had spiritual awakenings throughout my life, starting in college and then in Japan, and through books and everything I studied and did, but the spiritual deepening came because of Father Bede and Sister Pascaline. It was the depth of their embodiment — not their teachings — their embodiment. And because of the Forest itself. The Forest is an embodiment of deep peace.

In June 2006, Sr. Pascaline, who had broken her leg in the spring, asked Bob to go with her on a trip to California. She was one of the leaders of a conference: "Carrying Forth the Prophetic and Contemplative Vision of Father Bede Griffiths."

Sr. Pascaline and Sr. Judy Walter were going to Sky Farm Hermitage in Sonoma after the conference with a scholar who was studying Fr. Bede's life and work. Bob would spend a few days at Esalen Institute and meet them in Burlingame at the public conference. Sr. Pascaline, knowing that one of her favorite authors, Sam Keen, had taught at Esalen, asked Bob to buy her a copy of Keen's book *To a Dancing God* while Bob was there, because she had given away her copy. The book contained a story about Keen's father promising to carve him a little monkey from a peach seed, a promise his father only fulfilled years later, when he was dying. Sr. Pascaline had a similar story of her own. Her father had promised to give her anything she wanted when she finished college. She asked, jokingly, for season tickets to the St. Louis Cardinals and a red convertible. The tickets never showed up, but one day after she entered the BSPA convent she opened a little package from her father to find a tiny toy — a red convertible. Sr. Pascaline used this story and Keen's to illustrate the faithfulness of God to those whom she counseled — "The Good Father always keeps his promises."

The shop at Esalen, as it turned out, had no copies of Keen's book in stock. The four left Burlingame and headed to the Hermitage in Sonoma. At the gate to the Hermitage was a sign that read "Sky Farm Hermitage — Sam Keen." As they started up the hill to the Hermitage they saw a tall man in the yard nearby, who turned out to be Sam Keen himself. He soon joined the group at the Hermitage. When he heard Sr. Pascaline tell her story, however, he excused himself, went down to his home and returned with copies of his books that he gave to everyone. Then, he showed Sr. Pascaline a little box. Inside was the actual peach seed monkey, made for him by his father, which Sr. Pascaline held and gazed at warmly before handing the precious object back to Sam Keen.

As they left the Hermitage Bob said, "Sister Pascaline, you not only got the book you wanted, you met the author and held the actual peach seed monkey in your hand. *You are a manifester!*"

Indeed, the Osage Monastery Forest of Peace itself testifies to Sr. Pascaline's gifts as a manifester. In fall 2007, Bob Doenges, Sr. Pascaline, Edith Stein from the Friends of the Forest, and Father Brian Pierce made a pilgrimage to India, taking a donation from the Friends of the Forest to Saccidananda Ashram in gratitude for the gift of Osage. A letter they carried, dated September 6, 2007, reads in part:

> Today a few of us come with our dear friend, Sister Pascaline, on a pilgrimage of thanksgiving. We come to give witness to the miracle of God, for the seeds that Sister Pascaline carried back to Oklahoma — in the heartland of the United States — thirty years ago, and were planted and watered with much faith and hope. Those seeds became seedlings and the seedlings turned into another forest, another Forest of Peace.
>
> ... Father Bede visited the Forest of Peace many times over the years, and we believe that his spirit continues to live on in the person of our dear Sister Pascaline and in the wind and the trees, in the community and in the silent meditation of the Forest of Peace.[70]

---

[70] The letter is signed by Robert S. Doenges, Brian Pierce, Edith Stein, and others who were not along on the trip: "Sister Ramona Varela, OSB, Prioress General, Benedictine Sisters of Perpetual Adoration; Sister Benita Luetkemeyer, OSB, Superior, Forest of Peace Ashram; Friends of the Forest of Peace Ashram, Oklahoma; Benedictine Oblates, Forest of Peace Ashram; The many friends touched by the Forest of Peace Ashram these thirty years." It is held in the BSPA archive, Clyde, Missouri.

About what happened after that trip to India, Bob recalls:

A few days after Sr. Pascaline returned home, while Fr. Brian and I were still in India, Sr. Pascaline sent us an email saying Sister Ramona, the Prioress General of the BSPAs, told her that there was going to be a "very important meeting of the Congregation" and the main subject would be the Osage Monastery. We knew that, with the Sisters diminishing in number, their Order would be closing some house. ... It looked like the handwriting was on the wall.

As soon as Bob returned home to Tulsa, Sister Ramona traveled from the motherhouse to meet with him. She asked if he would procure the Osage Monastery property from the BSPA. "It was a choiceless choice," Bob later recalled. "I felt it was too important as a spiritual center to just be closed. It was a great gift to the world that had come out of Father Bede's teachings and Sister Pascaline's vision. It was something that needed to be continued in this world."[71]

Bob immediately said yes.

Sister Pascaline shared the news of the changes at O+M in the winter issue of *The Golden String*, the bulletin of the Bede Griffiths Trust:

... O+M has celebrated its blessed birth and growth and life, and is now in the process of death and resurrection.

... There were 5 sisters at O+M until just recently when our eldest, Sister Priscilla, now 91, was transferred to assisted living at the motherhouse at Clyde. This May two of the present community will return to the motherhouse at Clyde, and two will be transferred to our monastery in Dayton, Wyoming.

SISTER PRISCILLA TROST

... Over the past 27 years hundreds of private retreats have been offered to those in the area and beyond, who appreciated the peace and quietness of the Forest's 45 acres of trails with white-tailed deer, singing birds and hungry squirrels munching on the smorgasbord of acorns.

... The ashram, true to its name, has also been a place of simple lifestyle with efforts to be welcoming to people of all religions, poor and rich alike. The Benedictine Oblates at Osage now number 93. A large group of Friends of the Forest have generously gathered to assist the community in any way they are able.

The Sisters have been very active in the Monastic Interreligious Dialogue efforts and have been involved in the eight exchanges with the Dalai Lama and his monks and nuns, visiting each other's monasteries and welcoming the Divine in the other.

---

71   Quoted in "The Next Peace," by Bill Sherman, *Tulsa World* Religion Writer, Saturday, April 26, 2008, *Tulsa World*. Copy held in the Clyde archive.

TOP : JOHN DOUGLAS, FR. BRUNO BARNHART / BOTTOM :   FR. JIM CONNER

After their basic dedication to Christ in the Eucharist, the main effort of the Sisters at O+M, besides keeping contemplative prayer and its atmosphere as their goal for themselves and retreatants, has been hospitality; "welcoming the Divine in the other"—all others—a perfect fit for their interfaith dialogue efforts. The sisters believe dialogue with other religions has always been important even though practiced by only a few, but now it is crucial for all.

… Osage Monastic ashram was also a Bede Griffiths Center with a collection of the latter's books, tapes and letters. Father Bede visited the community in Sand Springs some five times and called it Shantivanam of the West, hence the name Forest of Peace (shanti=peace; vanam=forest). The Bede Griffiths website was created at O+M some five years ago and had been maintained from there ever since.

Bob Doenges, one of the O+M Oblates desires to maintain the property as a contemplative ashram in the spirit lived by the sisters here for the past 27 years. The new name of this budding non-profit spiritual center will be: OSAGE FOREST OF PEACE.[72]

Bob contacted John Douglas, the Dallas attorney who had been Bede Griffiths' lawyer in the US and had helped draft the Bede Griffiths Trust. John established a nonprofit entity with a small board of trustees to oversee the Osage Forest of Peace. The BSPA Sisters living at O+M would leave in April of 2008, all except for Sister Pascaline. In order to aid the transition, she would be allowed to stay until the fall of 2009.

As Osage was about to change hands, one Friend of the Forest, Barbara Schneeberg, was working with a group of widows and others who had suffered loss. She recalls, "They were needing to tap into some inner resilience."

Near the site of the 1995 Oklahoma City terrorist bombing, a lone century-old American elm tree, with a taproot that went deep into the Oklahoma soil, somehow survived the bombing, despite the shrapnel blasted into its trunk. It had been shredded and burned, but bloomed again after the bombing and had become known as the Survivor Tree. Now, over a decade after that horrific event, saplings grown from seeds of the Survivor Tree had become available for replanting in new places. Barbara recalled:

The idea of the Survivor Tree being there is a reminder of the Sisters' presence and what would continue and survive … that resilience that would still be there to keep going, with all the changes. It also became a symbol for those women [in the grief counseling group at Osage]. They were survivors. All would still be well.

With each change of leadership in the Forest, I would get the person in charge and say, "Look, here is this tree. Would you promise me that you will make sure it gets watered?" And they do.

---

72   Sr. Pascaline Coff. "Osage Monastery, Looking Back." *The Golden String: Bulletin of the Bede Griffiths Trust*, Winter 2007-2008, pp. 1-3.

A final Mass under BSPA ownership took place on April 20, 2008. The O+M chronicle book records the day before: "A busy day of preparations for tomorrow and packing for those leaving on Monday. ... Ramona and Joan arrived about 3:30 and began putting Benita's things in the truck they drove down from Clyde."

The next day, Father Jim Conner, who had done so much to make the Osage Monastery possible and had been its devoted chaplain in its first decade, arrived from Gethsemani to celebrate the final Mass. The ceremony took place in the chapel, even though the crowd that attended overflowed the space.

The chronicle book recorded that:

> More than 100 people attended. The circle was cleared of all cushions, and chairs borrowed from St. Patrick's Church filled the area. Other chairs were set up in the outer room and, with an audio system set up by Charlie Pratt and Joe Farney, everyone could hear clearly what was going on. Father John Vrana went to Tulsa to bring Father Patrick and Father Skeehan for the Mass. All these priests have been so good to us. Joe F. made a video of the whole Mass and will send a DVD production to each of our monasteries.

Eight years later, Sister Pascaline, having recently watched the video, would recall:

> The chapel was packed — in addition to our own small community, many Benedictines Sisters from in Tulsa, and Red Plains Monastery near Oklahoma City were present, along with other friends. Many of our neighbors were also present for the last Mass.
>
> — Bob & other dignitaries were seated in the front row.
> — Sister Ramona, at the appropriate time, walked over toward the celebrant: Father Jim Conner OCSO.
> — Bob came up to both of them and Sister Ramona handed Bob the key to Osage Forest of Peace.

Gerri Fey had arrived with the perfect wine to accompany the BSPA Sisters' last supper there — Blue Nun. The supper itself, enjoyed by the "16 at our table" was prepared by Mary Heck. The chronicle book records:

> Father Jim Conner will even come Tuesday AM when Sr. Pascaline may be the only other one present. Tomorrow Benita leaves for Clyde with Jan; Sarah leaves with Rosetta and Hope for Dayton, and Kathleen leaves with Mary Virginia Statzer for Tucson via Grand Canyon.

So Osage Monastery becomes the new entity: Osage Forest of Peace.

After the departure of the BSPA community, the Osage Forest of Peace entered a period of transition, a self-discovery process that was reminiscent of its earliest days in 1980 and 1981.

The Osage Forest of Peace was set up as a nonprofit with a board of trustees to oversee the funding and management. The new Trustees were Bob Doenges; Sr. Pascaline; John Douglas; Father Brian Pierce; and Balbir Mathur, founder of Trees for Life in Wichita.

The board met every three months. John Douglas drove up to Osage from Dallas for the quarterly board meeting. "His expertise was important," Bob remembers. John combined crucial legal knowledge with a sincere desire to preserve the legacy of Osage. He would later say, "Bob has done a magnificent job of keeping faith with Osage over the years."

Fr. Brian remembers that: "Bob asked me to be on the board. I was living in Rome at the time, and I said, 'I don't know what I can do from Rome, but I'll try to come to one meeting a year if I can.'" He and the rest of the board stayed current through emails.

Balbir Mathur was a source of deep spiritual support for Bob as he and others worked to discern what the Osage Forest of Peace might now become. He and his wife drove down from Wichita to every quarterly board meeting to offer wise council. Bob remembers that Balbir told him to quit worrying so much. "It's already written what Osage is to be." This assurance buoyed Bob's spirit immensely; he never forgot it.

"I relaxed and got out of the way."

It was a challenging transition, for the board, the new community, the oblates, and others drawn to Osage with their own thoughts about spiritual community.

JoAnn Huber, a clinical social worker from Tulsa who had begun coming out to the Forest in 2003 to voluntarily help with the grounds maintenance, remembered those first months after the BSPAs left. "There were several people out here at first, living and operating things, several young people. They all said the same thing. They'd want to come to work here and then would be busy because they were working and couldn't be on retreat. That was a learning curve."

The original little community during Sr. Pascaline's last 18 months in the Forest was managed by Emily Cox for the first months and then by Mardana Jones.

Bob calls Mardana his "greatest gift during the transition. Mardana saw the need and stepped into it and provided the glue that held it together." He recalled that she used her Buddhist "skillful means" in dealing with the various personalities, including Sister Pascaline.

"Mardana nicknamed Sr. Pascaline's resolute nature 'Rascaline,'" Bob remembers. "Mardana could handle her just beautifully, and that was something, because the only people Sr. Pascaline would pay attention to would be some priests and me — and she ran over a lot of the priests." (One of Sister Pascaline's personal treasures is a poem written for her by her father, Ed Coff, in which he said of his daughter: "If she'd been a man she would have been Pope!")

Sister Pascaline's time to move from the Osage Monastery came in September of 2009, thirty-one years after she had arrived with her Sisters to live in the little house in Tulsa and look for land on which to build a monastic ashram. Sr. Pascaline remembers that her departure was marked by "a nice oblate gathering with others." They presented her with a book to treasure of Forest photography and quotes — a "Contemplative Close-up" of this beautiful place.

She went from Osage Forest of Peace to the BSPA Monastery in Tucson, Arizona, where she was — she would say with a smile — "recycled as Novice Director." It was a role she loved in the contemplative embrace of her beloved BSPA Congregation, while, at the same time, her heart was never far from the goings-on back in Oklahoma. She would return to the Osage Forest periodically for special occasions and oblate meetings, and she continued to keep up-to-date with it through Bob and others.

"Sr. Pascaline was a tough act to follow," Monseigneur Gier says. "She was internationally renowned. She had tremendous credibility in the post-Vatican II intermonastic movement, was held in awe, really, by a large group of people that were very involved in that. She was crucial to all that."

Now, without Sr. Pascaline's presence in the Forest, the little live-in community there continued hosting interreligous meetings and meditation retreats. The Eucharist continued to be celebrated monthly by a visiting priest.

Bob, for his part, worked to facilitate a new life for the Osage Forest that would carry forward Sr. Pascaline's and her Sisters' charism, one that he could not carry himself. "I was a bridge person. Here was this great vision out of India and Father Bede and Sr. Pascaline and Vatican II. Sr. Pascaline had the strength to bring it through, and I had to hold it together. I thought, I can't just let this thing collapse on its own."

"Bob sought councel on a regular basis from his good friend Monsignor Gier. He was a great help," Sr. Pascaline recalled.

Monseigneur Gier had visited and celebrated Mass with the community a few times over the years. He would now play a vital role for the Osage Forest of Peace. Monseigneur Gier recalls:

> Being a protestant convert, Bob was very aware that he might not understand the Catholic practices and he also wanted to maintain Sr. Pascaline's charism and the mindset of the monastery. That, for him, was Catholicism. Bob wanted to maintain it as an approved, authentic Catholic space, with any one of the bishops supportive of the whole thing. I came in as his advisor to make sure that whole thing happened.

Once Sr. Pascaline left Osage, there was, for a time, nobody there acting as a Spiritual Director, although Bob liked to say that the Forest itself is a Spiritual Director.

Sr. Pascaline had been living in the BSPA house in Tucson a year when Ruben

DEDICATION OF THE PEACE POLE. L–R : JUSTIN PEHOSKI, SISTER PASCALINE, SISTER JANE COMERFORD, PAIGE BRITT, DOG GITANO

Habito, who had been leading Zen meditation retreats at O+M for years, was named Spiritual Director for the Forest of Peace. While still living in Dallas, Ruben would oversee the spiritual affairs of the Forest, while Mardana Jones coordinated the day-to-day business.

Meanwhile, Sister Pascaline was far from being detached from this monastic ashram into which she had poured so much of her life. She must have sensed that, in addition to Mardana's capable management and Ruben's spiritual guidance, the Osage Forest of Peace needed an actual flesh-and-blood Spiritual Director living onsite, someone with Catholic, as well as East-West sensibilities — as she herself had been.

Jane Comerford, a Sister of St. Joseph of Carondelet, was living in Tucson, on the staff of a house of prayer as the Spiritual Director. She was also very much in tune with the kind of East-West spiritual practices for which Sister Pascaline and the BSPAs had founded the Osage Forest of Peace, since the World Parliament of Religions in 1993 had inspired in her a commitment to interfaith work. She had read Bede Griffiths' books and was very interested in his unique combination of Hinduism and Christianity.

Sister Jane remembers that in late 2010:

> I was living in Tucson, and I happened to meet Sister Pascaline at an event for the Religious of the Diocese that was held at the BSPA monastery there. I'd never met her, so I went over to introduce myself to her and told her that I had similar interests in terms of interfaith work … although I'd never been to Osage.
>
> She said, "Do you think you'd like to live there?"
>
> I said, "What?"
>
> She said, "Well, they're looking for a Director." And then she asked me would I go with her the first week in December. This was in 2010. The board was meeting that weekend and I would get to see the place and meet the Board of Directors. So I traveled with her that weekend and stayed at the Forest.

That same weekend, almost three years after Bob Doenges had procured the Osage Monastery, it was time to transfer ownership of the property to the nonprofit entity he had set up originally. Bob explains, "It is a spiritual place. An individual person cannot own a spiritual center. It belongs to the world."

Just before the Board took ownership of the Osage Forest, more Dallas people became involved as Board members and financial supporters. Among them were John Ockels, Elaine Heath, and Amy Garrett, whose support during the transition years was "crucial," Bob says. JoAnn Huber agrees, saying, "Amy was absolutely key. Without her the Forest of Peace simply would not be here today."

A new board with Ruben Habito as president took over in early 2011 and developed a Blueprint for the Osage Forest of Peace. Soon thereafter, Sister Jane began her residence there as Spiritual Director.

JOANN HUBER

During Sister Jane's years at Osage, the Board members from Dallas resigned one by one, and were replaced by Tulsans. Sister Jane remembers:

> Sr. Pascaline had an international reputation and people from all over the world came to Osage, but local people didn't even know Osage existed. To me it was imperative that Osage would have Board members from Tulsa and it would become better known within that community.
>
> JoAnn Huber had been a volunteer. She was always coming out to work on the grounds. She had a great interest, so I encouraged her to be on the Board.

JoAnn joined the Board in November 2011. She remembers:

> I would come in and eat and then just go back to work. It wasn't until Sister Jane came that Jane asked if I would be interested in being on the Board. Bob was just getting off the Board and he wanted someone from the Tulsa area on the Board before he was gone. Eve Abrams was also from Tulsa and she got on the Board, but the Board president, Amy Garrett, was from Texas. Eve and I would do things, but none of the others were here. The Board was very small; we didn't have workers. Then Amy resigned from her role, and that put Eve as the president.
> Now there were Eve and Jane and me, and I saw that the place needed support.
> I finally said, "Jane, Eve, we're coming up with some names of people and we are going to call a meeting." We called the meeting in April 2013, and told people the reality. Several people out of that meeting said they wanted to be on the Board. So we got crackin.'

JoAnn had been on the Board about two years at this point. What was needed was a bigger Board, with more local members. JoAnn became Board president, elected, she says, "Simply because I had the longest history, not because I had any great skill, other than I'm passionate about this place."

> It became clear to me over time that what we had to do was figure out who we are now. It's not a monastic community any longer, yet we still wanted to live in community. It was a huge challenge, because it takes a long time to figure out who you are and what God is calling you to be. And then finding the staff people who can flesh that out.

The changes in the Osage Forest of Peace's leadership structure began a new period of development that was both an outgrowth and realization of the Osage+Monastery's original charism. "I think it's been marvelous — the development that's taking place — the direction of the Osage Forest," JoAnn said in 2016. "The Osage Forest is just unique. There are a lot of retreat centers where you can rent space, but there aren't a lot of retreat centers that have a live-in staff, where you can come and meet the Forest Dwellers and share prayer with them and have someone to talk to. That's a rare bird. I love that we can offer that."

In addition to her administrative and fund-raising service, JoAnn continued working in the woods and around the grounds. Any visit might find her trimming trees, clearing away brush, or sanding old paint and grime off the picnic table.

> I'm like the guests. I like the peacefulness. As soon as I hit that gravel turning down into here I feel myself just settle. The prayer permeates this place, the holiness of all these years of prayer here and the people that have been here, so just working in the woods is good for me and being able to join in the community and still serve as a board member as well was just a gift — an excuse to be here.[73]

Sister Jane's tenure ended in early 2015, and when the Board learned Sister Jane was leaving, they began to look around for a new director. The position was advertised in the email newsletter sent out regularly to all retreatants and supporters under the subject line "News from Osage Forest of Peace."

One response to the newsletter ad came from Don Chatfield, an interfaith minister in Tucson. Don had grown up not far from Sand Springs in Ponca City, Oklahoma, but had left Oklahoma as a young man, feeling spiritually at odds with the place of his childhood. The summer before, Don and Karen Chatfield had found the Osage Forest of Peace on a website: retreatfinder.com. Karen recalled:

> We came here in May of 2014, we fell in love with the Forest, and while here got on their email list so that we would get updates. We started getting their newsletter, and then in January of 2015 Don saw the announcement for an opening for an executive director here in the Forest.

---

[73] JoAnn would serve on the Board until 2021 and acted as Interim Director during periods in 2019 and 2020 when there was no resident director.

KAREN AND DON CHATFIELD AND THEIR DOG, LILY

He said, "I'm thinking of applying for this. What do you think?"

I said, "Well, throw your hat in the ring and let's see what happens." The next thing you know he gets called for a telephone interview, and then they wanted to bring both of us out for an in-person interview.

For the Chatfields, the move from Tucson to the Forest involved getting rid of "a lot of stuff" as they moved from a 2200 square-foot house in Tucson into a 630 square-foot cabin in the Forest of Peace. "It's amazing how freeing that is!" Karen said.

Don and Karen built on the visions of their predecessors and the explorations in spiritual life that began at O+M decades before. Expanding on O+M's tradition of offering spiritual direction for people of all faiths, in 2016 they founded Forest of Peace School of Spiritual Direction as a resource for people who want to serve as Interspiritual Directors as well as deepen their own spiritual lives. Karen and Don had trained as spiritual directors at the Tacheria School for Spiritual Direction in Tucson, where they had developed a deep interfaith background that respected the spiritual paths of all traditions.

The Osage Forest of Peace library began with books that publishers sent Sister Pascaline to be reviewed in the NABEWD Bulletin. It has grown over the years and is now a treasure trove of spiritual writing, audio and video materials. The library had never been indexed until Jeni Enns, one of the Forest residents, identified a software package and cataloged the 2500 books in an index available online.

The needs of the Forest of Peace would continue to be met; it was an article of faith. Karen Chatfield spoke of "manifesting abundance." She published a wish list of needed articles, many of which were quickly donated by Forest supporters and friends happy to help out. "It's been very gratifying, and I think the board will take the same approach for capital campaigns, or other fundraising activities … just upholding the belief that the people really want this and, 'if we build it, they will come.'"

As the Chatfields and the Board talked about manifesting what was needed for the Osage Forest of Peace, they were following in the tradition of the BSPAs — the method by which the Sisters built and furnished this unusual monastic ashram / retreat center / house of prayer. People who loved the idea of such a place — first the BSPAs and then Tulsa-area lay and religious Catholics, the Bishop, Sand Springs Catholics and other neighbors and many others—caught the Sisters' spirit and came forward with donations of money, skilled labor, furnishings, food, transportation, and many other needs to make the Forest dream into the reality it became.

Don and Karen moved from the Forest in the summer of 2019, and an online search brought Laurie Larson to Osage, to lead the residential community through the difficult early years of the Covid-19 pandemic. While the Osage Forest could not operate as a retreat center, the little community there continued daily meditation in the chapel and shared it with all who wanted to join on the Forest of Peace's Facebook Live channel. Teaching videos from the Forest were also posted online. "Whenever I encountered challenges," Laurie said, "I would pause in Sr. Pascaline's cabin to call in the spirit of the founders, asking, 'What would Sr. Pascaline do?'" The one cabin without a shower, where Sister Pascaline slept and prayed for 30 years, has now become the Chapel of the Blessed Sacrament, while Mass continues to be celebrated in the main Chapel every month.

A sense of the sacred has never left the Forest. Visitors say, "Just driving into the parking lot, I felt the peace descending upon me and enveloping me." Workmen inspecting the roofs would find themselves whispering to each other. "There's something about this place—it almost feels like you walked into a church." Many have sensed the Osage Forest of Peace as a "thin place" in the Celtic sense of having a palpable connection with the world of Spirit.

Laurie Larson said, "There is a healing energy in the Forest. I think that it has been magnified by the meditation that has been going on here two or three times a day for the last forty years. And that happens no matter what's going on with the staff."

Michaela Lawson, who became Board president in 2021, agrees. "I've seen what happens to people who come here — the peace, calm and hope they gain from being in the Forest."

Indeed, all the years of meditation and prayer here, both before and after the construction of the chapel and cabins, have created a sense in this place of a spiritual

MICHAELA LAWSON

aliveness that is at once peaceful and energizing. People find joy and direction here, their connection to the loving Heart of Spirit restored.

On a May afternoon in 2022, over a hundred friends from around the world gathered in the Forest and on Zoom to honor the remarkable memory of Sr. Pascaline Coff. She had passed away at the age of 95 the preceding December 16 at the BSPA retirement center in Clyde, surrounded by her beloved BSPA Community.

The crowd in the Forest of Peace filled the little chapel and expanded out through the Main House for a tearful and joyful Eucharist celebrated by retired Monseigneur Gier. During the dinner following the service, speaker after speaker took the mic in front of the crowd and Zoom camera to share memories of Sr. Pascaline and the Sisters of the O+M and the Osage Forest of Peace.

Through their work and prayers, and those of the community members that followed them, the Osage Forest of Peace has truly come to embody the same spiritual power and peace that flowed from the heart of Sr. Pascaline herself. This same Spirit is carried to all who enter here on each breath of wind that plays and prays through the leaves.

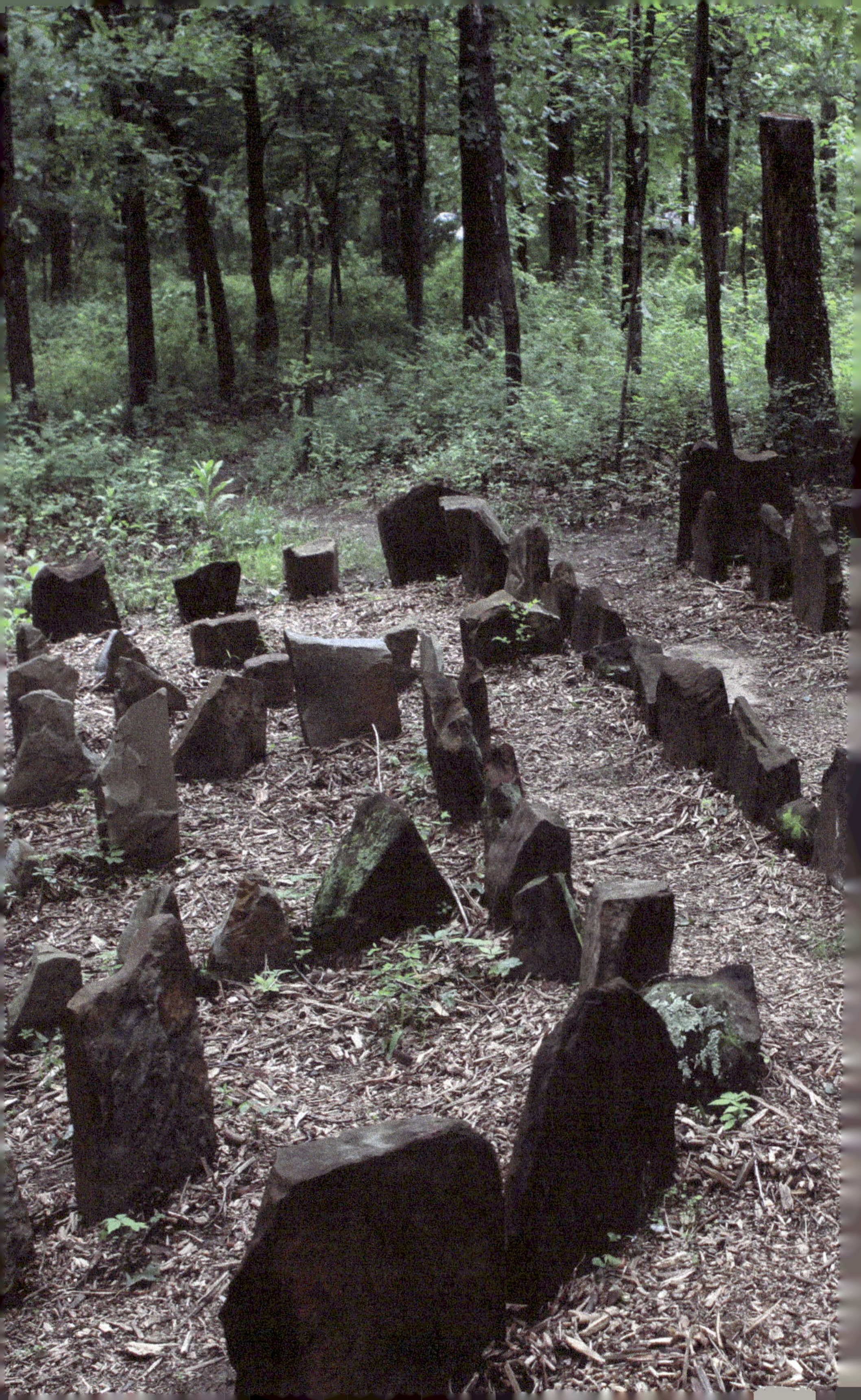

EPILOGUE

From the unreal lead us to the real
From darkness lead us to light
From death lead us to immortality.
Lead us from falsehood to truth
From despair to hope
From fear to trust.
Lead us from hate to love
From war to peace.
Let peace fill our hearts, our world, our universe.
— Osage Forest of Peace Prayer

A retreatant walked up the gravel path from the little cabins to the Main House in the Osage Forest of Peace as a cool spring rain pattered down on fresh leaves that spread like a green umbrella above her. Morning meditation would begin in the chapel soon, to be followed by breakfast in silence. The birds did not observe silence, she noticed. Even in the rain, their songs echoed among the tree branches with a harmonic woodsy fullness.

She had slept the night before in a cabin with a photo of Fr. Bede Griffiths on the wall, the same cabin where he was visited once by a vision of St. Mary as he struggled through a restless night. Now, however, she was not thinking of Fr. Bede, but of Sr. Pascaline, and Sr. Priscilla, and of all the BSPA Sisters who planned and built this place. She was thinking of all the people who loved this place, who helped transition the Forest after the Sisters had left a decade earlier.

Some things here had been added over the years — the labyrinth through the ancient oaks, the Cave of the Mothers, the white pole proclaiming Peace to the four directions in four different languages and scripts. There would be more changes, perhaps, welcoming future retreatants to bathe in the numinous peace beneath the trees. New residents, new leaders would come. A new generation was discovering this place, even as they discovered their own deep need for such a place and the spiritual sustenance to be found here.

As today's Forest Dwellers look to the future of our ever-smaller planet, and the builders and keepers of the Osage Monastery Forest of Peace remember its past, the need for such a place as this has become ever more pressing. The message painted on the Peace pole encapsulates the prayer that this place makes from every leaf and

© 2015 ROSEMARY DELUCA ALPERT

birdsong and hour of meditation: "May Peace Prevail on Earth."

Bob Doenges says that the mission of the Osage Forest of Peace is "to meet and greet the Christ consciousness, Buddha nature, infinite potential in everyone who shows up."

The Board has stated the mission more officially this way: "To create sacred space to nurture spirit in support of a more peaceful world."

Michaela Lawson says simply, "We're planting seeds of peace."

The name Sister Pascaline was given in India, with which she always signed her correspondence, might also be seen as a mission statement of sorts — a summation of what she and the BSPAs built here and what this place is to the many who have been and will be here: One+Heart.

This center — this centering place — has brought together people from all over the world as One Heart. As long as that heart center at Osage stays true to its universal principle — the Love that underlies all — peace will remain here, offering refuge, renewal and enrichment from the world's treasury of spiritual traditions to all who come.

Sr. Pascaline's benediction still speaks blessing from every rock and tree:

> For all that has been, yes;
> for all that is, Yes;
> for all that will be, YES Christ!

© SCOTT THOMPSON

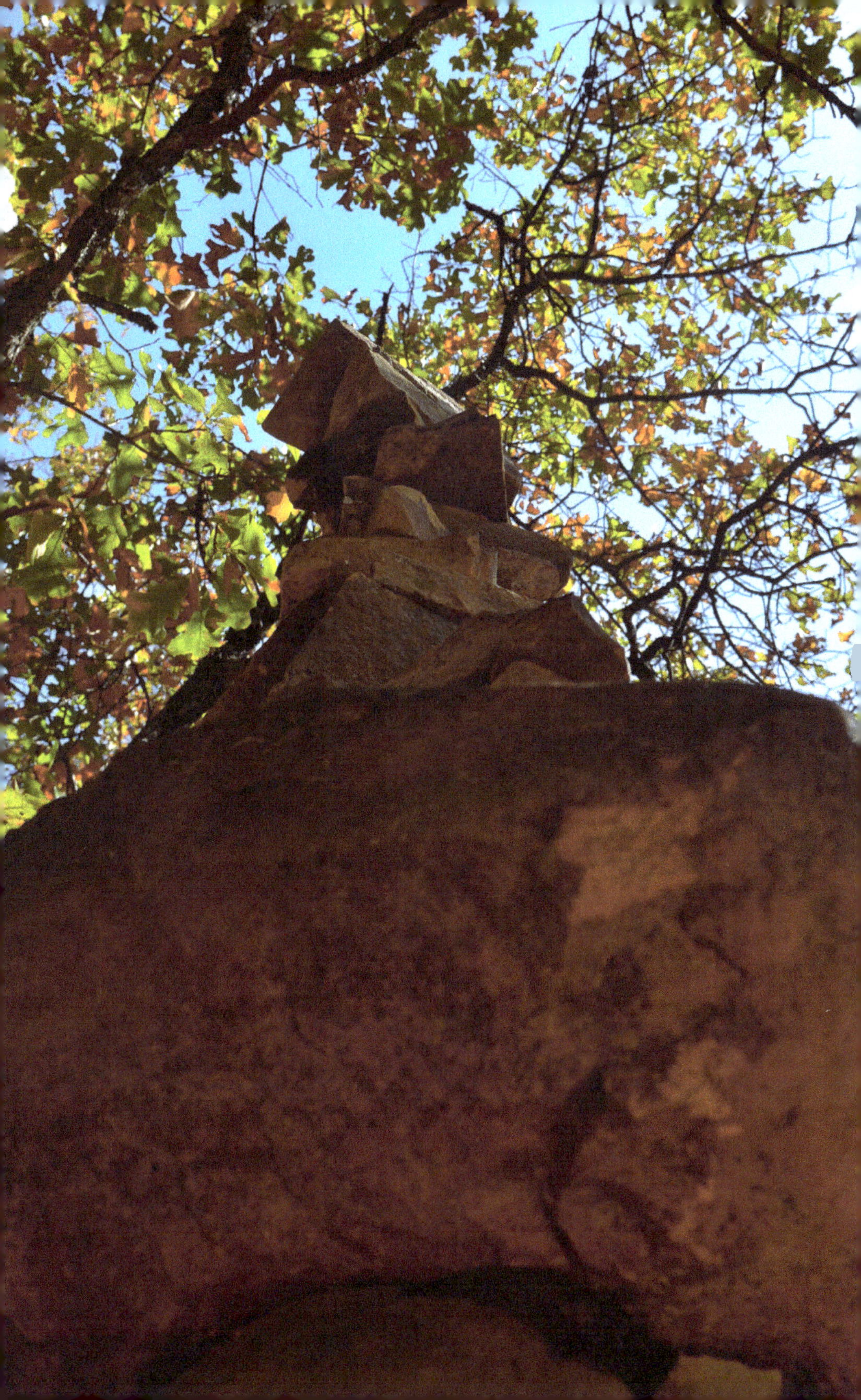

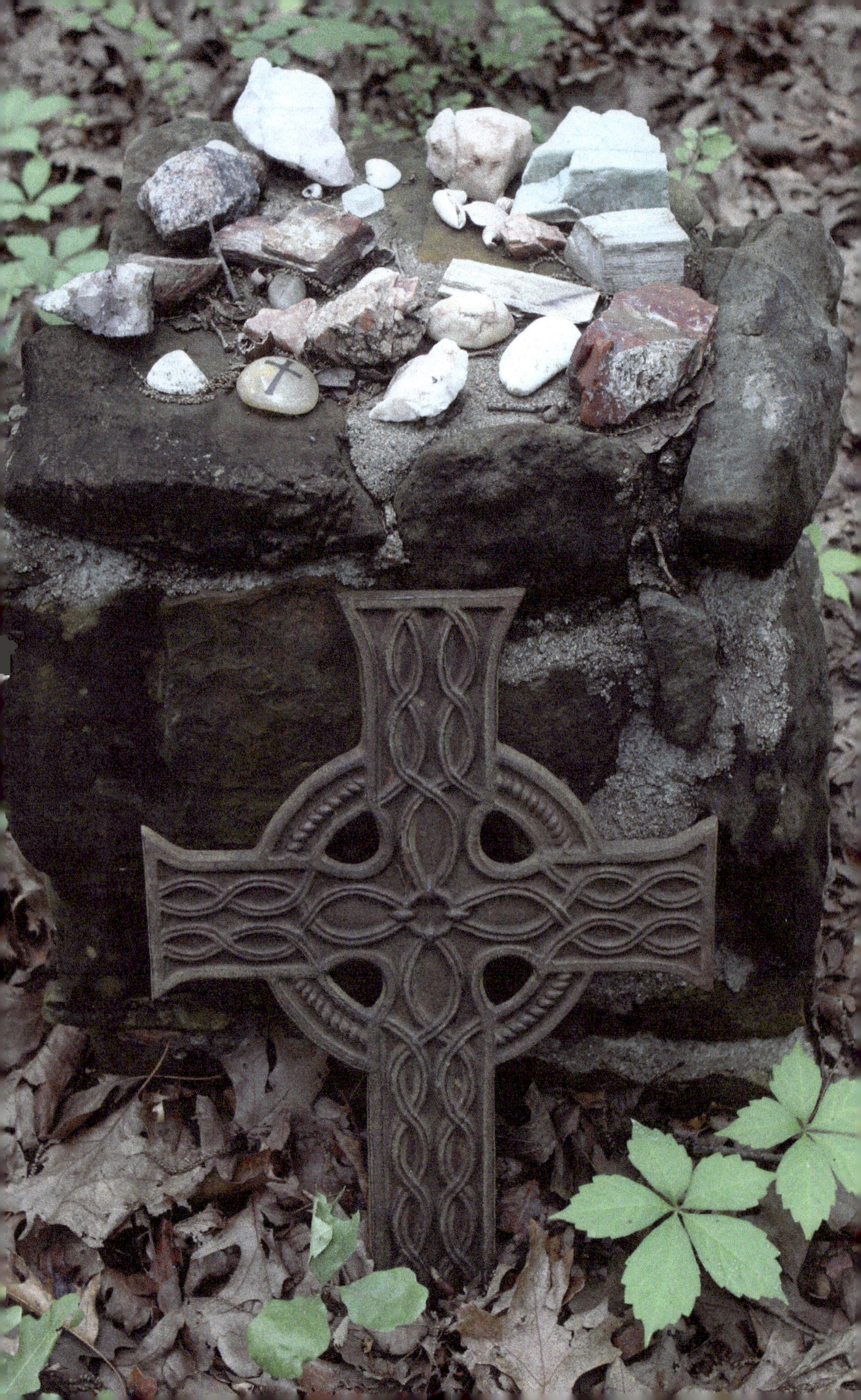

INDEX

22nd Place 40, 42, 44, 45, 48, 49, 52, 54, 58, 81, 83, 87

Abhishiktananda 18, 29, 96, 97
Abhishiktananda Society 96
adoration 8, 9, 51, 72, 78, 100, 103, 105
Advaita 110, 143
Advent 61
"A Human Search" documentary 153
AIM 29, 30, 35, 37, 48, 52, 144
AIM Secretariate 29, 30, 31, 49, 50, 128
Alaska 118
Allen, Sr. Maurus 7, 8, 10, 11, 13, 14, 19, 21, 25, 118, 153
Allred, Dick 61, 62
Amaldas, Bro. 49, 54, 55, 153
American Benedictine Review, The 13, 153
Anderson, Edward 52
Anderson, Joan 100
Andrea, Sr. 61
Ann, Sr., CSJ 66
Anselma, BSPA Sr. 73
arati 21, 22, 28, 62, 126, 140, 143, 144, 148, 155
Archibald, Sr. Marie Therese 59
architect 57, 58, 61, 70, 73, 100
Arizona 17, 170
Arnold, BSPA Sr. Regina 28, 109, 110
Asha 148, 149, 150, 152, 160
ashram 2, 7, 10–14, 16–19, 22, 28, 29, 30, 34, 35–37, 39, 43, 45, 47, 49, 51, 54, 57, 60, 65, 71, 87, 99, 100, 109, 118, 131, 140, 143, 147, 153, 155, 164, 165, 167, 170, 172, 176
Ash Wednesday 21, 68
Association of American Benedictine Prioresses 12
Atwood, Dr. 135, 153
Atwood, Virginia 134, 153, 159
Audrey, Mother, BSPA Prioress General 26, 28, 30–33, 35, 36, 40, 41, 45, 50, 51, 53, 54, 57, 59, 65, 68, 70, 78, 82, 83, 87, 100
Australia 150, 152

Ballman, Sr. Marie 60
Bangalore, India 10, 14, 22, 91
Bangkok 12
Baptist 41
Barbara, Sr. 126
Barnhart, Fr. Bruno 109, 155, 166
Barrow, Helen, Sr. 17, 18, 65, 70, 82, 91, 96, 99, 101, 103, 105, 109, 113, 114, 115, 132, 133, 144, 160
Bartlett, Jim 88
Baumer, Odette 96, 97
Bede, BSPA Sr. 110
Bede Griffiths literary archive 156
Bede Griffiths Trust 140, 155, 156, 165, 167
bell for O+M 70
Beltran, Bishop (now Archbishop Emeritus) Eusebius viii, 1, 35, 36, 39, 40, 45, 46, 49, 53, 59, 63, 65, 83
benches 42, 87, 91, 100, 101, 103
Benedictine vii, 1, 7–14, 17–19, 22, 27, 29, 32, 35, 40, 44, 50, 52, 61, 63, 70, 78, 87, 109, 111, 113, 118, 123, 125, 135, 153, 164, 165
Benedictine Convent of Perpetual Adoration in Oklahoma, Inc. 61
Benedictine Sisters of Perpetual Adoration 27
Benita, Sr. 35, 36, 41, 53, 60, 91, 110, 164, 168
Bertilla, Sr. 60
Bhagavad Gita 20, 21, 140
bhajan 51, 62
Big Sur 155
Bilderback, Barbara 90, 134
birdbath 162
Blée, Fabrice viii, 29, 125
Blessed Simplicity: The Monk as Archetype 96, 126
Blue Nun wine 168
Bly, Robert (n) 162
bond (performance) 60–63
Bonneau, Sr. Christine 35, 36, 40–44, 54, 55, 57, 58, 63, 65, 66, 72, 73, 75, 81, 87, 88, 91, 96, 97, 99, 109

© 2015 ROSEMARY DELUCCO ALPERT

INDEX

Booth, Christine viii
Bristow, Oklahoma 49, 50, 72, 91, 100, 103
Britt, Paige 171
Brück, Michael von 96, 110
BSPA council 96
Buddhism 1, 124, 126, 140, 159, 162
Bulletin of the Bede Griffiths Trust 140, 167
Bulletin of the NABEWD 33, 35, 54, 63, 96, 103, 105, 123, 155, 175
Burne, Abbot Martin J. 32
Butz, Jack 57, 58, 60, 61
Butz, Pat 100

Campbell, James 116
Carthusian 110
Cascia Hall 61
Catherine of Sienna 117
Catholic Charities 133
Celtic 176
cement 61, 63, 65, 68
center 1, 8, 120, 180
chalice 66
chalkboard at O+M 118
Chancellor 39, 40, 41
Channel 6 Eyewitness News 87
chapel vii, 1, 41, 44, 57, 58, 60, 63, 65, 68, 71–73, 75, 78, 81–83, 88, 91, 92, 96, 100, 103, 111, 113–116, 149, 151, 152, 168, 176, 177, 179
chapel pit 68, 75
Chaplain 34
Charleston, Nona viii
Chase family 100, 103, 105, 144
Chatfield, Don viii, 149, 174
Chatfield, Karen viii, 174
Cherokee 41
Chittister, Sr. Joan 12
Choephel, Geshe Lobsang 125
Christian ashram 12, 14, 28, 155
Christian Unity 150
Christ in the Desert monastery, Abiquiu, New Mexico 18, 36
Christmas letter 31
Christ the King Church 68, 133, 160
chronicle book 2, 59, 60, 62, 70, 72, 81, 105, 150, 168
Cistercian 44, 50, 128, 135
Clyde archive 133
Clyde, Missouri vii, 1, 8, 17, 18, 26, 27, 30, 32, 33, 39, 46, 54, 59, 60, 70, 118, 133, 164, 165, 168, 177
coconut 20
Cody, Cardinal 32
Coff, Agnes Newsham 26
Coff, Ed 27, 169
Coff family 9
Coff, Margaret Mary 8, 9, 26, 27
Coff, Sr. Pascaline iii, vii, viii, 1, 2, 7, 8, 10–14, 16, 17–37, 39, 40, 41–45, 47–55, 57–63, 65, 66, 68, 70–73, 75, 78, 81–83, 87, 88, 91, 92, 96, 97, 99, 101, 103, 105, 109–11, 113, 115–18, 123–26, 128–35, 137–40, 143, 144, 145, 147–150, 152, 153, 155, 156, 159–65, 167–73, 175–177, 179, 180
coincidentia oppositorum (coincidence of opposites) 147
Cole, Joan 110
Coless, Fr. Gabriel 130
Collegeville 130
Colossians, St. Paul's letter to 151
Comerford, Sr. Jane viii, 133, 172
common house 50, 57, 58, 59, 71, 82, 87, 91, 92, 113, 143
communication skills 18
community formation 31
Conception Abbey 54
Congregation for the Doctrine of the Faith 137, 140, 152
Conner, Fr. James viii, 18, 36, 41, 45, 47, 50, 115, 133, 145, 155, 166, 168
Conner, Joe 103
contemplation 1, 9, 11, 12, 28, 34, 109, 118, 127, 140, 149
contemplative 34
contract to purchase Forest land 54, 61, 62, 69
Cooper, Vincent 19
Corps of Engineers [Army] 61
Corpus Christi, Feast of 8, 9, 53, 63, 70, 82, 83, 84, 87

INDEX

cosmic wheel 83
Cox, Emily 169
Curtain, Bonnie 82

D

adul, Ven. Kalsang 125, 128
Dalai Lama, HH, the 109, 110, 117, 123, 127, 128, 130, 133, 134, 139, 150, 152, 153, 165
Dalai Lama Taking the Geshe Exam 127
Dalai Lama 129
Dallas, Texas 115, 150, 155, 167, 169, 172
Daney, Stephen 115
Daniel, BSPA Sr. 109
Darden, Sr. Miriam 36, 41, 53, 68
Daughtery, Rex 87
David, Bro. [Steindl-Rast] 145
David, BSPA Sr. 36, 40, 53, 66, 81, 82, 100
Davis, Howard 73
Dawn, BSPA Sr. vii, 78, 81
day hours 92
Dayton, Wyoming 165, 168
Dechen, Sr. 134, 135
dedication day celebration (for O+M) 63, 84
deer 55, 81, 92, 165
Denise, BSPA Sr. 68, 70, 100
Dennison, Gene viii
Denver, Colorado 83, 123
Desel, Sr. 134, 135
desert fathers 131
desert mothers 131
Devananda, Fr. 144, 145
dharma lessons 2
Dharamsala, India 128, 130
dining table 97, 113
discernment 18, 25, 31, 60, 83, 99
dishwashing 44
divine feminine 147
Divine Milieu 31
Divine Mother 147
Dobbins, Cheryl viii
doctorate 10, 110
Doenges, Bob (Robert S.) vii, viii, 117, 159, 162, 164, 167, 169, 172, 180
Doenges family 160
Doenges, Liddy 159, 160, 162

dogwood trees 70
Dolores, BSPA Sr. 17
Dominican 16, 116, 117, 160
Dorney, Fr. (Chancellor) 41, 44
Douglas, John viii, 150, 155, 156, 167, 169
Dunsang, Tensing 131
duplex 59, 71

E

asement 68
Eastern Fathers of the Church 11
Eastern Oklahoma Catholic (EOC) 48, 55, 59, 71, 91, 92
East Germany 110
Eastman, Fr. Patrick 115
Easton, Kansas 39, 44
East-West Bulletin 49
East-West dialogue 26, 29, 30, 44, 45, 49, 61, 96, 123, 138, 155
East-West liturgies 52
East-West monastic experience 114
East-West monasticism 70
East-West Monastic Symposium 110
East-West symposium 66
East-West Symposium 96
Eckhart, Meister 117
elections 12
electricity 47
electric (utility) 66, 68, 71, 73
Elva 52, 62, 73
Enns, Jeni 175
entrance sign 71, 73
Episcopal ministers 114
Episcopal Seminary of the Southwest, Austin, Texas 137
Epistle 20, 21
Esalen Institute 163, 164
Eucharist 1, 8, 19–22, 41, 44, 45, 50, 51, 53, 55, 58, 60, 61, 65, 66, 68, 71, 73, 75, 78, 81, 83, 88, 91, 96, 97, 99, 115, 116, 125–27, 144, 145, 148–52, 167, 170, 177
Evagrian the Solitary 114
evil, the problem of 152

INDEX

Fabian, Sr. Ludwigis 110
Farney, Joe 168
Feast of St. Michael 58, 59, 91
fence 47, 81
Fey, Gerri 168
fibrillation of the heart 148, 151
fire 2, 21, 22, 68, 75, 81, 88, 92, 100, 103, 120, 138, 140, 148, 153, 155
fireplace 68, 75, 103
first Christmas 100, 103
First Communion 9
first Eucharist in the Forest of Peace 44, 55, 60, 65
first Mass 75
first night in the Forest 44, 75, 78
fixtures 58, 71, 75
floor / flooring 21, 22, 34, 42, 43, 49, 55, 58, 60, 68, 71, 73, 82, 88, 103, 131, 149
Fontebonne University 26
food shower 78
Forest of Peace School of Spiritual Direction 175
Forfang, Eleanor 110
four directions 55, 179
framers 63
Franciscan 51, 59
Friends of the Forest viii, 164, 165
fundamentalism 140, 156
funeral 27, 40, 160
Funk, Sr. Mary Margaret 29
Fusche, Neil 71
Futrell, Sr. Janice 35, 49

Gabriel, Father Vincent 91
Gardner, Sue 110
Garrett, Amy 172, 173
Garrett, Bob 100
Garrett, Mr. and Mrs. Bob 78
gas 96
gas lines 47
gas (utility) 69, 91, 96
Gayatri mantra 22
Gemin, Sr. 150

General Chapter of the BSPA 37, 39
Geshe Exam 127
Geshela 124, 127, 128
Gethsemani Encounter 133, 134
Gethsemani (Kentucky) Abbey 12, 16, 18, 36, 115, 128, 133, 134, 155, 168
Gibson, Ed 65, 103
Gier, Monsignor Gregory viii, 160, 162, 170, 177
Gilcrease Museum 133, 147
goals for O+M community 51, 99
Goethe, Johann Wolfgang von 159, 162
Golden String, The 140, 156, 165, 167
gong 111
Gottwald, Bishop George 26, 27
Grand Canyon 168
Grant, BSPA Sr. Josetta 109, 110
Grant, Harold 110
Grant, Kathryn 143
Greenwald, Sr. Maryann viii
Greyhound bus 52, 62, 91
Griffiths, Fr. Bede vii, viii, 11, 13, 14, 16, 18, 21, 22, 32, 36, 39, 44, 49, 52, 54, 55, 109, 110, 114, 118, 123, 127, 139, 140, 142–44, 146–49, 152, 153, 155, 156, 159, 160, 162, 163, 165, 167, 172, 179
GTU (Jesuit Graduate Theological Union, Berkeley, California 36, 156

Habito, Ruben 110, 115, 159, 170, 172
Halloway, Paul 73
Harold, Brother 152
Harvey Lectures 138
Hays, Fr. Ed 39, 44
Heath, Charles (n) bequest 105
Heath, Elaine 172
Heck, Mary 168
Helen, Mary 126
Heller, Mr. 66
Hermitage 96, 100, 114, 115, 164
hermit day 105
Hindu 11, 12, 13, 22, 28, 29, 99, 110, 118, 120, 126, 139, 140, 153, 156
Hindu temple in Tulsa 153
hip injury, Pascaline's 26

INDEX

Hoblitzelle, Harrison 148
Hoey family 61
Hoey, Geralen 83
Hoey, Paul 50, 58
holidays: 4th of July 118; Christmas 30, 31, 60, 61, 62, 100, 103, 133, 137; Easter 8, 52, 65, 68, 70, 134, 160, 162; Halloween 145; Labor Day 57; New Years 31, 44, 49, 133; Thanksgiving 48, 61, 97
Holy Communion 8, 73, 83, 99
Holy Longing, The 159, 162
Holy Mother 159
holy offices 8
Holy Spirit 30, 31, 148
Holy Trinity 18, 148
holy water 92
Holy Week 52, 66
homosexuality (n) 152
Honduras 116, 117
hospitality 34, 66, 87, 113, 114, 118, 125, 135, 139, 140, 167
Howard, Sr. Katherine 152
Huber, JoAnn viii, 169, 172, 173
Hume, Cardinal Basil 78

Immaculate Conception Church / Parish, Pawhuska 47
incense 22, 68, 148
Incorporation of O+M 60
India 7, 8, 10, 11, 13, 14, 16–18, 22, 23, 25–30, 32, 34, 36, 39, 44, 49, 54, 55, 109, 110, 118, 123, 126–28, 130, 131, 137, 140, 144, 147, 148, 152, 153, 155, 160, 164, 165, 170, 180
Indian music 160
insulation 50, 63
intercommunion controversy 125
interfaith conference 12
interfaith dialogue 167
interiority iii, 1, 8, 11, 22, 23, 28, 31
intermonastic movement 170
Iran 62, 105
Israel 25, 41, 45, 138

Jager, Father Willigis 110
Jaiharikal 147
Jensen, Joli viii
Joe, Bro. from St. Procopius Abbey 123, 124
John Main lectures, New Harmony, Indiana 149, 150
John of the Cross 68, 75, 91
John Paul, Pope 40, 137
Johnstone, David 99
Jones, Mardana 169, 172
Jordan, Sr. 150
Joseph, Jim 88
Joy, BSPA Sr. 70
Jude / Judy, BSPA Sr. 62, 81, 83
Judith, BSPA Sr. 40, 51, 62
Judy Walter 163
Jungian 1

Kansas City BSPA convent 1, 10, 13, 14, 25, 26, 27, 34, 35, 42, 43, 46, 47, 50, 63, 65, 82, 91, 92, 96, 100, 144, 147
Kansas City, Missouri 1, 10, 13, 14, 25, 26, 27, 34, 35, 42, 43, 46–48, 50, 63, 65, 82, 91, 92, 96, 100, 103, 143, 144, 147
Kathleen Margaret, BSPA Sr. 82, 100, 168
Kathryn, BSPA Sr. 53, 81
Kavery River, India 7, 14, 20, 21, 22
Keating, Fr. Thomas 109, 138
Keefer, Katherine 162
Keeling, Bro. 127
Keen, Sam 163, 164
Kelly, Abbot Timothy 130, 134
Kelly, Alice 134
Kelly, Father Timothy 130
President John F. Kennedy 27
Kevin, Fr. 152
Keystone Lake / Dam 51, 100
kitchen 21, 40, 43, 44, 57, 71, 75, 82, 101, 113, 118
Korean, Sr. Theresa 110, 127
KTUL televison station 133
Kulithalai, India 7, 10, 14
kumkum 21

INDEX

Laity 2, 127, 140, 150
Larson, Laurie viii, 176
Lawson, Michaela viii, 116, 176, 180
Lazier, Sheila viii
LeClercq, Fr. Jean 109
lectio divina 111, 114
Le, Dung 110, 162
Lekshi, Sr. 131
Lent 8, 52, 68, 115, 134
Leocadia, BSPA Sr. 91
Le Saux, Fr. Henri 18, 29
Le, Sr. Lucia Anne 110
Letts, Rev. Thomas ("Reverand Tom") 118
Lhakdor, Ven. 128
library at Osage Forest of Peace 49, 143, 175
Liddy's Garden (Zen Garden in the Forest of Peace) 162
lifestyle 28, 30, 31, 43, 44, 45, 48, 58, 165
light fixtures 71, 73, 78, 81
Lillian, BSPA Sr. 60
Linda from Erie, Pennsylvania 118
Linda, Sr. 151, 152
Lioba, Sr. 63, 70, 91, 100, 109, 143, 144
liturgy 83, 99, 148: dedication 63; evening 41; Indian 149; "midnight" 61; Roman 92; Vedic 92
Liturgy of the Hours 1
Lodoe, Ven. Losang Sonam 125
Louisiana Purchase 46
Luetkemeyer, BSPA Sr. Benita 168
Lupita, Sr. M. 51
Lutheran 110, 133

Mahasamadhi (Fr. Bede's death) 153
Mahe, Sally viii
Mallon, John 110
Mannford, Oklahoma 100
Mannford (Oklahoma) News Eagle 126, 127, 144
mantra 22, 46
Margaret, BSPA Sr. 82
Margot, Sr. 75
Maria Kannon Zen Center, Dallas 115
Marie, Sr. Paul 82
Marquette, Fr. Jaques 46
Marriage of East and West 22, 126, 152
Martin, Fr. John 145
Mary Jane, Sr. iv, viii, 41, 136
Mary, Mother of Jesus 151
Mass 2, 7, 8, 21, 27, 44, 75, 83, 103, 111, 116, 117, 126, 127, 128, 148, 150, 162, 168, 170, 176
Mass of the Sacred Heart 150
Mathur, Balbir 169
Matthews, Mary Jane iv, viii, 136
Matthias, BSPA Sr. 52, 81
Matyniak, Kevin 149
Matyniak, Teresa viii, 110, 156, 162
McGlinchy, Fr. James viii, 115, 116
McGoldrick, Fr. 70, 75, 78
McGrane, Sr. Colleen vii
medicine wheel 82
meditation 1, 2, 11, 14, 22, 23, 29, 68, 92, 97, 114, 115, 118, 128, 131, 137–40, 144, 149, 150, 164, 170, 176, 179
Meehan, Frances 110
Melchesidech, the Order of 148
Mercer, Sr. Helen 17, 114
Mercy, BSPA Sr. 100
Merton Commemoration 44
Merton, Thomas 12, 16, 18, 44, 99, 133, 145, 155
Michael, BSPA Sr. 88, 150
Michael, Fr. 91
MID 29, 134, 155
Miller, Hubert 60, 69
Millichap, Paulette vii
Moan, Betsy 110
monasteries, Tibetan 127, 130, 131
monasticism 49: ashramic 92; Christian 11 East-West 70; Hindu-style 13; interspiritual 17
Monchanin, Fr. Jules 18, 29
Monte Casino 39, 75
Morgan, Jack 81, 103
motherhouse 53, 165
Mother Theresa 25
Moving day 75
Mt. Holyoke, Massachusetts 96, 97, 110
Mundelein (BSPA house) 28, 36, 60, 70, 71

INDEX

NABEWD 29, 30, 32, 33, 35, 44, 49, 54, 63, 70, 72, 88, 96, 103, 105, 109, 123, 130, 134, 137, 144, 152, 155, 175
NABEWD Board 32
NABEWD Bulletin 33, 35, 54, 63, 96, 103, 105, 123, 155, 175
NABEWD Secretariate 128
Nalanda University 139
Namgyal 131
Nandi / Ananda, O+M monastery dogs 54, 90, 92
Naropa Institute 123
Nataraj 54
National Catholic Reporter 139, 140, 152
Native American 1, 70, 82, 120
Nelson-Atkins Museum of Art, Kansas City, Missouri 145
New Creation in Christ, The 150
New Jersey 130
Nicholas, Cardinal of Cusa 147
night prayers 73, 152
Noh, Soo 110
Nordhaus, Sr. Trinitas 35, 36, 41, 42, 43, 50
North American Board for East-West Dialogue 29, 30, 45, 61, 96, 123
North Dakota 123
Nostra Aetate 16
Novice Mistress / Director 12
novitiate 62
nuns, Tibetan 109, 123, 130, 131, 134, 162
Nuong, Ferus 100
Nyingma Tantric Monastery 130

Oakland, California 162
 oak trees 156
oblate viii, 134, 167, 169, 170
Oblates, Benedictine 164, 165
oblates, O+M 134
Ockels, John 172
Office of Tibet 127
Oklahoma City, Archbishop of 75
Oklahoma City, Oklahoma 73, 115, 168
Oklahoma City terrorist bombing 167
One+Heart 1, 65, 70, 180
ordination 22, 134
Osage allotment 52
Osage allottees 47
"Osage Cathedral" 47
Osage County, Oklahoma 17, 45, 46, 52, 53, 54, 127, 156
Osage Forest of Peace viii, 49, 92, 107, 133, 143, 149, 159, 167, 168, 169, 170, 172, 174, 175, 176, 177, 179, 180
Osage hills 131
Osage Monastery 168
Osage Monastery Forest of Peace i, vii, 1, 23, 29, 53, 54, 91, 162, 164, 179
Osage Nation 46
Oshida, Fr. Shegeto 97, 110, 114, 116, 160
Our Father, the 66
outhouses 48, 49

Painting cabins 87, 91
 Panikkar, Fr. Raimundo 7, 92, 96, 97, 109, 126
Parliament of the World's Religions 133
Passover 52, 128
Patrick, Fr. 168
Paul Marie, Sr. from Hogan 82
Paul, Russill 148, 149, 150, 151, 152, 155, 160
Pawhuska, Oklahoma 45, 46–50, 52, 69, 71
Payson, Arizona 17, 18
peach seed monkey 164
Pehoski, Justin 171
Pentecost 75
Pentecostal 110
Perfectae Caritatis 17
Permanent Working Group 31
Peru 151
Peter, Bro. 126
Petersham, Massachusetts, conference 29, 125
pickup (truck) 63, 70, 71, 75, 78, 81
picnic 62, 65, 75, 78, 127, 174
Pierce, Fr. Brian viii, 116, 164
pilot lights 91
Piscopo Construction Company 58
Piscopo, Don 58
Pittman, Daniel 110

INDEX

plumbing 48, 62, 73, 96
Ponca City 174
Pope Benedict XVI 137
Pope John XXIII 27
Pope Paul VI 69
Potter, Dr. Robert 145
pottery 1, 88
poverty 17, 25, 31, 47, 87, 117, 127, 151
power (electricity) 73, 96
Prasad 21
Pratt, Charlie 168
prayer beads 124, 128, 130
Presbyterian 1, 110, 113, 118
Prioresses Council of BSPA 17, 18, 30, 47, 57, 59, 92, 96
Prioress General vii, 1, 10, 12, 17, 18, 26, 28, 43, 45, 87, 100, 118, 164, 165
privacy 52
progress report 37, 59, 65, 78
Propps, Fr. Joseph 144
Protestant 2, 39, 41, 110, 118, 125, 170
Pruitt, Bernadette 131
Psalms 92

Quaker 110

Rachel, Sr. 36, 68, 70, 91, 96, 99, 103, 105, 109
Rackley, Dennis 110
rainbow 68
Ramey, Joe 83
Rachel, Sr. 165
Ramona, BSPA Prioress General 168
Ramona, BSPA Sr. 82, 168
Raphael, Sr. 62
Ratzinger, Cardinal Joseph 137
Ratzinger letter 137, 140
Raymund, Br. 146
RCIA (Rite of Christian Initiation of Adults) 160, 162
Red Plains Monastery, Oklahoma City, Oklahoma 168
Reed, Brook 110
Reed, Greta viii, 110, 111, 113, 144

Reparata, BSPA Sr. 100
resurrection 31, 54, 165
Return to the Center 22, 52
Richardson, North Dakota 123
Rickenbach Center 30
"Riches from the East" audiotapes 145
Rigveda 22
Rishikesh, India 29
road 7, 47, 52, 60, 69, 71, 81, 83, 96, 97, 103, 148
road fill 96
Rosetta, Sr. 168
Roshi, Yamada Kuan 115
Rule of St. Benedict 11
Rymondraj (Raymund), Bro. Joseph 143

Saccidananda Ashram 11, 18, 164
    Sacred Heart Convent, Cullman, Alabama 13
Feast of the Sacred Heart 53
Sacred Heart of Jesus 8
saffron robe 11, 23, 156, 160
Salary from AIM / NABEWD 30, 35
Salvation Army 41
Samten, Acharya Ngawang 131
Sanders, Sr. Monica 35, 40–42, 50, 54, 55, 57, 58, 61, 66, 72, 88, 91, 92, 96, 97, 99, 100, 103, 105, 109, 132, 133
San Diego, California 1, 35, 40, 41
Sand Springs, Oklahoma 52, 53, 57, 61, 66, 70, 71, 75, 78, 82, 87, 96, 97, 100, 128, 147, 167, 174, 176
sannyasi 23, 25, 44, 156, 162
sannyasi renunciant 11
Saranath, India 131
satsang 134, 137, 145, 148
Schneeberg, Barbara viii, 167
School of Dialectics [Tibetan] in North India 128
School of Spiritual Direction 175
scorpions 88
Sellers, Barbara 82, 83
Sellers, Bob 57, 58, 60–63, 65, 68, 71, 73, 78, 81, 83, 96, 100
septic tank 65

INDEX

sesquimillennium 63
sesquimillennium of St. Benedict's birth 78
sesshins 159
Shantideva 139
Shanti (dove) 92, 96, 97
Shanti Niyalam 14
Shantivanam 10, 11, 13, 17, 19, 28–30, 39
Shantivanam of the West 159, 167
Shantivanam prayer farm (in Kansas) 44
Shawnee, Oklahoma 133, 135
Sheridan, Sr. Mary viii, 18, 21, 26
Sherman, Bill 165
showers 21, 58, 60, 63
Sikh 118
silence 1, 22, 31, 51, 62, 92, 103, 111, 115, 117, 179
Sioux Indian 59
Skaggs, Donald 68, 71
Skeehan, Fr. 168
Sky Farm Hermitage 163
Slickman, Ruth 82, 83, 97, 110
slide presentation vii
snakes 88
"Snow Jewel" 133
Snowmass, Colorado 41, 70
Solomon, Sr. Gloria 44
South India 7, 13, 14, 130, 144, 147, 148, 153
spiritual: advisor 160; aliveness 176; awakenings 162; center 165, 167, 172; community 169; development 8; direction 1, 39, 49, 50, 92, 99, 160, 175; director 99, 116, 162; enrichment 180; exercises 140; experience 97; growth 31, 149; guidance 25, 172; life 22, 175; masters 138; materialism 109; path 120, 135, 159; place 172; point of view 139; practice 11, 16, 17, 49, 114, 115, 140; readings 148; retreat 2, 25, 59; revival 97; seekers 19; support 169; surrender 153; sustenance 179; teachings 2; traditions 34, 139, 180; treasures 31, 34, 138; writing 175
stationery 151
Statzer, Mary Virginia 168
St. Bede's retreat house at O+M 162
St. Benedict medal 63
Stein, Edith 164
St. Elizabeth 160
Stendl-Rast, Fr. David 109
St. Gregory's Abbey, Shawnee, Oklahoma 133, 135
St. John's Abbey, Collegeville, Minnesota 130
St. Joseph's convent, Tulsa, Oklahoma 39, 44, 50, 58, 63
St. Louis, Missouri 1, 8, 10, 12, 18, 26, 29, 35, 37, 46, 48, 49, 52, 53, 58, 61, 62, 72, 78, 81, 83, 97, 114, 128, 144, 149, 164
St. Mary's Abbey 130
St. Mary's at Notre Dame 10
St. Michael's Day 40
St. Monica's parish, Tulsa, Oklahoma 88
St. Patrick's parish, Sand Springs, Oklahoma 70, 71, 78, 87, 168
St. Procopius Abbey, Lisle, Illinois 123
Straub, Linda 118
stroke, Father Bede's 147, 148, 149, 153
Sullivan, Bishop John 35
Sullivan, Maggie 99
Sullivan, Paula 91, 92, 99
Sundance Circle 68, 83
surgery, Pascaline's 109, 149
survey (land) 49, 55
Survivor Tree viii, 167
"Susie Van" 66

Tabernacle 41, 51, 61, 69, 81
table prayers 120
Tacheria School for Spiritual Direction 175
Takamori, Japan 114
Tamil Nadu, India 11, 14, 18
Tannirpalli, Tamil Nadu, India 14, 18
Taylor fellowship 113
Teasdale, Wayne 148
telephone 32, 81, 88, 175
television 133
Teresa of Avila 68
Tholens, Abbot Cornelius 52, 97, 99, 109, 125
Tibet 126, 127, 130, 133, 160
Tibetan Institute for Higher Studies, Saranath, India Studies 131

INDEX

Tibetan Institute of Performing Arts 130
Tibetan monks 109, 123, 128, 130, 131, 134
Tinker, Alice 69, 127
Tinker, Chief Sylvester 69, 144, 146
To a Dancing God 163
toilets 58
Toward a True Kinship of Faiths 150, 153
trails in the Forest of Peace 92, 143, 162, 165
Trapnell, Judson B. viii, 13, 153
Trappist 12, 18, 36, 58, 70, 133
Trichi, India 22
Trinity 18, 83, 110, 148
Trost, BSPA Sr. Priscilla vii, viii, 18, 35, 36, 39, 41–44, 49, 50–52, 54, 55, 57, 58, 62, 66, 71–73, 75, 78, 81, 88, 91, 92, 96, 99, 100, 103, 109, 128, 132, 134, 165, 179
Truland, BSPA Sr. Maureen 18, 109, 110, 132
Trustees, Bede Griffiths Trust 155
Trustees, Osage Forest of Peace viii, 167, 168, 169
Tsering, Geshe Konchok 131
Tucson, Arizona vii, 1, 22, 35, 42, 75, 168, 170, 172, 174, 175
Tulsa, Diocese of 1, 35, 37, 40, 41, 48, 62, 78, 91, 115, 140
Tulsa five 48, 50
Tulsa, Oklahoma 1, 2, 26, 35,–37, 39–46, 48–54, 57–60, 62, 63, 65, 68, 70–73, 75, 78, 81, 88, 91, 110, 115, 117, 122, 124, 126, 131, 133, 134, 140, 143–45, 147, 149, 159, 160, 162, 165, 168, 169–73, 176
Tulsa Tribune 126
Tulsa World 131
typewriter 43, 44, 70, 71

Unitarian 159
United Nations 29
universal priesthood 148
University of Tulsa 110
Ursuline Academy 8

Vance, Mary 52, 62, 65, 81, 83
Varela, Sr. Ramona 164
Vatican 137, 138, 139, 140, 152
Vatican II 1, 12, 13, 16–18, 43, 125, 140, 170

Vedic Experience 92
Veilleux, Fr. Armand 109
vespers 20, 21, 62, 75, 78, 82, 88, 91, 100, 103, 105, 118, 124, 143, 144, 148, 153
Vicar General 40
Vice-Chancellor 39
Vietnamese Buddhists 133
vigils 103
Virginia Anne, Sr. 91
vision quest 59
Visitation Monastery 8
vocation 8, 10, 27, 34
Von Brück, Michael 110
vows 1, 62, 127, 152
Vrana, Fr. John 116, 168

Wagner, Abbot Lawrence 123
Wagoner, David 109
wagon wheel light fixture 81, 82
Wakeham, Nancy 110
Wallace, Mr. 73
Walter, Judy, Maryknoll Sister 110, 144, 147, 148, 150, 165
Warnken, Charlene 71
Warren, Kay 110
Warren, W.K. 73, 78, 81
Webster College 26, 32
West, Juanita 66
white scarf gift from Tibetan Buddhists 128, 130
Wichita, Kansas 169
Wilkinson, Carrie 73, 83
Wilkinson, Ruth 58, 62, 65
Williams, Grant 126, 144, 145
Wilson, Roy 65
Wiseman, Fr. James 134
WK Warren Foundation 73
Woolaroc Museum 127
World Community for Christian Meditation 150
World Peace Day 62

Zen 114, 115, 117, 140, 159, 162, 170
Zendo 116

Printed in the USA
CPSIA information can be obtained
at www.ICGtesting.com
CBHW080033230224
4613CB00005B/13